DIVERSE BODIES, DIVERSE PRACTICES

TOWARD AN INCLUSIVE SOMATICS

EDITED BY DON HANLON JOHNSON

North Atlantic Books
Berkeley, California

Published by
North Atlantic Books
Berkeley, California

Cover photo © 2018 by Rosalyn Driscoll
Cover design by Rob Johnson
Book design by Happenstance Type-O-Rama

Photos of Stephanie Francis-Ecoffey, Don Hanlon Johnson, Roger Kuhn, Jules Pashall, Antoinette Santos Reyes, Kurt Wagner, Nick Walker, Alyssa N. Zelaya, and group photo of authors by Rockwell Creative

Photo of tayla ealom by Michael Wellman
Photo of Haruhiko Murakawa by Ako Murakawa
Printed in the United States of America

Diverse Bodies, Diverse Practices: Toward an Inclusive Somatics is sponsored and published by the Society for the Study of Native Arts and Sciences (dba North Atlantic Books), an educational nonprofit based in Berkeley, California, that collaborates with partners to develop cross-cultural perspectives, nurture holistic views of art, science, the humanities, and healing, and seed personal and global transformation by publishing work on the relationship of body, spirit, and nature.

North Atlantic Books' publications are available through most bookstores. For further information, visit our website at www.northatlanticbooks.com or call 800-733-3000.

Library of Congress Cataloging-in-Publication Data

Names: Johnson, Don Hanlon, 1934- editor.
Title: Diverse bodies, diverse practices : toward an inclusive somatics / edited by Don Hanlon Johnson.
Description: Berkeley, California : North Atlantic Books, [2018] | Includes bibliographical references and index.
Identifiers: LCCN 2018015024 (print) | LCCN 2018019036 (ebook) | ISBN 9781623172893 (e-book) | ISBN 9781623172886 (pbk.)
Subjects: LCSH: Mind and body. | Mind and body therapies.
Classification: LCC BF161 (ebook) | LCC BF161 .D58 2018 (print) | DDC 616.89/1—dc23
LC record available at https://lccn.loc.gov/2018015024

1 2 3 4 5 6 7 8 9 SHERIDAN 22 21 20 19 18

Printed on recycled paper

North Atlantic Books is committed to the protection of our environment.
We partner with FSC-certified printers using soy-based inks
and print on recycled paper whenever possible.

CONTENTS

ACKNOWLEDGMENTS

To Rosalyn Driscoll for her generous contribution of her sculpture for the cover design, and also for the many contributions to cover art that she has made in the past to the volumes in this series of somatic texts edited by North Atlantic Books.

To Scott Hoag for his offer of many of the photos in this book.

To the many people at North Atlantic Books, especially Richard Grossinger and Lindy Hough, who have supported our somatics community's body of literature for nearly twenty-five years.

INTRODUCTION

Borderlands

Don Hanlon Johnson

1. From Division to Creation

For my colleagues and myself, the juice in crafting this volume comes from the joy that arises from joining with an Other to create something new. The great cellist Yo-Yo Ma inspired both my conception of this project and helped me appreciate the deep joys and illuminations that I received in the process of following it through with this idiosyncratic, intricately thoughtful, and wildly creative group of people who are so different, one from another. At the end of the last century, Yo-Yo Ma created The Silk Road Ensemble, gathering musicians, singers, and songwriters from the entire length of the first Silk Road, which crossed the Eurasian landmass from Kamchatka to Prague. He took on the project when he was struck by finding that all along that endless route, musicians had for centuries relished playing with one another, even though their instruments and words were strange to each other—and while the religious and secular leaders along those same paths were engaging in endless bloody conflicts, which they continue to this very day. In fact, the words "even though" do not do justice to the significance of his insight. What he grasped, thanks to these various artists, is that in the case of creativity and the imagination, "difference" is an essential component, moving the creative person out of the already-done into the fresh world of the not-yet-explored.

Over the past fifteen years, I have attended many of the gatherings of these musicians, where you can witness a living model of a creative community of radically different people, where the differences are transformed from problems into stimuli for a soul-wakening freshness. What makes their work possible in a world riven by conflict is that they are operating on the subconceptual, nonideological level, where the sensations of rhythm, movement, sound, and words felt in the throat and mouth take precedence over the ethereal philosophies and theologies that are used (or misused) to support violent struggles for wealth and power. In doing so, these artists penetrate to the heart of those deeper impulses and longing to create a more humane and just world. In their emphasis on the nonconceptual realm, their work is not so different from ours, which is based in silent touch, moving, sensing, and sounding. As I worked with each of the gifted authors in this book, I kept finding myself in that joy that comes from working with others to create something genuinely fresh: the unexpected insights and formulations, the move toward new layers of understanding how our lives together might be more satisfying. A clear hope emerges that perhaps we might make some contribution to efforts to turn diversity from a source of strife into a nudge toward creating the new.

In crafting this work, one question that has motivated us is: How do we create a community that not only tolerates the inevitable crossings of so-called secure borders, but welcomes the ever-fluctuating tides of peoples moving here and there, while feeling the enormous creative possibilities of joining with those with radically different perspectives to create a more intricate and interesting social order? The seemingly simple solutions to the tensions that arise in the encounters with the margins, like the old great walls of Hadrian and Genghis Khan, and the anachronistic walls now abuilding in various tension points around the world, are clung to in the old fears of the Other, with little lasting success. In the chapters that follow, you will find people building their strategies of creating a more just and satisfying world by openly sharing intimate details of the suffering that they have endured and shaped into capacious adult selves, creating an atmosphere of recognition for the struggles we all make to become human. An honoring of each trail of tears has the potential to transform our fears of the Other into compassion for one like ourselves, helping create an effective community of resistance and transformation.

2. Shared Suffering

An unanticipated common theme emerged as we worked together: that we each arrived at this particular conjunction of people and task from histories of intense struggle—physical and emotional. In writing together about the different textures and colors of that struggle, we found ourselves closer in our shared creativity and more effective in succeeding at the difficult task of this production. It shouldn't have surprised me, knowing that grief is a turning point in the process of healing. And yet, because we each are so different, one from another, in so many categories—gender identification, color, age, dysfunctions, neural capacities, religious backgrounds, and current ideologies—this closeness came as a surprise.

Many years ago, I had received a grant from the UN Commission on Human Rights to develop in San Francisco a healing center for survivors of political torture. I had come into that work knowing that the worldwide network of physicians, psychotherapists, and healers dealing with this tragically widespread phenomenon had come up against a daunting challenge. They knew that the very nature of torture required addressing not only the medical and emotional aspects of it, but also the residues of direct assaults to the flesh. And yet, the conventional methods of medically based physical therapies and other well-known methods like chiropractic evoked traumatic memories of the torture itself because of their invasive nature.

In my own work of gathering the various training institutes of body practices, I knew of many that were oriented toward the kinds of sensitive, respectful, and noninvasive touch that the organizers were looking for. In an early meeting exploring how to structure our work, I met with six men who had been imprisoned and tortured in Cambodia during the terror of Pol Pot's regime. Their legs bore the deep marks that chains had left on their calves. One man articulated their plight in these words: "Because of this torture, our souls were driven from our bodies. Only our shamans know how to retrieve them. But they are all gone."

In that pregnant moment, I grasped with utter clarity the challenge that any system of healing would have to resolve. We can indeed each help one another with the resources we each have, both individually and as members of one or another community. In the case of these survivors, the kinds of sensitive respectful hands-on work we made available have been significantly effective in helping them create active lives again in this new country. And yet some regions of their souls still wander. That experience brought home to me what I had long known more conceptually, that individual and communal healing could not do the whole job without addressing the larger social structures within which we live, whose powers to shape us are so much greater than any of our smaller interventions. This book is a small move in that direction, both in its content and in its modeling of how a radically diverse group of people can have an impact on the shaping of our larger world to recognize the assaults on the souls of so many displaced peoples.

The terrain in this book is one of borderlands: the often uncharted regions between "Us" and "Them"; the "Healthy" and "Not-" "Normal" and "Not-" "White, Brown, Black." It's a dangerous territory populated by wanderers who are often disoriented and vulnerable, constantly vigilant so as not to be gerrymandered into one or another sequestered compound by those who live in the center. Wanderers are in these territories not by some version of choice, like adventurous tourists or emigrants in search of a better life, but because of their bodies of birth, like those Cambodian refugees who were born into the killing fields.

One author in this volume, Nick Walker, is an autistic person who found himself growing up among caregivers who had no real sense of how he experienced the world. Another chapter is by Jules Pashall, a fat person who, from infancy, was faced with a culture that shamed them. Other chapters recount the struggles of people who are born at the intersections of cultures and ethnicities, where healing and microaggressions were mixed. In my case, a congenital spinal dysfunction spurred a long history of being charged with stiffness and rigidity by people who thought of themselves as highly skilled in "body-reading." What brings us together is that we share a focus on how an emphasis on our bodily, nonverbal, subverbal, and preverbal worlds of experience has enabled us to move out of our isolations into communities of learning and service. Our passports into communal creativity were our shared discoveries of breathing together, truly seeing each other in careful detail, listening, feeling, and moving responsively with one another. It is that crucial shift from making words and ideas the forefront of our interactions toward giving ever more attention to the vast realm of direct experience. As this book testifies, we are not giving up on words and ideas, but righting a serious imbalance in which the weight of the verbal and conceptual has all but snuffed out the recognition of the enormous wisdom in the experiential, and especially how that imbalance makes it difficult to widen our community to include those seemingly very different from ourselves.

3. A Democratic Sensibility

We authors are working in a neglected dimension of this struggle, the preparation of a sensibility for a cooperative model of communal organization, in between personal healing and social activism. On the one hand, we must attend to physical and emotional wounds, those of others and of our own. But at the same time, at least some of us need to attend to the larger institutions of education, medicine, community organizations, and all the rest whose failures to negotiate among our differences may cancel our small efforts at personal relief. Just as those damaged Cambodians needed a sensitive touch to allow their souls to return in at least a partial way, so too our institutions need the recovery of a densely embodied sensitivity so as to create a welcoming atmosphere to those living on the margins, helping them to feel truly situated within the communities of healing.

With so many self-described democracies around the world struggling to survive, it is now more obvious than ever that the creation of a truly just and inclusive social order is not automatic but the work of intense self- and communal transformation. Nor is it primarily a matter of intellectual debate.

One inchoate dream of a more just society originated in fifth-century BCE Greece, where it represented the rebellion of the *demes*—the neighborhoods in the various city-states—against the tyrants. In Plato's *Republic* and Aristotle's *Politics,* democracy was not simply a system of voting and governing, but a goal that required the thoughtfully organized training of young men to learn how to consolidate their communities when their turns at governing arose. It started out with gymnastic training that was not only for health and vitality, but also for shaping scattered youthful sensibilities into capacities for clear perceptions of the movements and strengths of their companions. In that sense, "democracy" is not as much a reality as an ideal of mutual respect and collaboration that continues to urge people throughout the world to keep bending the arc of history toward the inclusion of more kinds of different people into the category of "citizen," a person worthy of the full rights, respect, and care structured within this particular social order.

The contemporary social philosopher Susan Griffin puts it this way in her aptly entitled book *Wrestling with the Angel of Democracy*:

> I am aiming at neither a definition nor a catalogue of qualities. It is the inner states that generate and are generated by democracy that interest me, and the purpose lies in the journey itself too. At this pivotal moment, the idea of navigating my own life as an American citizen seems to satisfy a longing whose meaning I cannot quite fully articulate yet.[1]

Her book's dust-cover vividly captures the notion that democracy represents an ideal achieved only by long struggle: a reproduction of a nineteenth-century French painting of a naked man wrestling a half-naked winged angel, both erotically super-muscled, struggling,

---

1 Susan Griffin, *Wrestling with the Angel of Democracy: On Being an American Citizen* (Boston: Shambhala, 2008), 6.

reminiscent of Plato and Aristotle wrestling naked with their students in the Palestra on the Acropolis, debating about the nature of governance. Looking at this, one gets a feeling not only of how muscularly hard it is to bring about a just society, but also how sensual it can be: making love, having meals together, singing and chanting into the long nights, engaging in sparkling conversations, marching together in solidarity through the streets, and shaping a society that is not only just, but also pleasurable in its network of sensual and creative connections.

Widespread dialogues over the last 2500 years around the ideal of democracy and its social offshoots took for granted a certain commonality of embodied practice that grounded abstract thought in sensual intersubjectivity: wrestling in Athens, meditation and ritual in medieval Europe and India, sports, marching in time, music, and song, and thickly embodied tribal practices throughout the world. There was no question but that a bodily felt consensus that aimed to integrate the welfare of others in one's community with one's own welfare was recognized as the foundation for egalitarian forms of government.

By the time of the European Enlightenment, however, the bodily preparation for democracy had been subordinated to an emphasis on abstract thought and intellectual debate. Medicine, education, psychology, and government were each put into separate conceptual silos, masking the fact that they are inextricably interlinked in how they affect us. Our founding political thinkers tragically failed to take into account the fact that people who have not learned how to successfully attune to each other, especially to those in other *demes* in the midst of intense differences, cannot successfully collaborate in the enormous project of creating an intricate and just set of democratic structures. This neglect has become even more tragic in its consequences as we enter a planetary era when it is clear that we are all sustained by this Earth, breathing common air, and nurtured by common waters, soils, and food, even though we agree about so little intellectually and spiritually, and are often so afraid and dismissive of one another. Although many creators of modern attempts at socialized forms of governance knew the need to form collaborative attitudes among citizens, their strategies veered upward into mental constructs. They became so dissociated from direct bodily experiences that their good-willed desires to create more effective communities were unable to withstand the inevitable pressures that promote conflict rather than creative resolutions.

Vincent Harding, a leader of the Civil Rights Movement and historian of the Middle Passage, put it this way in a monograph he published shortly before his death, inspired by a phrase of Langston Hughes:

> So my initial approach to the challenge of the American dream and its meaning comes in the form of the question ... "Is America Possible?" For it seems to me that any exploration of a national experience of deepening, of maturing and honing, must urgently fold into itself the search for this nation's capacity to discover and give witness to its own unique and hard-won gifts for becoming "the land that never has been yet." This America was Langston Hughes's stillborn child, waiting for the breath of life to rise from some deep place within us, daring to create and harbor great visions of redemption for us all. This is my historical and spiritual context for wrestling, dancing with the prospect of deepening the American dream.[2]

We in this volume share works designed to evoke that capacity of "waiting for the breath of life to rise from some deep place within us," suggesting practices of movement, touch, sensing, and feeling as methods for laying the bodily foundation for a more effective democratic way of life.

Nearly a hundred years ago, John Dewey articulated this arduous task with great clarity, which he and others were using to formulate the structures of the then-newly established public school system, whose central goal was to shape active and thoughtful citizens:

> Democracy is much broader than a special political form, a method of conducting government, of making laws and carrying on governmental administration by means of popular suffrage and elected officers. It is that, of course. But it is something broader and deeper than that. The political and governmental phase of democracy is a means ... for realizing ends that lie in the wide domain of human relationships and

---

[2] Vincent Harding, *Is America Possible? A Letter to My Young Companions on the Journey of Hope* (Kalamazoo, MI: The Fetzer Institute, 2007), 2.

> the development of human personality. It is, as we often say, though perhaps without appreciating all that is involved in the saying, a way of life, social and individual. The key-note of democracy as a way of life may be expressed, it seems to me, as the necessity for the participation of every mature human being in formation of the values that regulate the living of [citizens] together: which is necessary from the standpoint of both the general social welfare and the full development of human beings as individuals.[3]

These words, appearing in a book which would help shape the course of the public school system in America, articulate a spirit that drives us to craft this book: the notion that a democracy that is capable of nurturing both individual and collective healing is not primarily a system of institutions built on ideas and texts and certain abstract values, but "a way of life," requiring "the participation of every mature human being in formation of the values that regulate the living of [people] together: which is necessary from the standpoint of ... the full development of human beings as individuals." Democracy is not a reality but a hope, like somatics itself, a regulative ideal that sets us on paths of struggle to imagine what is not yet, and requiring a profound reshaping of our narcissistic proclivities.

4. Making Bodies and Social Change

This collection is primarily practical in that it aims at learning how to change things—bodies, ideas, institutions—by way of specific experiential strategies, but with a heightened awareness of the many differences among the participants that require attention. Ideas emerge from bodily practices in two very different forms:

1. from what is done to us, and what we do, both just going about our lives—infant handling, walking, sitting, breathing, studying; and
2. deliberately chosen activities such as exercise regimens, dance, diet, and meditation practices.

---

[3] John Dewey, *On Democracy.*

This seems at odds with the more conventional notion that ideas emerge from reading books, listening to lectures, speculating about things in interior conversations, and doing controlled experiments. An older meaning of "body" in Anglo-Saxon carried this meaning. *Bottich* or *bodig* was derived from the term used for brewing vats, the containers in which spirits were distilled from grains and fruit. Before the eviscerating assaults by Descartes, Galileo, Newton, and others, which cleaved the interiority of the imagination, feeling, and sensation from empirically isolated biological mechanisms, the word referred to the whole person within whom images, thoughts, values, words, speculations slowly emerge, purged of the weight of muscles, bones, and intestines.

The older image grounded the once-prevalent notions of education, which required disciplines of meditation, music, exercise, and other embodied practices laying the foundation for later stages of adult development in philosophy, science, and theology. "Cultivation" is an important term in that it implies a work with living beings. Too often, the metaphors used in experiential work are based on computers and engines: "regulation," "control mechanisms," "triggers," and so on. But as with gardens and crops, effecting positive outcomes in humans requires a feel for the ever-changing climate, the shifts one way and another brought about by a single intervention where one person reacts very differently from another, and especially the infinitely complex life systems at play in humans in contrast to the mechanisms of an automobile.

As the dualistic models of Enlightenment Europe began to take hold of the institutions of medicine, education, science, and philosophy, the "body" was put off into the realm of inert objects, connected in some ways (if at all) to what came to be thought of as a spiritual soul or mind, detached from materiality. In this more recent model, within which we have been shaped, the various body practices were thought to be useful indeed for relaxation, vitality, good health, sexuality, and such peripheral pursuits, but not intrinsically related to the quality of one's thinking and decision-making.

The late Japanese scholar Yuasa Yasuo, throughout his many books on this topic, argues that, based on his lifetime practice of Qigong, Western thinkers are making very large claims about the nature of reality based on untutored sensibilities. It's not so much that they are logically in error, but that they are immature; their ideas are the distilled speculations of a teenage sensibility.

> In the East, one starts from the experiential assumption that the mind-body modality changes through the training of the mind and body by means of cultivation or training. Only after assuming this experiential ground does one ask what the mind-body relation is. That is, the mind-body issue is not simply a theoretical speculation but it is originally a practical, lived experience, involving the mustering of one's whole mind and body. The theoretical is only a reflection on this lived experience.[4]

In chapter 8 of this book, Haruhiko Murakawa develops this radically different notion of intellectual development that is embedded in Eastern educational models.

In a similar vein, many European and American social scientists have initiated studies of cultural practices that form a foundation for understanding the values and ideas that those practices give rise to. Marcel Mauss's brief 1933 essay "*Les techniques du corps*" launched many studies of culturally different body practices by identifying the wide range of activities that shape the protean body of the infant into that of an adult, ranging from styles of infant-handling to gender formation, styles of play and work, exercise, sexual postures, dance and ritual, medical procedures, and to such everyday practices as walking, sitting, and eating.

Following the logic of these various lines of social science studies raises the question of the significance of seemingly trivial everyday practices of discourse. For example, when ten or fifteen people assemble in a room for a working meeting, what exactly happens? What is the arrangement—around a table, and if so, what kind? What is the

---

4 Yuasa Yasuo, *The Body: Toward an Eastern Mind-Body Theory*, trans. N. Shigenori and T. P. Kasulis (Albany, NY: SUNY Press, 1987), 18.

design of the seats and their ordering? What is the lighting like? How is the scheduled time for the meeting allocated?

The architecture of comings-together—from private offices to legislatures and courts—shapes our common sensibilities to ourselves and to others. But significantly all of this is subverbal, under the radar, rarely attended to. Add to this all the human forces: tones of voice, facial expressions, size, forcefulness, passivity. Such banal details become meaningful in their repetition over long times. Unwittingly, our organisms are literally being shaped by these kinds of factors: negatively, when they exaggerate curvatures in our bones, webs of restriction in our muscles and ligaments, and restrict our digestion and respiration; and positively, when they augment our liveliness, expand our ranges of movement, and comfort our eyes, etc.

In this volume, you will find several different trains of cultivations. Some are embedded in the narratives of those authors from ancient cultural currents not taken into account in mainstream somatics—the African diaspora, Native Americans, Meso- and South Americans, Japan, India, and China. Other narratives of cultivation come from authors whose bodies are on the margins of so-called normality—autism, weight and size, ability, erotic attractions.

5. The Body and the Body Politic

Two important models for the early formation of the somatics community were Wilhelm Reich and Mohandas Gandhi. Intimations of the kind of work we are addressing in these chapters are found in the works of these two revolutionaries. Even though they were from radically different parts of the world, both geographically and ideologically, both shared the notion that the body and its sensibilities are central factors in social change. Despite dramatic social changes since the era when they shaped their works, they laid down the kinds of inquiries that we even now can develop to address today's unique challenges. Most significantly, they differed from many other revolutionary theorists in their focusing on the "how to" of social change, not simply the theories about it. Much of their work is a seamless web of theory and practice, a synthesis that we seek for in this volume.

In Gandhi's long struggles in South Africa and India to invent an Indian identity of freedom and social justice, he kept bumping up against the bitter resentments that turn us against one another even while we desperately seek to consolidate. It was for this reason that he was virtually obsessed about seemingly minor personal issues of diet, exercise, and sexual control.[5] It is astounding to go through his writings and discover how much he devotes to the smallest details of self-cultivation in the midst of world-changing activities with thousands of people. Water cures, mud-packs, herbalism, Western gymnastics, vegetarianism, and other body disciplines are the stuff out of which *ahimsa* was derived and made possible in the face of colonial domination. Gandhi's notion of nonviolence—born of intense work with the self, pruning automatic reactions, toughening fibers, learning to bring into clear, useful focus the people's wild impulses—was far from passivity. The truth of being that flowed from these practices—*Satyagraha*—was truth enfleshed, full-bodied truth, whose bearers stood firmly in that truth against the violent purveyors of illusion.

A secondary motivation in Gandhi's somatic thinking was to discipline the hard edges of emotional reactions that fragment the revolutionary community and keep it from harmonious and effective action, activities which he thought of as purging the body of the effects of colonization. He perceived that diet and standard medical practices, on top of wanton sexual behavior, had weakened the Indian population. His pleas for vegetarianism and celibacy were aimed at increasing capacities for freedom.

While Gandhi was working to change the conditions of Indians in apartheid South Africa and colonized India, Wilhelm Reich was addressing the social devastations in Europe resulting from the Industrial Revolution, pogroms, and World War I. As a young physician,

---

[5] Mohandas Gandhi, "Letter to Shankarlal Bankerr," 1918, *Collected Works* (72: 380), quoted by Joseph S. Alter, *Gandhi's Body: Sex, Diet, and the Politics of Nationalism* (Philadelphia: University of Pennsylvania Press, 2000), 3.

Reich was shaped by both psychoanalysis and Marxist humanism. Freud made him aware of the roots of impotence within the fluids and nervous channels of the psyche. He saw that the innate energies of the organism became so distorted by the family and religion that they lost their capacities to energize a truly free adult, producing instead passive citizens subject to manipulation by charismatic leaders, like Hitler, Franco, and Stalin. Marx made him aware of how the conditions shaping mass populations of factory workers and soldiers robbed their bodies of an internal sense of agency molding them for submission to national and industrial goals formed by others. Like Gandhi, he understood that the struggle for freedom required intense practices of transforming the body.[6]

In the early 1930s, Reich wrote a hauntingly prophetic analysis of how Hitler succeeded in rapidly mobilizing hordes of ordinary citizens to engage in a mass movement that seemed obviously contrary to the most basic human values. In response to the question of why it was that countless thoughtful and seemingly virtuous Germans were unable to stem the tides of the apocalyptic tragedies they could see bearing down upon them, he argued that the missing piece in social thinking, that doomed them to repetitive failure, was the social evisceration of the body: "the miscalculation that all freedom-fighters until now have made: *The social incapacity for freedom is sexual-physiologically anchored in the human organism.*"[7]

Scarred by his long experiences of being hounded by psychoanalysts, Marxists, and capitalists, he eventually came to realize that fascism is not a peculiar characteristic of ephemeral political movements in Germany, Spain, Italy, and Japan. It is a universal phenomenon precisely because it is rooted in the human body. When the multiple layers of bodily movements, impulses, and perceptions are not creatively transformed into creative movements in the directions of freedom, feelings for others, and purpose, people become easily subject to

---

6 Wilhelm Reich, *The Mass Psychology of Fascism*, trans. Vincent R. Carfagno (New York: Farrar, Straus & Giroux, 1970), 319.

7 Reich, 346. (Italics are Reich's.)

mass media and ideologues who foment populist movements fueled by fear and disorientation.

Though somatics have developed inspired by these two men and many others, we recognize that we now know more about these realities, even though we carry forward their foundational insights. Their shortcomings illuminate what we now have to reset. For example, even though they intellectually recognized the equality of men and women, that recognition was not embodied in their patriarchal stances. In addition, they held unquestioned assumptions about sexuality—ideally penis in vagina with simultaneous orgasms—which we now have opened for complex discourses, as addressed here by Kurt Wagner. They were both highly critical of racism, but were not able to succeed in engaging ethnically diverse comrades with different voices, like the ones in this volume articulated by Antoinette Santos Reyes, Muriel Vinson, tayla ealom, Stephanie Francis-Ecoffey, Alyssa Zelaya, and Roger Kuhn.

The results of the movements initiated by Gandhi and Reich are ambiguous. Their large marks on the contemporary world are obvious in the many communities that continue to develop the institutions that they seeded. And yet, Gandhi was painfully aware that his constant experiments with various strategies to change himself and change the nation enjoyed only modest successes. There were his personal failures in his attempts to regulate his sexual desires, and his larger failures to forge an alliance with the Muslim communities in India, leading to the tragedies of the Partition. Reich was ousted by every community he tried to join. In 1956, he was imprisoned in Lewisburg, Pennsylvania, on spurious charges of transporting so-called medical equipment across a state border. Shortly before he died there in 1957, the United States Food and Drug Administration held a medieval-style book-burning of everything he had published.

Although their great hopes are dashed in the ruins of fragmented India and Pakistan and in the depredations of the West, Reich's analysis of fascism and Gandhi's of colonialism are crucial in getting beyond the tragic patterns of revolutions in which the formerly oppressed, when they succeed in getting power, regularly become the new oppressors. Reich argues that it is not possible to break this oppressed-oppressor cycle without getting at "the social incapacity for freedom rooted in the human organism." Our repetitive good-willed efforts to create a just social order keep foundering on the shoals of closed-off bodies, with dulled senses and weakened capacities.

6. Somatics

Reich and Gandhi are but two of the many who have inspired those of us who have been working with the intersections between our bodies and our institutions. They include early pioneers Trigant Burrow, Carl Rogers, and Eugene Gendlin, who articulated clearly effective strategies for working on the relation between direct bodily experiences and democratic groups. Many of my contemporaries—Arnold Mindell, Joanna Macy, Staci Haines, Anna Halprin, Gabrielle Roth, Susan Griffin, and others—have created body-based methods for work with groups in a sociopolitical context. Our aim here is to contribute to those many efforts toward realizing the dream of a more egalitarian society. Arnold Mindell writes of his version of this dream:

> In a conference call, leaders of many cities were talking to one another. People in Vladivostok, Anchorage, Seattle, Chicago, Montreal, New York, London, Berlin, Helsinki, Stockholm, Warsaw, and Moscow were saying, "We have tried everything else. Nothing has succeeded. Let's try this new worldwork. Let's open up to what is happening in communities. Perhaps we can begin a new world order." In my dream, people actually learned to work with one another.[8]

Nearly fifty years ago, a handful of us joined in using the Greek-rooted term *somatics* as an umbrella designed to coax together a fragmented community of innovative and revolutionary teachers who had managed to craft methods of sensory awareness, touch, breathing, sounding, and moving to address the healing of old and widespread

8 Arnold Mindell, *Sitting in the Fire: Large Group Transformation Using Conflict and Diversity* (Portland, OR: Lao Tse Press, 1995), 12.

traumas, and to enhance human functioning. The unique characteristics of each method evolved from particular locations in history and geography. They shared the common goal of addressing a very peculiar virus originating in Paris, London, and Athens dividing "mind" from "body," a virus that was harmful not only to infected individuals but to larger communities when it became a weapon used to justify colonialism, slavery, displacement of tribal peoples, and ravaging the earth. We always knew that different viruses were alive in other parts of the world, and that wise people were crafting other ways to deal with them—the innumerable practices of healing dance, music, chant, massage, martial arts in Africa, India, China, the Amazon Basin—addressing different kinds of suffering and spiritual yearning. But we could only do what was available to us in the circumscribed limitations of our times and places.

Since that time, many of us have used this umbrella to organize conferences, develop study groups, start clinics and graduate degree programs oriented toward professional licensing, initiate research projects, join with medical and psychological practitioners in healing works, and craft a body of literature about the various methods participating in this movement—how they work, and their results. The rapidly growing field has had discernible impacts on the psychological and physical well-being of thousands of people in pain, contributed to the understanding of how to bring these practices into various group activities such as recovery from war and natural disasters, eldercare, early childhood education, and wilderness-based therapy. North Atlantic Books has played a significant role in this development by publishing a large body of literature on which the intellectual basis of the work can be articulated.

At the same time, ominous forces in our current world situation—environmental destruction, recurrence of nuclear threats, displacements of populations, rise of totalitarian and racist politics, and rampant greed—are calling upon us to develop our works within a broader, more inclusive social arena. This volume represents an update of our ever-growing collective works in response to these emerging challenges. The original innovators of somatics emerged in the climate of two World

Wars, the Holocaust, and the residues of slavery in the United States and the devastations of our indigenous populations. Most of them were fully aware that personal and small-group healing, though necessary, was not enough to assure a truly human life within institutions that were sources of widespread suffering. They saw their methods of touch, sensing, breathing, feeling, and moving not only, or even primarily, as aimed at personal well-being, but as methods for reshaping the institutions of a sick social order. Ida Rolf many times lamented that we misunderstood her work as a remedy for physical suffering when she saw the healing as a consequence of working to transform an unbalanced society. Charlotte Selver argued in a similar way about Sensory Awareness that it was aimed at bringing the world to its senses.

And yet, how do we truly come together in a sustained way that becomes effective enough to stem the tides of destruction? How do we heal the divisions that make them compete with each other rather than unite against the Darth Vaders of the world? An obvious fact also needs to be acknowledged, because it is a principal motivator behind the design of this collection. In the now-many volumes of literature in this field, it is hard to locate a single voice of color or radical bodily difference. And the underlying assumptions of what constitutes "normality" in such basic regions as neural functioning and musculoskeletal structures are extremely narrow. The authors of this volume represent a model of how voices from various places in the world and diverse bodily capacities might interact creatively with each other to imagine fresh solutions for the daunting questions we all face.

Somatics has many contributions to make to the disorientation that diversity consciousness brings in its wake. I am sitting … my fingers tapping … hearing the sounds of the furnace and seeing the sunlight break through the clouds I see outside my window. I am here now breathing, aware of the sensations of sitting in my chair. As I developed the capacity to turn easily to paying attention to this here now, when I was one time incapable of doing so, I am able to find a similar space with you, where our ideas become something like the clouds I see floating by, not intruding on the reality of you and me—a fertile ground for making a new world.

Ursula K. Le Guin died just as we were completing this manuscript. One of our authors found this passage about her, which articulates so clearly one aspect of what we are trying to do here. I offer it in memory of her robust thoughtfulness and that imaginative body of literature that she left.

> On the whole, social science research articles and monographs are confined mainly to what Le Guin (1986) refers to as "the father tongue," a high-minded mode of expression that embraces objectivity. Spoken from above, the father tongue runs the risk of distancing the writer from the reader, creating a gap between self and other. What is missing from most social science writing is "the mother tongue" (Le Guin, 1986), a binding form of subjective and conversational expression that covets "a turning together," a relationship between author and reader. Voiced in a language of emotions and personal experience, the mother tongue exposes rather than protects the speaker through a medium that can bring author and reader closer together. The absence of a mother tongue in social science literature reflects the conventions of disembodied writing that extol the virtue of objectivity. As Le Guin (1989, p. 151) notes, "People crave objectivity because to be subjective is to be embodied, to be a body, vulnerable, violable." The real discourse of reason, she claims, is a wedding of the father to mother tongue, which produces "a native tongue."[9]

Our hope, in the ways that we have crafted these chapters, is to help recover this native tongue, with its ancient healing wisdom.

---

[9] Patricia Levy, ed., *The Oxford Handbook of Qualitative Studies* (Oxford: Oxford University Press, 2014), "Practicing Narrative Inquiry," 209, quoting Ursula K. Le Guin, "The Mother Tongue," Bryn Mawr Alumnae Bulletin, Summer, 1986, 3–4.

Chapter 1

Fieldwork: Seeking Balance through the 5Rhythms

Roger J. Kuhn

Beginnings

I consider myself a soma-cultural therapist. I am interested in the body and its relation to culture, which helps shape, challenge, and ultimately influence our experiences. My therapeutic approach and my research are informed from this soma-cultural perspective. I believe in asking questions that evoke an emotional response. These questions are explored through a constructionist worldview. A constructivist viewpoint explores the subjective experiences of the subject(s) and the meanings they make of them. From a soma-cultural perspective, this view invites me (as therapist or researcher) an opportunity to examine what I call the triple Ps—power, positionality, and privilege. These triple Ps color the lens in which I am able to engage in critical analysis of my work, and further challenge the discourse around the cultural and social phenomena that is at the core of my inquiries.

When I was approached to contribute a chapter to this book about diverse bodies and practices, I wanted to share how I think about diversity. From my soma-cultural perspective, I believe diversity welcomes and validates the unique perspectives that are present in the world. It is the thread that ties together the human experience and creates pathways for deepening our connections with multitudinous identities. Diversity encompasses age, gender and gender expression, race and ethnicity, religion and spirituality, national origin, sexual orientation, and socioeconomic status. It is also inclusive of disabilities, immigration status, learning styles, levels of education, nontraditional families and partnerships, body size, as well as various expressions of personal identity. Diversity establishes the foundation for which we build both equality and equity, and ensures all people, from all cultures of the world, are granted acceptance and inclusivity.

Diversity also includes intersectionality and the reflection of one's positionality. I identify as a mixed-race Native American of European descent. I also identify as Two-Spirit and gay. My senior year in high school, I was voted most likely to have an out-of-body experience. I am sure the intention behind this recognition was not malicious. I have convinced myself over the years that my graduating class was just as confused about my identity as I was. I was one of four students of racial minorities in my grade and one of two mixed-race people. My fellow students were perplexed by the rocks, crystals, and sage I carried around with me and placed on my desk during tests and quizzes. They didn't understand that I wasn't wearing a fanny pack, I was wearing a medicine bag, and the items held within were sacred to me. The joke was on them though, as I had already left my body many times before. I had mastered the art of disassociation from an early age spurned by the secrets, abuse, and trauma that complicated my young life.

The irony in the award I received in high school is that I now work as a somatic psychotherapist and my work focuses on helping people connect with and stay centered in their bodies. I hear phrases such as "I feel disconnected," "I don't know how to feel into my body," and "Everything below my head feels numb." Clients express these views from varying perspectives relating to trauma, anxiety, depression, or issues relating to sexuality. Together, we explore how this disconnect has challenged their lived experiences, and also how being disconnected has benefitted them. When I ask about how being disconnected from their mind/body experience has been helpful, I most often hear, "It hasn't been helpful, that's why I'm here." I ask them to not judge their experience, but rather invite an inquiry into understanding any benefits a disembodied experience has granted them. This inquiry does not take place in the course of one session; it is an evolving knowledge that grants clients an insight to their experiences they may have previously numbed. Through this inquiry, clients begin to recognize how a disembodied experience has created a false sense of safety and security in their day-to-day lives.

I too have struggled with understanding my mind/body connection. I have struggled with understanding what it means to be biracial and bicultural. I have struggled with knowing that the blood of the colonizer and the colonized runs through my veins. I have struggled with what it means to be gay, sexually fluid, and Two-Spirit. I have struggled with what it means to be a survivor of trauma. My positionality and epistemology are constantly evolving, creating new opportunities to challenge my worldviews, my trauma, and ultimately my healing.

According to Bowen, "greater awareness enhances the capability of a person to feel the embodiment of the self (what is called 'the somatic sense of self')."[1] When we work with the somatic sense of self in the moment (working with what is in the now), the projections of self in the past can be brought to the surface in an effort to remove any boundaries or limitations we have placed on ourselves in regards to different ways of expressing embodiment. This creates a capacity for transformation. Transformation is an internal process, which can lead to both internal and external bodily shifts. I am on a continuing path to recognize the doorways of my own life and the areas that must be explored in order for my healing to expand. According to Takacs, "when we develop the skill of understanding how we know what we know, we acquire a key to lifelong learning."[2] My process of lifelong learning involves connecting with my body through dance, movement, learning, sexuality, and community. These modalities play an intricate part in my pleasure and my pain.

---

1 Bill Bowen, *Somatic Resourcing: Psychotherapy through the Body* (Portland: PPT Publishing, 2009), 22.

2 David Takacs, "How Does Your Positionality Bias Your Epistemology?" *Thought and Action Journal* 19, no. 1 (2003): 28.

I encountered my first out-of-body experience at birth. I have vivid memories and dreams where I am floating above my body, looking down at my mother as she is screaming for me to breathe. I was told that during my birth, my heart momentarily stopped. The imprint of my mother's screaming face has been with me every time my heart has been broken, been tired from exercise, or pained from heartburn. I am always wondering if this is the time my heart is going to stop again. I see a heart specialist from time to time to help ease my anxiety and am told upon each visit that I am fine and to continue exercising, eating well, and to not smoke. The second time I remember having an out-of-body experience, I was four years old. I witnessed the rape of a close family member, jarred awake by her screams. I was lying on my right side. To this day I still experience pain and loss of sensation in my right hip. My next out-of-body experience also involved violence, this time blacking out after receiving a physical beating from my father, so severe that it left scars on my body. At this point in my story I was only eleven years old and already had a life's worth of trauma that I was carrying around in my body.

The violent episode that I am reminded of whenever my finger traces the scar just below my bottom lip was also a catalyst for change in my family life. I made the choice to no longer hide my father's abuse and allowed my mother and sisters to see my bloodied face after the beating. It's not that my mother did not know the abuse was happening; she herself was victimized by my father's alcoholic violence and felt helpless and alone. The last time my father beat me, I remember looking into the bathroom mirror, bloodied and swollen in my face. I told myself, "No more." I remember my mother's expression when I walked into our family kitchen afterward. She too said, "No more." All transitions begin with blood.

Homecoming

Those first hours of the morning, as the crepuscular light rises above the horizon, have always been inspiring to me. I am reminded of a time in my childhood at seven years old when I first visited my tribal nation's reservation in southern Alabama. There was a field on the reservation that I felt called to explore, enraptured by this land that I had heard my mother speak about so many times before. I vividly recall the morning light seeping through the trees as the wind carried the songs of the morning birds. I remember taking off my shoes, my feet connecting to the bare soil, my toes mingling with the earth. I was aware of new sensations coursing through my body and I began to stomp my feet. I stomped my feet and moved my body in ways I had never moved before. The dancer within me was suddenly born. I connected not only with the earth, but also with the wind through the trees, and the cacophony of bird songs in the air. This next part feels dreamy, as if I were lifted on a cloud and gliding through a landscape of my ancestors who walked this land before me. I see horses running and five people watching me; they resemble my maternal grandparents who are Native Americans. This vision does not last long, it was over shortly after it began, and it remains clear to this day. The vision that I had on the reservation was my first understanding of my somatic sense of self.

I learned many things on my first trip to the reservation, including some of the differences between Native Americans and European Americans as well as some of the differences between Catholics and other Christians. Up until that point in my life, I did not have memories of traveling outside of my home state of North Dakota, which was a beautiful and also sheltered place to be raised. However, to say that my childhood was innocent would be a disservice to the traumatic parts of my story, a narrative I believe is steeped in what I call a soma-cultural crisis.

Though I have never identified as white, I recognize that to some I am perceived as white. Perception is powerful and can impact how safe people feel with others. Perception also plays an integral role in how I am received in the world. The name I was given at birth is Roger Jason Kuhn. I was named after my father's brother, though my mother tells me she wanted to name me David. At the age of twelve I underwent the ritual of Roman Catholic confirmation and was rechristened Roger Jason John Stephen Kuhn. I have never resonated with my birth name, nor my confirmed name.

Names have the power of conjecture. They can persuade our minds into believing something about people, places, or things before we know anything about them. My first name, for example, is Germanic in origin meaning "famous spearman." My last name is also of Germanic origin, meaning "bold." The name "Roger Kuhn" speaks to my Euro-American ancestry but says nothing of the Indigenous blood that also courses through my veins. I am the child of a white man's lust to relive the cowboys and Indians fantasies of his youth. I am also the child of a Native woman seeking to escape trauma, only to enter into another traumatic relationship.

My existence is based upon a narrative rooted in the heteropatriarchy and heteronormativity of settler colonialism. In many ways, I view myself as a poster child for white settler colonialism and the subjugation of Native bodies. In particular, Native women's bodies, which (as legend tells) is the savior of the savage Indian because of her desire for white males. My white father is the John Smith to my Native mother's Pocahontas. It was my father's land I inherited after his death from an alcohol-induced car accident.

Sharing Knowledge

There are 567 federally recognized American Indian and Alaskan Native tribal nations within the United States, and over 200 unique Indigenous languages spoken. The 2000 United States census estimated approximately 4 million American Indians/Alaska Natives (AIAN) with 1.6 million people claiming AIAN identity plus one or more additional races.[3] The 2000 census also marked the first time that people could identify as more than one race. Any person who belongs to a federally recognized AIAN tribal nation is American Indian/Alaska Native and therefore can be counted on the United States census and is eligible for certain benefits through the Bureau of Indian Affairs (BIA). Within Indian country, the term American Indian is interchangeable with Native American, and/or Indian. Native American is "a term that arose after the Civil Rights Movement

---

[3] Stella U. Ogunwole, *The American Indian and Alaska Native Population: 2000* (Washington: US Census Bureau, 2002), 1–12.

in response to a need for unbiased terminology regarding historically maligned ethnic groups."[4]

Native Americans, including mixed-race Native Americans, are subjugated to others questioning their identity, their authenticity, and their citizenship. How much Indian are you? Are you enrolled? Do you have a CDIB card? What is your clan name? What is your Indian name? When is the last time you did a sweat? Can you make a dream catcher? Do you speak your Native language? Do white people find you attractive? Questions like these are steeped in settler colonial narratives that seek to delegitimize Native people and support blood quotient levels that have been established by tribal and federal governments. In order for white settlers to claim the land from its original habitants, they had to either erase those inhabitants through genocide, or they had to make those inhabitants as much like them as possible—through forced assimilation, boarding schools, and the decimation of Native language and culture. When whites had sexual relations with Native people that resulted in children, "the child although racially half Native, through white supremacy and patriarchy becomes white, since inheritance under patriarchy is passed on through the father."[5] How tribal nations identify varies, as does identification from an individual perspective. Some AIAN people use their tribal nation as an identifier as opposed to, or in addition to, AIAN (i.e., Poarch Creek, Muscogee, Crow). The official term used by the United States government is American Indian. I identify as Creek, and my tribal identity is Poarch Band of Creek Indians. I also identify as Two-Spirit, an umbrella term used to signify gender and sexual orientation variance in Indigenous communities of North America, specifically Canada and the United States. The word associated with Two-Spirit

4 Roxanne Dunbar-Ortiz and Dina Gilio-Whitaker, *"All the Real Indians Died off": And 20 Other Myths about Native Americans* (Boston: Beacon Press, 2016), 146.

5 Qwo-Li Driskill, Chris Finley, Brian Gilley, and Scott Morgensen, eds., *Queer Indigenous Studies Critical Interventions in Theory, Politics, and Literature* (Tucson: University of Arizona Press, 2011), 36.

in my tribal language (Muscogee) is *ennvrkvpv* (pronounced "ee-nuth-ka-ba"), which translates to "in the middle."

Terms such as *berdache* and Two-Spirit exist as a counterpoint to perceptions of normative gender and/or sexual orientation behavior favored by Europeans. *Berdache* has appeared in ethnographic literature since the late sixteenth century.[6] The linguistic origins of the word are Arabic, from a Persian word that translates to male sexual slave.

Within social science fields, such as anthropology, it was a term to describe American Indians who did not fit dichotomous gender categories, and first appeared in colonial ethnographic literature in the later part of the sixteenth century.[7] Despite over 130 tribal nations already having language to describe gender and sexual orientation that falls outside Eurocentric heteronormative perspectives, *berdache* continues to be used in academic discourse. In 1990 a group of Native activists chose the term Two-Spirit to represent gender and sexual orientation variance in Native American and First Nations people. Two-Spirit was derived from the Northern Algonquin word *niizh manitoag*, which translates to "two spirits." Two-Spirit represents gender and sexual orientation expression and also applies to Two-Spirit people who perform traditional roles in their Native communities. Two-Spirit is an identity for Native American and First Nations people to use as best resonates with them. To claim Two-Spirit identity is to claim an Indigenous identity, and be inspired by traditional ways that may inspire their continuation, or their transformation into contemporary ways of knowledge, community, and healing. To claim a Two-Spirit identity is also to claim ownership of one's body and to claim sexual sovereignty.

I remember the first time I heard the term *berdache*. I was having a conversation with an older white male, Ed. He inquired about my racial and ethnic background, and I shared with him that I have a

---

6 Will Roscoe, "Bibliography of Berdache and Alternative Gender Roles among North American Indians," *Journal of Homosexuality* 14, no. 3–4 (1987): 81–171.

7 Roscoe, 81–171.

Native American mother and a white father. Ed stated, "Oh, so you're a *berdache*." I remember asking him what that means, and he said it means you're a gay Indian. When I went home that evening, I searched the term *berdache* online and found a variety of definitions from kept boy to male sexual slave.

I did not know about the term Two-Spirit until the early 2000s while living in New York City. Since I can remember, I have always experienced a sensation of both masculine and feminine qualities enveloping my identity, and I have also experienced sensations of sexual attraction to varying gender expressions. My otherness did not stop at my racial and ethnic identity. Rather, it found its way into almost every area of my life, rejecting binary classifications of identity.

I recognize terminology such as masculine and feminine is often subjugated to strict binary classifications. I also recognize that I have been socialized since childhood with Eurocentric values in regard to the expression of masculine and feminine tropes. Early in life I did not feel as balanced in my body as I do today. I felt the constant pull of white and Native, gay and straight, male and female. I felt the need to get close to homeostasis. I needed balance.

The 5Rhythms

When I was twenty years old I left North Dakota and moved to New York City. I did so to have an adventure and to also escape from the fear and trauma that was present at home. I worked various jobs: bookstore clerk, assistant, office manager, musician. Though I loved New York, I experienced a culture shock and struggled with feeling connected to my body. To find the balance I was seeking, I tried a variety of outlets. I started taking yoga classes and going to meditation workshops. I took part in spiritual communities, Two-Spirit community, performed music around the city, and experimented with sex, drugs, and rock and roll. These things were helpful, and yet I recognized there was room for more. I felt a shift in my life when I was introduced to the 5Rhythms practice.

The 5Rhythms is described as a moving meditation that involves people engaging their bodies to release emotional energy. A typical class is structured around what is called a wave, where people move through each of the five rhythms: flowing, staccato, chaos, lyrical, and stillness. Gabrielle Roth (1941–2012) created the practice. She developed the practice at the Esalen Institute in Big Sur, California, where 5Rhythms workshops continue to this day. She believed our bodies were key to connecting with our authentic self, what Bowen would call the somatic sense of self. Engaging with the 5Rhythms offers the mover an opportunity to let go, and then let go of letting go, and finally let go of letting go of letting go.

When I took my first class, Gabrielle's son, Jonathan, was leading the practice. I entered the room and watched as bodies of all shapes, sizes, ethnicities, and sexual expressions moved to Middle Eastern string instruments and light percussive beats. I closed my eyes, surrendered to the rhythm, and began a dance that would forever change my life. Two hours later, covered in sweat, feeling lighter and freer than I had in ages, I knew why I had moved to New York City. I came to free myself through dance. In the dance, I did not feel conflicted or restrained by any of my identities. I was there in all of my totality. Every part of my being was welcomed on the dance floor. Years of shame, aggression, heartache, and fear were released in that first class. It was the greatest therapy I had experienced.

After experiencing my first 5Rhythms class in New York City, I set out on a peregrination of consciousness. I longed to find a way to break down the walls that I had built, and the 5Rhythms practice became the heart-opening guide I had been searching for. I read the books that Gabrielle had written[8] and listened to the music[9] she had created. I took workshops with her and other instructors in an effort to deepen my understanding of each individual rhythm. The

---

8 Gabrielle Roth, *Sweat Your Prayers: Movement as Spiritual Practice* (Dublin: Newleaf, 1989); *Maps to Ecstasy* (London: Thorsons, 1999).

9 Gabrielle Roth and the Mirrors, *Endless Wave*, Vol. 1, (1996); *Trance* (1992); *Bones* (1988); *Jhoom* (2008).

5Rhythms became the interlocutor on my epistemological journey of self-understanding. To borrow a sentiment from Mary Whitehouse,[10] I felt alive because I moved, and I moved because I was alive.

The 5Rhythms are broken down between flowing, staccato, chaos, lyrical, and stillness, but "the rhythms don't only exist in the dance; they infuse every aspect of our lives."[11] The rhythm of flowing invites a sense of fluidity and yin energy. Movements in flowing are circular, each gesture evolving into the next. The rhythm of staccato is percussive, yang energy, which evokes sharp, linear movements. Flowing and staccato merge to form the rhythm of chaos in which the dancer begins the real work of letting go, "swept up in some primal rite; falling deeper and deeper ... plugged into something bigger than yourself, vibrantly alive."[12] Once you have danced through chaos, the mover is greeted by the rhythm of lyrical. In lyrical the movements are light, springy, grounded yet free. Finally, the dancer comes to meet stillness where the attention is drawn to the inner dance and the process of letting go of letting go takes place. Together these 5Rhythms create the framework for a movement meditation that I, and countless others, have also used as a movement therapy.

In ways that are practical, subtle, profound, and deep, the 5Rhythms have woven their way in my day-to-day life. One of the greatest lessons I learned from the practice is the ability to find space in crowded environments. When I feel overwhelmed by crowds walking down the street, or in airports and the like, I take a deep breath and look for the spaces in between the feet. Once I find the space, I begin my own rhythmic dance with those around me. I allow my shoulders to dip and my torso to turn. My feet move, light as air, and reach into

---

[10] Mary Starks Whitehouse, *Authentic Movement: Essays by Mary Starks Whitehouse, Janet Adler and Joan Chodorow. Vol. 1.* ed. Patrizia Pallaro (London: Philadelphia, 1999), p. 37.

[11] Roth, *Sweat Your Prayers* 33.

[12] Roth, 33.

the open spaces. I weave in and out of these human traffic jams until I break free from the chaos, and am once again held by the stillness.

Since I began working with the 5Rhythms over fifteen years ago, I have been drawn to certain rhythms more than others. Each rhythm holds different mysteries that we unlock when we inquire to the moment. Given what I am experiencing at any given time in my life, a rhythm will dominate my thoughts and expressions. I like being able to name particular experiences I'm having and using the rhythms as my guide. From a rhythms perspective, I can recognize that I am in a particular state such as flowing or lyrical. I will know this by the way my body responds to the space around it. My awareness as my body relates to other bodies is also indicative of what rhythmic state I feel I am in. The 5Rhythms helped me process various challenges that I have had in my life. I have used and been inspired by Gabrielle's work to heal from the disembodied feelings I had while growing up. In the 5Rhythms, I found the safety and support to explore issues concerning my sexuality, my perceived failures and accomplishments, my biracial and bicultural identity, and the trauma that impacted my body, mind, and spirit. When I am engaging in a 5Rhythms practice, I feel connected to my seven-year-old self, dancing with my ancestors. The 5Rhythms differed from other movement-based modalities, such as yoga, because the movements were of my own creating. There is not a prescribed way that the flowing, staccato, chaos, lyrical, or stillness is supposed to look like. Unlike asana practice, I have never been given an adjustment during my practice, only permission to allow myself to go deeper and deeper in the wave.

Flowing

Flowing: soft, feminine, circular, forgiving, inhalation.

When I think of my mother, I am immersed in the rhythm of flowing. In this rhythm, I am reminded of the time on the reservation when my feet connected with the soil and I had a vision of my ancestors. The rhythm of flowing starts in the feet, rooting down into Mother

Earth. As you let go and allow your body to surrender to flowing, you will feel the rhythm in your knees, your hips, elbows, shoulders, neck, and head. Here the movements of the body are wide, circular, steady, and connected. The rhythm of flowing has always had an ease in my somatic experience, and perhaps my Two-Spirit identity is the reason this ease has always been present, as I do not live my life in a gendered binary expression, though I do identify with male pronouns.

I remember when I came out as gay to my mother in the summer of 1997. I was twenty-one years old and living in New York City. I had not yet discovered the 5Rhythms, yet dancing was already a part of my creative expression. My mother took the news of my sexuality well, not asking many questions at the time, and she stated that as long as I was happy, she was happy. I did not anticipate her not accepting me; she always had.

My mother and I had formed a close bond over the years and remain close to this day. In the early years of my life my mother tried to help me understand my mixed-race identity. While my white father insisted my sisters and I were raised as Roman Catholics, my mother was nonpracticing and during church would sit in the pew while the rest of us performed the rituals familiar to Catholics around the world. My mother's refusal to convert to Catholicism was an act of resistance that would inspire my social justice activism. I remember many times after Sunday mass when my mother would take me to the woods on our family farm and share a differing viewpoint than the one I had just encountered in church. My mother offered my sisters and myself a combination of Indigenous spiritual views with a small dose of Christian ideology. Her worldview was the one that resonated with me more than what I was learning in Catholic mass and the Sunday school teachings that would follow. My mother's spiritual views always included the earth and our ancestors. No guilt was associated with her teachings, nor was I required to do penance for sins I had committed. There were no Hail Marys or Lord's Prayers. Instead, we burnt sage and danced and laughed and sang. We gave thanks to the breath maker, to the animals, and to our ancestors for keeping us safe. My mother made it a priority that I understood and connected with my Indigeneity. She instilled pride in our Native culture and told me to always stand up for myself and to never abandon our ancestors.

When I began to show a proclivity for the arts, she encouraged me to follow my passion. When my parents eventually split up, she would drive me to dance class or to theater rehearsal, usually on little sleep as she was working the graveyard shift as a nurse at a local hospital. I never heard her complain, though I could tell she was tired, not just from working as hard as she did, but also from the recovery from her own trauma she experienced at the hands of my father.

I think of the rhythm of flowing as a celebration of my mother. I think of the rhythm of flowing as gratitude for the life that she gave me and for the passion she inspired in me. I think of the rhythm of flowing as an acknowledgment to my mother and to all the mothers of the world (including Mother Earth), for their selfless acts of unconditional love and continued support. It makes perfect sense to me that the 5Rhythms begins with the feminine. Without the influence of the feminine, I would be lost. Without the love of my mother, I would be lost.

When I am dancing the rhythm of flowing, I am able to begin the process of releasing my soma from the constrictions it has been holding. The trauma that had been buried in my right hip since that tragic night years ago is able to slowly release itself as it is held, supported, and loved in the rhythm of flowing. I do not have to hide my emotional and physical pain in this rhythm as I am supported by the divine feminine and held close to her heart. In flowing, I am guided by the ancestors.

Staccato

Staccato: sharp, angular, heated, percussive, exhalation.

My father was raised in a rural farming community in North Dakota. After serving in the Navy, he married my mother, who had recently been divorced with two children. He adopted my older sisters and they took his surname after my parents' marriage. He had two children with my mother and raised four. He died on November 18, 1999, five days after his fiftieth birthday. I remember at his wake I went off into a side room and began to cry. My aunt found me and said it was okay to be sad. I told her I wasn't crying because I was sad. I was crying because I was finally free.

My father embodied all the things I detest about male privilege. He was arrogant, selfish, unaware, and ignorant. When his physical abuse toward me happened the first time, I had already accepted that I would eventually be the receiver of his rage. My father told me to always tell people that I was German American. He valued white male privilege. If I identified as white, I would further validate his whiteness. His role as colonizer continued in how he tried to make me identify in the world. When I would get in trouble, he would make cruel jokes about my sexuality and my ethnicity. Years of living in a constant state of hypervigilance had given me a tight torso region. I had shaped my body as if it were an armor to protect me from his perceived and real threats of violence toward me.

In the rhythm of staccato I began to explore the boundaries I had created around my relationship to my father. I explored how I held myself rigid whenever he was near, always needing to be ready to defend myself. In the rhythm of staccato I learned how to use my exhalation as repudiation of his toxic masculinity. I used my body to release the rage and fear I felt about him. My elbows yielded shields that protected my heart. My arms were swords that cut through my fears. My legs acted as spears piercing the lies, shame, and aggression my father evoked in my life. My body organized to protect myself while also letting go of pain.

I have always struggled with the rhythm of staccato. Grief has no time line and though I have accepted certain truths about my father, I continue to grieve what he stole from our family. Flashes of my father are always with me in staccato. I never want to stay in this rhythm long. Yet, over the years I have been able to recognize there is also beauty in this rhythm, and alongside struggle there is love for staccato. Thoughts of my father while I am dancing are rare these days. Dancing staccato helped me to release and let go of a lot of the metaphorical armor that I had been wearing. I had to release as much of the armor as possible so that I could experience the ecstasy of chaos.

Chaos

Chaos: energized, connected, releasing, cathartic.

In the rhythm of chaos your body, mind, and spirit surrender to the moment. In this rhythm, the binaries of feminine and masculine energies meet. Here, yin and yang combine in the realm of connectivity. We move from one end of the spectrum to the other, reveling in all the sweet spots we meet along the way. If we can free the body to connect to both the feminine and the masculine energy within all of us, we can continue to move toward homeostasis.

The rhythm of chaos is where I have taken the deepest dive into the exploration of my sexuality. When I think of the term *ennvrkvpv*, I think of the rhythm of chaos. Chaos offered the space for me to explore not only gender binaries, but also tropes of Native American and European American identity. I also explored sexual orientation variance and discovered that I identify as sexually fluid in terms of whom I am attracted to sexually (in behavior and thought). In chaos, there is an exploration of my sexuality, and chaos is the gateway to freeing my body into a state of ecstasy.

The feeling of ecstasy in my sexual experiences and sexual expression is important. I value sexuality as an integral component in understanding the totality of my being. I define ecstasy as a state of release that leads to euphoric feelings throughout the mind, body, and spirit. Ecstasy often is thought about in relation to sexual behavior, yet I use ecstasy to express all aspects of sexuality. When I think of Two-Spirit identity, I think of ecstasy, a state of connection to the totality of one's spirit. In the rhythm of ecstasy, I do not feel the conflict of biracial identity. The complexity my biracial identity adds to my sexuality is not present in the rhythm of chaos because of the feeling of ecstasy this rhythm evokes. When I move through the rhythm of chaos, I explore all aspects of my identity. It is through this exploration of the intersections of my identity that have helped me gain acceptance of my uniqueness in the world. Through the rhythm of chaos, I understand how catharsis feels in the body. In my experience, chaos leads to catharsis.

The breakthroughs I was having while moving in the rhythm of chaos were profound. I learned to trust my instincts and to not judge my past and current experiences. In chaos, I found mindfulness. I could connect to the here and the now because it was in this rhythm that I found balance. I ceased to be the labels I had been given, and the ones I had given to myself. In chaos, I was free to be who I was; all of my flaws and all of my joys were welcome.

Chaos is like Grand Central Station during rush hour on a Friday afternoon. Chaos is like a looming deadline that is both exciting and exhausting. Chaos is like the first time you are with a new lover, somewhat awkward, but also uninhibited. Chaos is pain, and rage, and bliss, and love all moving together. Chaos is two spirits connecting as one.

Lyrical

Lyrical: ethereal, jovial, light, patient, free.

When I first started to practice the 5Rhythms, I found myself called to the rhythm of chaos. In chaos, I would scream, undulate my body, and fall on the floor writhing around. I would dance with my darkness and be cradled with love in my pain. Chaos would lead to catharsis, which would lead to the rhythm of lyrical. Gabrielle Roth states, "If we don't completely let go of all the stuff that we carry ... we get stuck in chaos."[13] I recognized this was a problem I was encountering. I wanted to continue holding onto chaos, because it was the only time I felt confident to confront the obstacles in my life.

---

[13] Roth, 157.

Chaos grants us the opportunity to break free, yet I was not allowing myself to welcome freedom fully into my life. I had interpreted letting go of chaos as a letting go of my capacity to fight. If I let go of chaos, I would also let go of courage. This hypervigilance consumed my body and armored me from years of trauma in my past. It took many years of dancing the 5Rhythms before I understood that letting go does not mean *gone.* Letting go does not mean packing everything up and burying it as if it doesn't exist anymore. Letting go means that we shift our response to the triggers in our life, because that is all we can do. I have realized the triggers I have in my life aren't going anywhere. That does not mean that I have to react toward them as I always have. I can be the change I want to see in the world and with conscious choice that is possible. If problems I have in my life are reminiscent of a rhythm, then lyrical is now my chosen way to shifting my reaction to them. I see the triggers for what they are and instead of rebelling against them, I welcome them into my life. I take back the power I have given to them. I am patient with my triggers and no longer struggle with my window of tolerance disappearing and being pulled back into fight, flight, or freeze. Lyrical helped me understand what it means to be free: it simply means letting go.

Stillness

Stillness: quiet, complete, grounded, whole.

Across from my childhood home there was a large field. One of the few positive memories I have about my father involves a conversation we had about that field. I remember asking him why the field was not producing new crops. He told me the field had gone fallow. The earth needed to maintain its richness and needed to become still for a few years. He said the earth needed to slow down, that it was a good thing, and in a few years, we would see the results of our patience. I would never see those results as my parents separated before the field was planted again. Perhaps that is one of the reasons why I struggled with the rhythm stillness when I first started to practice the 5Rhythms. I hadn't learned to trust a fallow field.

Years later I was in graduate school studying somatic psychotherapy and one of my professors mentioned the fallow field. Memories of my childhood and my father danced in my head and I realized this was a full circle moment. Now in my private practice, I often talk to clients about the concept of the fallow field as an example of patience and growth. This does not come without stillness. Stillness does not mean standing still or lying down. Stillness does not mean thanatosis.

I have feared slowing down because I have always been on the move. My body feared stillness because of the vulnerability I would encounter. I slowly began to trust the feeling of letting go in my physical body, as well as my mental and spiritual bodies as well. Thich Nhat Hanh says that when we let go we are letting go of something. What was it that I was not allowing myself to let go of? Anger? Fear? Sadness? Shame? Yes, all of those and more. These emotions were my security blanket. They had protected me for years and still had work to be done. I began to question all the congestion I felt in my life. I questioned why I was holding onto beliefs and behaviors that no longer served me. The rhythm of stillness gave me a space to explore the fear I had in making a radical shift in my life. I had to learn that I was the fallow field.

The greatest shift did appear in my life, I fell in love, and he loved me back. I believe because I practiced the 5Rhythms and had investigated each rhythm on its own I was ready and open to sharing and receiving love. Accepting love into your life feels radical, almost dangerous. I'm still working on myself and now I have to trust someone else too? Yes, you do and it is a wondrous experience. Do not fear the stillness; allow it to envelop you and gently prepare you to move through the rhythms again.

Applicability

The 5Rhythms introduced me to a new epistemology, rooted in the symbiosis of mind, body, and spirit. I applied this understanding to my studies in somatic psychology. Later, I would apply the theories behind the rhythms to how I would think about my clinical work. Using body tracking, I sense into the rhythm that I feel is present in the session. Knowing my rhythmic structure informs how I can remain present during sessions. It also informs interventions that are presented during sessions. I also believe knowing my rhythmic structure gives me security. Sometimes I find myself needing balance after a session. If I know my rhythmic structure, I can move for a few moments in that rhythm. In my experiences, movement has always been a welcome way to attain homeostasis.

Though I do not teach the 5Rhythms to clients, I use the philosophy of the rhythms as part of my soma-cultural perspective. For example, in my work as a somatic sex therapist I am often helping people navigate their relationships and how they view love, intimacy, sex, and pleasure. With the advent of technology, clients are also learning how to navigate dating and relationship applications that are on their computers and mobile devices. The rhythms have inspired what I call the cycle of inquiry, a relational model that uses five areas of exploration of the somatic sense of self. These include initiation, engagement, intimacy, rejection (or acceptance), and shame.

Initiation mirrors flowing as it is the space in which we enter the relational dance. Initiation is about crossing the threshold of fear, acknowledging our desire for connection, and opening to the possibility of vulnerability. Engagement is like staccato as it is the space where we challenge our resistance. Engagement is about trusting our instincts and pushing ourselves to go after what we want. Intimacy is an extension of chaos as it is the space where our fears, joys, passions, and desires come together. Intimacy is about meeting our anxieties and our excitation from a place of nonjudgment. Rejection (or acceptance) reminds me of lyrical as it is the space where we have broken free from our fears and joys and are able to reflect. Rejection (or acceptance) is about knowing your truth in the moment. Finally, I think of shame like I think of stillness. Though shame has a negative connotation for most people, I view shame as an opportunity for surrender, to grow still, to dance within the fallow field. When using the cycle of inquiry, we can spend multiple sessions on just one aspect of this relational model. Similar to the 5Rhythms, clients may feel more at ease or more trepidations about different branches of this modality. My role as clinician is to help them move between these branches in all their challenging, beautiful, engrossing, clumsy, graceful, and evocative movements.

There are numerous ways a clinical practice can be informed from the 5Rhythms. My example of the cycle of inquiry is just one intervention that has been inspired this modality.

In my office, I keep copies of Gabrielle's books *Sweat Your Prayers, Maps to Ecstasy,* and *Connections.* I have her music on my mobile device at all times. In between sessions I find myself drawn to the highlights and notations I have made throughout these books or I will listen to one of her songs when I need to feel balanced. If I am feeling disembodied after a session, I sense into the rhythm that I am feeling, move with the rhythm for a bit, and then read a highlighted passage from one of Gabrielle's books focusing on the particular rhythm. Over the years I have appreciated how the rhythms are always present; I do not need Gabrielle's words or her music to connect to the rhythms (though I do appreciate them). I need only to use my breath to connect the rhythms for they are always a part of my life.

One of the aspects of the 5Rhythms I value is their continuation. The rhythms are like the waves of an ocean, always shifting. I have been moving through the 5Rhythms for fifteen years and each wave has always been different. I have had the pleasure of dancing next to Gabrielle, learning from her son, Jonathan, and being welcomed by a diverse community of people who celebrated the pleasures and pains of life. In 2012, Gabrielle Roth transitioned to her final stillness. Her work will continue through the dedication of 5Rhythms students and practitioners across the globe who will continue to move their way through flowing, staccato, chaos, lyrical, and stillness on the dance floor, and perhaps more importantly, off the dance floor.

What I have discovered is the importance of understanding my bodily experience in the world. The way that I think about my work as a somatic psychotherapist is informed from this body-based somacultural perspective, of which the 5Rhythms is just one avenue of exploration. Through the rhythms I found a form of communication that helped me to let go and inquire about my somatic sense of self.

I have moved to a place of comfort with the multiple ways I identify in the world. I feel less conflicted about my biracial identity. I also feel less triggered when I think about the trauma I have experienced in my life. The 5Rhythms helped with working through the complex feelings associated with the struggles I endured. Having moved through the rhythms, I am confident I can help others move through the various struggles in their life, one rhythm at a time.

Conclusion

I'd like to take you back for a moment to the two fields that I mentioned earlier. First, the field in Alabama on the Poarch Band of Creek Indians reservation where I had a vision of my ancestors while dancing. Second, the fallow field that was a part of my childhood farm. These fields held such wisdom that I was not aware of until I started to move through the 5Rhythms. The power of the earth to evoke the ancestors, and the power of the earth to rejuvenate itself through patience and stillness serve as powerful reminders of what my body, my totality can also do. When I begin my 5Rhythms practice, I always evoke my ancestors and my family. I call on my grandmothers Dorothy and Elda to guide me through flowing. I call on my grandfathers JB and John to guide me in staccato. I call on my mother and my father to join me in chaos and dance through our trauma and our pain. I call on my sisters to break free and join me in lyrical where we can heal together. Finally, I call on my husband to join me in stillness where we can enjoy our love, celebrate our freedom, and patiently await the next chapter of our lives. I leave you with an excerpt from a song I wrote called "2 Nations."[14]

The blood of the women who have died courses through my body
The blood of the men who have died courses through my veins
I run with the horses as I fly in the helicopters

14 Roger Kuhn, "2 Nations" in *Proof*, Roger Kuhn, 2006, CD.

I know what I'm not, but I don't know who I am
Raised off the rez, does that make me white instead?
Can I finally claim my brown blood, now that my daddy's dead?
So tell me am I free because I have sovereignty?
Yeah, I have my CDIB, I have the four directions within me
So what do you see, brown or white?
Or do you see the berdache in me?
I have my own philosophy, and it's so easy
But I have reservations
I have reservations
I come from reservations
I come from reservations

Those words continue to be true, but no longer bear the emotional weight they did when I first wrote them. Today, I have a better idea of who I am. I know that I identify as a mixed-race Native American of European descent. I know I identify as Two-Spirit, gay, and sexually fluid. I know I identify as a dancer, artist, activist, a husband, son, brother, and friend. I know I am loved and seen by those who matter to me, and I know I love them as well. I know my power, positionality, and privilege are fleeting moments in time. I know my epistemology continues to evolve. I know my body holds wisdom and truth. I know that I have a lot more to learn about life, and love, and pleasure, and pain. I know that whenever I am in doubt, whenever I have fear, whenever I want to express joy, or anger, or anxiety, I have the 5Rhythms to guide me through the wave. Thank you, Gabrielle.

Bibliography

Bowen, Bill. *Somatic Resourcing: Psychotherapy through the Body.* Portland: PPT Publishing, 2009. http://www.psychophysicaltherapy.com/ppt/publications.html.

Driskill, Qwo-Li, Chris Finley, Brian Gilley, and Scott Morgensen, eds. *Queer Indigenous Studies Critical Interventions in Theory, Politics, and Literature.* Tucson: University of Arizona Press, 2011.

Dunbar-Ortiz, Roxanne, and Dina Gilio-Whitaker. *"All the Real Indians Died off": And 20 Other Myths about Native Americans.* Boston: Beacon Press, 2016.

Katz, Jonathan Ned. *The Invention of Heterosexuality.* Chicago: The University of Chicago Press, 2007.

Kuhn, Roger, "2 Nations," in *Proof,* Roger Kuhn. 2006, CD.

Ogunwole, Stella U. The American Indian and Alaska Native population: 2000. Washington: US Census Bureau, 2002, http://www.census.gov/prod/2002pubs/c2kbr01-15.pdf.

Roscoe, Will. "Bibliography of Berdache and Alternative Gender Roles among North American Indians." *Journal of Homosexuality* 14, no. 3–4 (1987): 81–171.

Roth, Gabrielle. *Connections: The Threads of Intuitive Wisdom.* Cork: BookBaby, 2014.

———. *Maps to Ecstasy: Teachings of an Urban Shaman.* London: Thorsons, 1999.

———. *Sweat Your Prayers: Movement as Spiritual Practice.* Dublin: Newleaf, 1989.

Roth, Gabrielle, and the Mirrors. *Bones.* 1988.

———. *Endless Wave.* Vol. 1, 1996.

———. *Jhoom.* 2008.

———. *Trance.* 1992.

Takacs, David. "How Does Your Positionality Bias Your Epistemology?" *Thought and Action Journal* 19, no. 1 (2003): 27–38. http://repository.uchastings.edu/faculty_scholarship/1264.

Chapter 2

Multiple Paths: Intersectional Pneumasomatic Approaches to Mental Health

Alyssa N. Zelaya, AMFT

Introduction

In Lukumi practices—as in many traditional and indigenous spiritual practices that had to be hidden in order to survive and continue under the noses of colonizers—there is an air of secrecy in the what, how, and why we do what is done in ceremony. Lukumi ceremony is officiated behind an opaque white sheet signifying the entrance to the *igbodú* (meaning the womb of the forest/wilderness)—the sacred ceremony room where religious rites are being performed. It is done this way, both to discourage curious eyes that have not yet earned the right to know, as well as to honor the sanctity of the knowledge that is being earned behind closed doors. In order to step into that room and work any ceremony, a person has to be complete of their novice year (*iyaworaje*) and must be presented to the room by their godparents as a rite of passage. It is within the *igbodú* that a person's spiritual transformation takes place witnessed only by the priests participating in the crowning of the *orisha* to that person. If an *aleyo* or *aborisha* (an outsider or non-practicing follower of the religion, respectively) were to take a peek, they may not actually understand what they are seeing although it may seem obvious. Knowledge and perspective are key.

I begin my chapter here because many of my ideas and approaches stem from within the *igbodú* and from the space of my personal transformation from *aborisha* into *iyawo* (novice), and *iyawo* into *olorisha* (priest). I hope to explain and describe what, how, and why this perspective—and the foundations of other disciplines and practices described throughout this chapter—inform my approaches to somatic work without letting anything out from behind the white sheet of knowledge. My truth and my belief is that when you are initiated into and committed to any path, you are unofficially in ceremony all the time. I silently represent the many paths that I have come into contact with that have shaped me and my movements through space and time—everywhere I walk, I am a crowned priestess of Shango; *soy danzante*; I am a Reiki master; I am Mea Hula—it's something I wear on my skin that no one can see, but I've been told many times that it is felt. It is somewhere between philosophy and faith that I find myself writing this chapter about the practical somatic psychotherapy applications of ancient ways of belief and movement. I am in no way an expert in any of these ways that influence me, but this work that I do is an extension of all of the working knowledge I have earned. It is soul work that gets filtered through these many bodies that carry me, namely Catholic, Lukumi, Hula, *danzante* (Aztec dancer), Reiki, *bruja* (witch), and *milagro* (miracle).

Sometime in 1995, I wandered into a newly opened storefront up the street from my house. It looked like a bookstore, but turned out to be a religious shop, a *botanica*. I would spend hours in there asking questions about the herbs in jars, wondering about the fascinating objects I was looking at, reading about Afro-Caribbean religions, buying dressed candles, and learning what I could from observing the owner working with other customers. I may have thought at the time that this was a welcome distraction from my life, just a fun way to spend my time—learning, being curious, submitting to an energy in that space that seemed to be attracting me. I bought my first book on Santeria (another name for Lukumi)—an Afro-Cuban religion based on Yoruba beliefs and traditions mixed with Roman Catholic elements—and I was excited to read it as soon as I got home. The distraction that felt essential at this time in my life was getting away from feelings of emptiness, a sense of being lost and unwell without truly grasping what I was needing to feel better. On the surface, I was going through the motions that everything was as it should be. Although not all things were perfect, I was in school; I was a faithful *danzante*; I lived at home with my family; I had all the reasons to be grateful and, yet, I felt so disconnected from myself.

A few years later, through some twists and turns and with the help of my now-Madrina, I found myself sitting on a short stool on top of a grass mat facing a man I'd never met, dressed in all white. He said, "Call me 'Padrino.'" I sat in silence as he began reciting prayers in another language, throwing and analyzing the up-turned and down-turned cowry shells, then confirming random but true facts about my life, pausing only to continue throwing and counting the shells again and again. He sat there verbally pointing out the holes and pains in my soul that had never been spoken out loud. It was like being seen and understood for the first time, yet I hadn't shared anything more than my name and my date of birth. The floodgates opened and I sobbed. I suddenly felt less crazy, less alone, less misguided. He prescribed what was needed for me as assigned through the numeric formations of the shells that represent the mouthpiece of the many *orisha*.

A *diloggun* reading (cowry shell divination), as I have come to understand it, assigns an *odun* (a sign/pattern) to your current situation through the number of the cowry shells facing up or down on the mat. Each *odun* is determined to come in either *iré* (blessings) or *osogbo* (misfortunes), and the *pataki* (fable-like story) that accompanies each *odun* reveals the purpose of your visit from the point of view of the *orisha*. The blessings from the sign being in *iré* are never truly permanent, nor are the misfortunes of a sign being in *osogbo*. Advice from the *oriate* (the shell diviner) is given on how you can hold on to those blessings for longer, or they give you a prescription (*ebbo/ebó*) on what can be done to shift the energy of the *osogbo* and receive the *iré* of that odun. Examples of *ebbo* prescriptions or advice can be anything from you lighting candles and praying for your ancestors who may feel abandoned, cleaning yourself with herbs, or perhaps being directed to seek out medical advice or make a lifestyle change for the betterment of your health. An *ebbo* can also include being given the option to participate in and receive ceremonies that are suggested only when there's a need to make more drastic or urgent shifts. Just as a Western doctor determines what can be done for your health—whether they prescribe medication or have to set bones back into place or suggest surgery—the *oriate* uses their knowledge and expertise to assign, or mark, the *ebbo* needed just for you. In my case, I was told that I was living my life with "one foot in the grave, like a ghost," perhaps not due to physical illness, but because death followed me. I was told that although I was not actively seeking danger, I was constantly making choices that encouraged my possible demise. It was true on so many levels. I was, in fact, living a secret life and making literally and figuratively bad choices in deciding where I wanted to go and whom I brought into my life to take me there. Perhaps I made such deviant choices to fill that indescribable emptiness.

I was advised that what was necessary in my case, if I was willing, was to partake in a day-long ceremony to receive the *eleke* (consecrated beaded necklace/flag) of Babalu Aye/Asojano (the *orisha* synchronized with Saint Lazarus in Catholicism). Among other things, Babalu Aye teaches humankind the concept of limitations, self-discipline, repercussions, and mortality. It is through our conscious lifestyle choices that we either choose to live longer or die earlier. It is said that he teaches us the importance of abiding by the laws of the universe and behaving accordingly; he then tests us to see if we have learned this lesson and issues a suitable consequence. For example, if humans have a natural and biological desire to seek out pleasure, Asojano may extend a test to see if this desire for pleasure-seeking can be easily turned into greed; he examines our willpower to see if we take only enough of what we need and not fall into the trap of spending our energies grabbing beyond what is necessary. The possible outcomes of failing this test of desire and greed, for instance, may be anything from being plagued by an illness/disease or living with an addiction, either one leading us to possible death. If you pass the test, Babalu Aye may send fewer obstacles and challenges your way and perhaps bless you with health after an illness.

It's believed among Lukumi practitioners, as in other Yoruban-based belief systems, that each *orisha* can be described as a living force, an energy, or a spirit that has its place in nature and in our surroundings. Eleggua is the energy of beginnings and endings, which guards the doorways, entrances, and crossroads taking you from one place into another; Oggun is the energy of labor and industry. With his brute force, he clears paths and invokes both destruction and progress. Yemaya is the energy of motherhood and familial relationships. She is all of the seven seas and the act of traveling to faraway lands; she is the rain and the ocean; she is Mother Earth and Mother Nature. Ochun is the energy of self-love and romantic relationships. She is the sweet and indulgent yet unbridled force of the river; she is our self-esteem, our ability to be in relationship with others, and our sense of love and happiness. In 1999, I chose to receive my first *eleke* as prescribed by Padrino, and at my own discretion, returned for many readings that led to many *ebbos* and, eventually, led to many other ceremonies, including my priesthood/crowning ceremony in 2002. I had found my place.

Again and again, I share space with clients whose life is not quite right at the moment; they are not feeling like their best self. They are seeking help to get back to a person who existed before whatever it was that occurred led them to feel this way. I sit with them … a person they've never met before, ready to discover all of their secrets and hopefully help them reconnect to their best selves. My approach is this: I tend to view clients and their current situations the way I tend to view the world. We are all in search of some form of balance, of centering, of discovering the heart or root of the pain that needs to be recognized and healed in order for us to move forward. In order to attain this balance within ourselves and with our surroundings, we must first know that it is attainable, and secondly that if we have not yet attained it, then the conclusion is that something is missing or blocking us from getting to it … and so begins my process of investigation. Being that I am not an *oriate* and therapy sessions are not *diloggun* readings, I am forced to use the tools, skills, and training accessible to me in the moment.

This conceptual philosophy of seeking to be or feel internally in sync with the external is an ancient one, and examples can be found in many, if not all, spiritual practices and thought. This external "universe" that we may be intending to connect to and be in alignment with can be anything: our immediate environment, nature, space/time, or a higher power. We create things outside of ourselves from an inspiration that seems to be happening internally; yet, all that is external may be the muse for that inspiration. What is art if it's not a need to express ourselves? And what is expression if it's not coming from a place of perspective? Perspective, by definition, is a position taken in relation to the "other." I contend that what manifests through creation and inspiration is actually reflection of the other. Following the saying attributed to Hermes Trismegistus, "As above, so below," I find that, within a somatic psychotherapy context, "As within, so without" rings true. Chakras, karma, yin and yang, Sufi whirlers, Mesoamerican pyramids, and Stonehenge seem to have a common theme of internal, psychological, or spiritual inspiration for expression, linking to something external and a need to physically manifest or reflect that inspiration with the purpose of finding peace or creating balance within the self and with the inspired-beings' surroundings. It is a gesture, it is a movement, it is a dance, it is stillness, it is a repetitive action or word, it is art, it is music, it is birth, it is death, it is divine connection, and it is choice.

Even down to our smallest body parts, something internal is constantly needing to maintain homeostasis and will act according to the needs of the whole. Every cell in the body has a micro-purpose that supports the system it functions within, and a macro-purpose of maintaining life (i.e., white blood cells multiply when the internal body temperature rises in order to heal the body). We are like that cell, outwardly reacting to changes within ourselves and shifting our environment to create or recreate what is on the inside.

East

The direction of the East is the direction of the sunrise, the birth of the light, and the element of fire. East is where movement is born and where everything (life) begins. Fire is an element that aids our survival by heating our bodies for warmth, heating our food for consumption, and providing nutrients to the earth for the growing of food and supporting life. For Indigenous people of the Americas, the eastern direction is represented by the color red and the energy of masculinity, extroversion, and physical strength. Red is the color of the root chakra that sits at the base of our spine bringing stability, identity, and survival. For practitioners of Lukumi, it is the color of *epó* (palm oil) used as a spiritual medicine to ward against malevolent spirits that can harm us. In Catholicism, the colors red as well as purple are worn to represent the Passion of Christ that leads to His rebirth, the blood of Christ, and the Pentecost—the descent of the Holy Spirit, often considered to be the birth of the Catholic Church and the emergence of the phenomenon of speaking in holy tongues (also called "tongues of fire").[1]

Red has its purpose and place in these many belief systems. There is a time, place, and purpose for everything, as suggested in Ecclesiastes 3:1-8. Catholicism was my introduction to ideas of mysticism, purpose, and ritual. I was eleven years old when I became an altar server for my parish church; I sometimes would serve two masses back-to-back since I loved being a participant in the ritual rather than an observer. I was fascinated by the customs and flowing movement of it all. Everything had its place, meaning, and intention. It was my earliest observation of the creation of sacred space. The altar with its white cloth linen overlay,

---

1 Katie Scott, "What do Liturgical Colors Mean?" The Arlington Catholic Herald. Catholicherald.com. December 14, 2017. https://www.catholicherald.com/Faith/What_do_liturgical_colors_mean_/.

the offertory table with its holy water and wine, ringing the bell in recognition of the Body or Blood of Christ, bowing heads, the memorized communal prayer, the genuflections made in reverence, receiving the Eucharist in the left hand and picking it up with your right. During mass, I would relish the comfort of the predictable and expected—now we stand, now we kneel, now we sit, now we sing, here is where we offer peace, we hold hands to recite the Our Father, and so on.

Meanwhile at home with my non-church-going-but-devoted Catholic family, an annual altar was built in devotion to the Virgin Mary of the Immaculate Conception where certain elements were considered necessary—a statue of the Virgin Mary placed high up as in ascension, burning of frankincense, a blue and white overlay for the altar, twinkling lights or stars as decoration. Sacred space was created by nine days of prayer and song, and food was made to share with the community of people who came in devotion to sing and pray with us. Ceremonies such as this made it obvious to me that ritual is everywhere, that creation of sacred space was possible anywhere.

Through about twelve years of weekly *Xitontequisa* (Danza Azteca) commitments to the discipline of presentations and ceremony, I was shown the importance of the physical and intentional placement of elements for the altar. I saw how the order of where things belong creates the connection and induces an embodiment of prayer. Each *danzante* is purified with copal resin smoke, and the drum beat invokes the dancers to move their feet in a sacred pattern, which creates the *chachayotes* (rattles worn around the ankles) to harmonize and be in sync with the drum. Each participant holds a responsibility in the circle as individual elements of the prayer, including those with assigned roles to lead in the dancers and mark the steps to create the sacred circle as well as distribute the order of prayers (calling each *danzante* out to lead a prayer). Another carries the end of the line and helps maintain the balance of space and harmony of the circle; another holds and carries the smoke and forms the altar for each gathering and the drummers who hold the heart of the circle.

As each *danzante* is asked to lead a prayer; everyone follows in community, undulating as one and contributing to the vibrational uplift and shift. It's an overwhelm of the senses to witness—the movement connected to the sound connected to prayer. But even beyond that, each *danzante* becomes the manifestation of energy with the movement of each unique prayer/*danza*. We and the elements become one. We are all part of the altar where the copal smoke sits and carries our intentions up to Creator, candles to give light to our ancestors, some water to commune with spirit, elements such herbs, flowers, or corn for grounding us, and feathers or wind-related objects to lift our energy and help transform us. The altar itself is intended to reflect balance and harmony out to the circle and each participant. The *huehuetl* drum and the main altar (in the middle of the circle) face the East—the doorway—inviting sacred energies in to commune with us. It is important to note that without one of the many pieces, the ceremony is considered out of balance.

As a therapist, I try to recreate the same intention in the room with a client by starting our initial sessions asking them to tell me what they need in order to feel safe in the room. Often, the initial response may be a shrug or "I don't know." I begin to name examples: Do they prefer to sit close to the door, or a window, and why; I ask them if I'm speaking too loudly, if the lights are too bright, etc. Where should I sit in relation to them, where do things need to go, what feels right? In this therapeutic process, I begin to make the adjustments needed while the parallel process helps us to create our sacred therapy space. Often clients are not able to verbally express what their needs are, but they will, indeed, let you know if something feels off for them. It is at these moments that I'm grateful to have tools that give me something outside the scope of psychology theory to work with and implement. It's where my training calls for me to be prepared to name what the client seems to be expressing.

Moises

A six-year-old client, Moises sat on the floor in a summer program classroom throwing a tantrum because he didn't understand the math being explained—and because someone gave the answer that he was going to give! Moises is the youngest of three boys and his mom let me know that he has anger issues. He was prone to feelings of powerlessness that sparked and escalated into a rage and aggression, although his biggest triggers were his two older brothers who would either leave him out or explain why he was too "little" for some things. Moises was usually angry at everyone. In the classroom, a situation got out of control rather quickly as the mentor teaching his section and the summer program director, both frustrated, urged him to get off the floor as a way to try and neutralize the situation and stop the disruption by telling him to sit in his chair and quiet down. This only fanned the flame, so to speak. Being expected to quiet down or "behave" was a call for Moises to force his emotions into containment, causing an imbalance that manifested as aggression and a need to take action—he would not be quieted down, but would lash out and be louder and more dramatic.

My opportunity presented itself for me to meet Moises where he was at—I sat with him on the floor next to him, let him know that I saw his anger, and encouraged it to be present.

> *Me: You're angry; that's okay. You can be angry. What do you want to do?*
>
> *Moises: (through tears) I hate math; I'm not going to do this stupid work (tears part of his paper).*
>
> *Me: You want to tear up that paper? Let's do it together....*

I let him do most of the tearing as I vocalized, in a playfully angry voice and scowling face, how much we hated this paper and how satisfying it was to destroy that paper with my/his anger. I would pause and check if he was done, and we continued until he was complete. I let him know that we weren't done. In my Reiki training, I learned that it's important to know that when you "remove" something negative for the enhancement of healing, a space is left open. Balance is created by filling the space back up, whether it's by replacing it with positive thoughts or healthier choices; otherwise that hole can attract other negative energies.

Moises now was given a choice about what he wanted to do with the small torn pieces of paper that represented his negative feelings.... Would we go outside to bury them, or perhaps drown them in a glass of water? He chose to bury them. While we found a stone to pick up and dig underneath as a spot to leave the paper, I asked him what it meant to bury something. He expressed his thoughts about how things get buried when they die. I asked him what would he like to feel instead of angry, now that it was buried, and he responded that he wanted to feel included and wanted to feel like he's being paid attention. So, in the space of his body where anger once resided, he was able to fill it with a new understanding of his own needs. It was a hopeful beginning to a change.

The approach may be based in harm reduction theory, but the choice of intervention was formed as a fusion of my Reiki and *danza* background noticing what truly seemed out of place and finding a way to release and replace or shift the energy within this person. The elements of fire (rage and frustration) seemed clear to me in Moises's actions. His movements were not submissive but attention-seeking, although within the normal range of behavior for a child who is in fear of not understanding and being left behind from his peers. Fire energy, itself, is not an imbalance; it is a form of communication to the outer world about your needs. What I felt was missing was the completion of his expression and action. His anger was not released and allowed to shine as it was deemed inappropriate behavior in the classroom. From my toolbox, I had made a plan for holding his rage and I offered a way to neutralize it with fire-reducing elements, like water or earth.

West

West is the direction of the shadow, of inner strength, introversion, and of the mother and femininity. It is the color blue or black (depending on the tradition) and is represented by the moon and the element of water. Water, in turn, is an element of fluidity, of cleansing, cooling, and replenishing. In Lukumi, blue/black represents the color of *omiero* —a hand-made infusion of water and sacred herbs that is prayed over and intended to be used to cleanse a person both externally and internally (only those priests knowledgeable about ingestible herbs will gather what is needed). The western direction teaches us containment, the power of silence, and the ability to see what is not showing itself, to believe in the unknown. It is the hidden, the subconscious, and the secret parts of ourselves that we keep quiet. It is where our inner magic lies dormant.

Perhaps a year before I was conceived, my mother, Noemi, who had given birth to my older brother, James, and had then undergone six miscarriages afterward, was suddenly expecting again with pregnancy number eight—a boy—and she was well into the second trimester. My father, Allier, often took business trips by train from his office in Managua, Nicaragua, to Guatemala City, with my mother and sometimes my older brother in tow. On this particular trip, while my father was in meetings, my mother took a walk through a marketplace and decided to stop into a local church to light a candle, kneel before the picture of the Virgin Mary, and say a prayer specifically asking for this new baby to survive.

Against the advice of her doctor, my mother was strongly determined to have more children after each miscarriage, and she wasn't going to give up, despite having suffered physical and psychological pain with each loss, each recovery, and years of medical experiments trying to resolve the mystery of why a perfectly healthy woman's body would reject so many pregnancies. Through the various pregnancies, my mom was given horrific-sounding treatments including live charcoal to drink "to kill bacteria," and a surgical procedure in which the doctors sewed her closed. Yet nothing worked. Becoming a mother again seemed impossible.

When my mother left the church and began walking down the street, a nearby vendor rushed up to her exclaiming that her dress was on fire. My mom looked down in shock and patted down the flames on her now-singed dress. She noticed that there were burns in a circular shape over her newly protruding belly. Had she set fire to herself while lighting the votive? The dress was burned, but not the slip she wore underneath. Baby Eight did not survive the pregnancy. My mother blamed herself quietly, wondering if she had done something to deserve this. Was it because of a curse? Was it because she had been abandoned by her own mother and perhaps wasn't fit to be a mom?

Later, even after being told this miscarriage was caused by toxoplasmosis and being given the correct medicine and treatment from a small clinic in Diriamba, twenty-five miles away from Managua, and after successfully giving birth, not only to me, but also my younger brother, Allier Jr.—both successfully carried to term and healthy overall—the trauma from this loss in a stillbirth and the six miscarriages beforehand was a secret pain my mother never really shared with any of us. We tried to imagine what she had gone through: a pain that she must have held on to in her scarred and sacred womb, the source of so much of her pain and sadness. She was a jovial woman who was loving, present, protective, and attuned, intuitively and nearly psychically so, to each of her children and to her husband. Mom's womb became aggressively cancerous in November of 2007; we lost her eight months later to uterine leiomyosarcoma. Losing her, we have felt like no one on Earth will ever truly know us or love us in the same way she did.

John Bowlby's attachment theory suggests that children come into this world hardwired to create attachments (connections and relationships) with others for the purpose of survival. Attachments to our caregivers, though, are the most essential relationships we create as infants. Psychological experiments and studies have been done since the 1940s regarding the importance of touch and nurturing, especially by caregivers. Some of these studies have cruelly resulted in deaths, forcing us to take seriously the thought that touch is crucial to our development and survival.[2,3]

Norma Jean

Norma Jean (NJ for short) is a five-year-old girl referred to me because of complex trauma she had experienced at the hands of her father when she was three years old. He is now out of the picture and

---

2 Alice Sterling Honig, Hiram E. Fitzgerald, and Holly Brophy-Herb, *Infancy in America: An Encyclopedia*, Vol. A-I (Santa Barbara, CA: ABC-Clio, 2001), 489–90.

3 René A. Spitz in collaboration with Katherine M. Wolf, 1947, *Grief: A Peril in Infancy*, film, 24 min.

her custody is shared among both grandmothers and her maternal great-grandmother. Little NJ was angry, bossy, mean, and cruel when she began seeing me. She would often play tricks on me, such as telling me that she wanted to tell me a secret then screaming loudly in my ear. Other days, she would come in and create chaos, being completely forceful and unrestrained in the room. Whoever dropped her off would often tell me that she had gotten in trouble during the past week for cussing at school or at home or for hitting and fighting.

When her treatments began, I was told that the family's goals were to get her to stop hitting kids at school and to help her with her nightmares, which were about "monsters." In the therapy room, NJ needed to be in control; she role-played as the teacher, as the mother, or the big sister, always taking satisfaction in getting her way or telling me what to do. Everyone was working under the assumption that her behavior was all about what her dad did to her. So I carefully examined her play themes over months and tried to figure out which patterns fit the trauma she had endured, and, once I had built enough rapport with her, I asked her about her dad. She told me that she missed him, but she wasn't supposed to talk about him because he had hurt her … "It's a secret." I ask, "Who told you that you weren't allowed to talk about him?" She responded, while coloring a Barbie's face with a purple marker, "Gamgam …" (her great-grandmother). Later in our treatments, NJ shared her sadness about all the kids in school making Father's Day cards while she refused to make one. I offered that we could make one that I would keep for her whenever she wanted to bring it home. She agreed and all was well that day.

Gamgam was a tough woman who never smiled. She often was sarcastic and she seemed to convey ulterior motives in what she reported every week, disapprovingly commenting, "Grandma One did *this*," or "Grandma Two did *that*." She hardly ever mentioned NJ's mom. Here's where the reality of NJ's intergenerational trauma gets complicated. Gamgam had two daughters, one being Grandma One who abandoned NJ's mother due to addiction. Gamgam raised NJ's mom while Grandma One got clean and sober. After ten years of sobriety, Grandma One still had a strained relationship with her mother, Gamgam, and her daughter, NJ's mom. In the next generation, NJ's mom also came to not be in the picture due to addiction and would only come to see NJ on weekends at Gamgam's house because she was not in a program and Grandma One would not allow her to stay. Gamgam also had issues with Grandma Two on the paternal side because she was the mother of NJ's dad. Overall, Gamgam was trying to figure out a way to gain sole custody of NJ and keep everyone else away. Although her intention seemed to be love for her great-granddaughter, it was also clear that NJ was being used as a way to create a wedge between family members. I begin to think that her monsters were actually everywhere, rather than just in her dreams.

Over the next few months, without any initiating from me, NJ began changing some themes in her play that surprised me. She began to experiment with being a baby in our roleplays. She wanted to speak in baby talk and wanted me to carry her to bed, then feed her. I would ask NJ if she wanted me to hold her in my arms like a baby; she would nod and crawl into my lap, where she would pretend to sleep. I thought of all the mother figures fighting over her, but not really attuning to her, and I spoke to her as if she were my child needing a mother's love and attention. I told her how beautiful and precious she is, and how loved she is by everyone around her.

By this time in treatment, the custody schedule had shifted, and Grandma Two was keeping NJ during the week. I shared with Grandma Two the constant need for affection that NJ was seeking out in therapy and was able to get her to commit to spending a little more time on using affection-based vocabulary, and rewarding NJ with hugs and hand-holding. NJ is now six years old and enjoying her quality time with Grandma Two, yet always seeking time with her mom and secretly wondering if she will ever see her dad.

North

The North is the direction of the ancestors and elders, represented by the color white and the element of air. It is the place where wisdom comes from and the direction that leads to the spirit world and the land of our the ancestors. The color white, in many traditions, represents peace or purity. In Lukumi practice, white is the color of mental clarity and represents the medicine of *efun*. *Efun* is a white powdery chalk made of pulverized eggshell and holy water that is used in ceremony for protection, for grounding and bringing tranquility, and for marking religious symbols and sigils within the ceremony spaces. White is also the color of the crown chakra where we connect to our higher selves or a divine and higher power. It is our consciousness, our awareness, and our sense of connection to the universe.

Ikú lobi ocha is a Lukumi phrase meaning "the death of ancestors gave birth to the Ocha," *ocha* being short for *orisha,* the title of Yoruban deities. This phrase, in the deeper sense of the translation, describes the concept of "before" and "after" and forces us to reflect on our state of current existence while acknowledging how we came to be and how we find ourselves in this moment. We each are the pinnacle of the intelligence, wisdom, and survival of every single person in our lineage that came before us. The ancestors birthed each of us and helped create the foundation of all that we do, believe, think, and choose. Without them, there is no "me."

Many ceremonies that I've attended begin specifically after asking permission of the ancestors. In *Danza Azteca,* the spirits of each of the four directions plus the center, the heart of the circle, are called into the space by blowing of a conch shell to each direction with the intention of asking permission and to announce the beginning and ending of a ceremony. In my Usui Reiki practice, I was taught to call not only upon my personal spiritual healer guides, but to also invite the client's guides to step forward and be present during the Reiki session to assist in whatever form they feel is necessary. In Hula Kahiko (an ancient-style Hawai'i dance) traditions, the protocol is to display your intention and begin with an *oli* (a chant) that is sung with the purpose of asking permission to enter [a space], since it is customary to announce yourself before any transition occurs—whether the oli is sung to the *kumu* (hula teacher) by the students before entering the dance space, or to the audience before a performance. I've heard that an oli is done to announce one's entrance into someone's home or to deities before entering the sacred dwellings of the gods as a way of exhibiting your honorable intentions. In Lukumi religion, a *mo'juba* prayer is done to invoke the spirits of our ancestors and the guiding spirits that grant us peace and knowledge; we ask permission for whatever we are about to begin.

I bring this tradition with me to session. *Ikú lobi ocha*, I must honor and please my ancestors before moving forward. I name as many ancestors as I can remember from my blood and spiritual lineages and the names of my teachers whose knowledge and teaching I am using to do the work/ceremony, and I ask for their blessings and guidance. I ask permission of those in the lineage of my client so they can allow me to see, hear, and understand what needs to be done in today's session. I'm now feeling grounded, present, and prepared. I like to begin some sessions with introducing the importance of being grounded to the client. In somatic psychotherapy, for example, it is of utmost importance to be "present," or connected to yourself and surroundings, or being "in our bodies" with awareness. As in anything in life, there is never really *one* way to achieve this awareness; there are many paths to finding our center, our groundedness, and our sense of neutrality.

The first law of thermodynamics, also known as the law of conservation of energy, states that energy can neither be created nor destroyed; energy can only be transferred or changed from one form to another. Something shifts on an energetic level; how is this new energy form experienced? Is it like when you're feeling positive and encounter someone feeling down and it results in a physical and energetic impact on your mood? Is it like having the exposure to witnessing physical violence that raises a hyperawareness of changes in the air or energy in your space that speaks to possible danger or an anticipation of a fight about to happen? Is it, rather, a positive change, like something that inspires or brings hope? I often think of it in this way: you know that feeling when you sense someone watching you, or someone walking closely behind you. It is what Eugene Gendlin calls the "felt sense." A felt sense comes. It isn't just there waiting. We have to let it form and come. That takes at least a few moments, sometimes longer. So we understand that a felt sense is a certain development, a certain bit of further life-process. What does it stem from? How can we think about ordinary events and experience in such a way that we could understand what a felt sense is and how it forms?

> A felt sense is distinctly there, something with a life of its own, which we attend to directly. If we attend to our bodies, in the middle of the body it comes, and then it is in an odd sort of space of its own. It brings its own space. In that space the felt sense is a direct object, *that, there.*[4]

This felt sense is something we each have; it is an unspoken wisdom or knowing that is experienced just outside of our physical bodies. In 2010, I completed my master/teacher-level training of Usui Reiki. The practice of Reiki (roughly translated as "sacred life force") engages and connects the outer layers of the body—where the felt sense happens—and channels *ki* energy (like *chi* in Chinese Medicine) in order to bring healing wherever it is needed. In yogic systems, there are seven layers in the human aura that correspond to the seven chakras: physical, etheric, emotional, mental, causal, spiritual, and divine. During a Reiki session, there is a sensation that happens to the practitioner when something is different in the client's energetic field. For me, I feel coldness or stagnation in an area in comparison to others. It could be physical or emotional injury, it could be a past trauma, or it could be a current dissonance creating conflict in the person's auric selves and physical self.

Sebastián

I sit in Sebastián's home; he is a well-spoken, mature, and polite eleven-year-old boy I'm assessing and for whom I'm formulating a treatment plan. So far in our conversations, I've noticed that he often mixes up fantasy and reality, idolizes Pokémon as deities or trophies (not just as cards or a game), and presents as a little odd and eccentric with a bit of a grandiose and inflated sense of self. I could easily assume

---

4 Eugene T. Gendlin, "Three Assertions about the Body." 1993. Accessed February 5, 2018. http://www.focusing.org/gendlin/docs/gol_2064.html.

that it's age-appropriate, this imaginative and magical thinking, but this client also has a history of psychotic episodes. The language that Sebastián uses in our conversations leads me to conclude that he thinks in terms of black or white, possible or impossible, righteous or evil, right or wrong—all of which give me a sense of his rigidness and minimal creativity. It feels like what I would describe as a crown chakra imbalance. It is for these reasons that I bring an abstract, right-brain intervention to our session. The stack of 120 postcards I place on the table are a random mix of images of nature, animals, art, celebrity still-shots, photos from various eras, and cartoons. I instruct him to pick any three cards that represent how he is feeling today, and after some time and distractions he eventually chooses three. The choice that stands out to me is a picture of a sea turtle swimming. Sebastián tells me that he sometimes feels like this turtle because it looks like it's flying the way he feels like when he is flying away into outer space. Curious about this response, I ask when exactly is it that he feels like he is flying away? He responds, "Mostly when I'm sleeping."

I instantly flash to being in Matanzas, Cuba, dressed in all white, sweating from the heat, my body kneading itself into the thick island humidity, making it difficult to concentrate and be still as I sit on a milk crate in a tiny room jammed with seven people. It's day two of five of the week-long *kariocha* ceremony—a crowning of the Obatala (owner of the white cloth and ruler of our heads) to the head of a new priestess. The thirty-year-old woman who is the reason we're in ceremony has traveled here from the United States for the first time. She has minimal Spanish-speaking skills attained from the inevitable interactions and conversations with Spanish-speakers while living in the San Francisco Bay Area. She sits in anticipation, in the midst of being initiated into a new family of non-English speakers who have never left Cuba. The *iyawo* (novice)—for ceremonial purposes—is in the center of a spiritual investigation being facilitated by the elders. The elders are well skilled and well developed in communicating with and receiving messages from the present spirits of the *iyawo*'s ancestors and guardian angels; such messages are conveyed and openly shared in order to prepare the necessary components for the next few days of ceremony. The *iyawo* is asked specific questions that they need to confirm. This process is to determine what is missing and what is needed. A question is posed: What happens to you when you sleep? The *iyawo* responds, "Well, I leave my body and I feel myself everywhere, like out in the universe and outer space." An involuntary astral projection was occurring. The danger in that case was that the *iyawo* was dealing with delicate health issues and it would not benefit her to continuously leave her body. The logical solution was to require the *iyawo* to wear something on her person that would keep her chained or tied to the earth while she slept.

Could it be that Sebastián needed to be weighed down in order to find a healthy balance in his life? The treatment could be translated into the family investing in a weighted blanket or his doing some mindful meditation focusing on the sensations of his feet and staying connected to his body. At a later session, and after two separate emotional breakdowns about the idea of his having to go to sleep early, I posed an idea to make something with him that would help him stay grounded and centered. His response to me was a doubtful, "Nothing that doesn't already have the energy to help is going to make a difference in my life," sounding very close to the law of conservation of energy.

I haven't given up on the idea that we can cocreate something to keep him grounded and that his crown chakra needs balancing. In the interim, his medication dosage has increased and he is calmer and having more coherent conversations with me.

South

The direction of the South is the direction of children, and the element of earth. It is represented by playfulness, exploration, creativity, and curiosity. It is also represented by flowers, herbs, fruit, tree resins, and basically any traditional medicine that blossoms from the ground. In many traditions, it is believed that children carry their own wisdom and magic since they are the closest beings (time-wise) to the Creator. South is yellow in color, and offers the wisdom of simplicity and the wonder of new growth. In

Lukumi, yellow is the color of oñí, honey (sweetness), the color of gold (riches), and represents the *orishas* Ochun and Obba Nani, who each bring the ideas of love and romantic connection into the world and to humankind in all its forms. Yellow is the color of the solar plexus chakra where our self-empowerment and self-love can be activated; it is the origin of our self-identity, our self-worth, and our core values.

It is said that Ochun is the youngest *orisha,* but one of the most powerful and glorious. Her greatness couldn't be seen right away. There are multiple stories of her that speak about her saving humankind from famine, floods, war, and near-destruction with her sweetness. They are stories of her ability to convince or entice the other *orisha* with her honey—never for the purposes of harm, only for the intention of keeping the world in balance as a reminder that we always have sweetness in the most bitter times. But there are also stories about the strength of her witchcraft and her knowledge of making powerful magic powders and medicines, which came from her inspired creativity and youthful curiosity. Eleggua, the trickster, is also represented by youthfulness and children, and he is often depicted to have child-like qualities. He is given toys, sweets, play-money, and is often given a *garabato*—a hook-shaped stick—as they are his wands that he uses to disperse his tricks and lessons onto the world.

My great-grandmother, Francisca Gutierrez, had a special table where she would talk to spirits. The table was reportedly small but heavy, made of all wood, no nails, and used for consulting important "yes" or "no" questions or to find a definitive direction. My father, as a young child, remembers that she would ask questions like, "Should we travel by plane or train? Knock one time for plane, twice for train." The table would slightly lift off the ground and slam down to create the knocking sound. He didn't believe in this "magical table" until he was asked to sit with her while she asked something. They sat with their hands in view on the table, the question was posed, and the table lifted and dropped to give the answer. He remembers that earlier, he and his brother tried to move the table, in hopes of proving that she was making the whole thing up and maybe lifting the table with her wiry legs on her small frame, but soon he realized that it was too heavy for the two of them to lift without help. Now, although he won't take a position to say that he believes that it was the spirits, my father believes that it was impossible for her to lift that table with her legs.

When my mother was about five months pregnant with me, the doctors finally were able to figure out the root cause of her constant miscarriages. She was being treated while pregnant and also being prepared for the worst—her newborn could have neurological and developmental challenges, blindness, and other physical ailments. Surprisingly to everyone, I was unexpectedly healthy, strong, and hit all of my milestones early or on time. I was my mother's ninth child, born on July 5, 1975. My parents baptized me "Milagros," which means "miracles." When I was nine years old, I became interested in different religions, traditions, the occult, and in the power of prayer. My first trip to the library in fourth grade with my Catholic school class resulted in me finding a book on Afro-Caribbean religions that fascinated me. I would create my own Ouija board out of binder paper and a Styrofoam cup then ask questions about my future; I desperately looked for tarot cards, I bought books about astrology, listened to Edgar Cayce recordings, and was constantly intrigued about psychic phenomena and anything having to do with the spirit world. My mom nicknamed me *"la brujita"* (little witch). When I came to be crowned as a priestess during my Saturn return (I was twenty-seven), I reflected on my story and how the *orisha* let themselves be known in my life. Seven is the number for Yemaya, the Mother of all *orishas* and humankind and represents motherhood; five is the number of Ochun, the *orisha* who heals with sweetness and with her strength, and represents pregnancy and all the struggles of womankind; nine is the number of Oya, the *orisha* guardian of the spirit world, the female warrior, and the avenger of her children from death (Ikú). Shango, the *orisha* I was crowned to, is the only *orisha* that was deified after his death as a king on Earth and is considered to be both Spirit and *orisha.* His skills include both acute knowledge of divining and having the highest esteem for his drumming and dancing.

My therapist once told me that no matter what I bring to talk about on any given week, it's really all to do with the same core issue that manifests in these different places in my life. It can often take a while to pinpoint what the core issue may actually be, and the reason for any client coming in for therapy is really about their finally feeling the end result of an emotional build-up that has now become unmanageable—like the outermost ring in the ripple caused by a stone thrown into a still body of water. The client is now feeling the nauseating rolling and pushing of rhythmic waves that keep permeating out from the source, throwing them off their center. The stone causes a sudden disturbance, and the client wants to return to the stillness. A decision to seek therapy is never for *one* thing; it's *all* the things, which inevitably intersect. My job as a therapist myself is to help my clients figure out what that stone actually was, where it landed, and when. It is in understanding these root issues that the unknown allows itself to become known and tangible so it can be shifted and be made useful to the client. Sometimes what happens is preverbal and cannot be easily identified, and often it becomes part of a person's personality and constitution. It is only when they have come to a point where their own natural disposition begins to hinder and affect their life in a negative way that this delving into finding out the root cause of their problems feels appropriate.

As a therapist, I try to train and teach new skills that will help clients create new patterns in their life that allow them to regulate, manage, and maintain this balance in their life, or at the very least to relieve some of their distress or emotional discomfort. When hearing the client's initial complaint, a series of theoretical frameworks and applied approaches help to further inform the therapist as to which direction we will take in therapy, like having access to tools in a tool belt. "Which one is right for the job?" I ask myself; will it be a focus on attachment, on family relationships, some inner-child work, play therapy, or psychoanalysis? Often, and as I continue developing in my approach, I'm growing new muscles and discovering which tool works best through constant trial and error, never really knowing which one will actually do the trick. It's in this very place of the unknown and the undiscovered that the real magic happens for me. On the surface, the strategy of finding and applying the best tool is what appears to be happening when I'm with the client. My natural impulse and approach has me dig deep into the multifaceted toolbox that I come into the room with, which are often nonpsychological frameworks that lend their applications to psychotherapy.

Tomás

Tomás is a nine-year-old boy referred to me by his mother for his anxiety. I see him every week at his home after school. She reports that he is overly attached to her and cannot seem to do anything without her. I gently spent time assessing him during our session and realized that he never really wants to be too far from home or his mother. Discussions with his mother resulted in her telling me that even when she was an infant, she would notice that if she left the room even for a moment to get his bottle or to do anything that took a few seconds, he would cry. She is frustrated with him but cannot bring herself, as his mother, to ask him to give her space, and he can't help trying to be closer to her so that he doesn't continue feeling pushed away.

Although there are many ways to work with both Tomás and his mother, the first thing I'm inspired to do is test his tolerance for being away from her. I test how far he wants to go to have a session with me and I hand him the reins to see where it will lead. He wants to go as far as his front yard, and when I get a chance to speak to his mother alone, he can't seem to help wanting to come and be near her. He reports that he often has thoughts of worry about her and his younger brother, wondering if they are okay, although he assures me that it doesn't stop him from doing his schoolwork.

We spend months in his front yard before winter and rainy weather loom. I take the bold step to explain that the front yard may not be sustainable in the cold weather and maybe we can decide on a new space to meet. Tomás suggests his kitchen; I suggest a nearby library. For weeks before the December holidays, we sit in his kitchen while his mother preps dinner for later. His younger brother constantly wants to be part of our session and we all play card games, always going back to the notion that finding another meeting space would work best for our purposes.

Over the winter break, while not seeing Tomás, I realize that he didn't want to get in the car with me, and I reflect on one of his previously revealed worries about being kidnapped. The titration between home and driving somewhere is too far of a leap for him and I need to find the half-way step.

When we resume our sessions, I take advantage of the unusually nice weather and propose a neighborhood exploratory walk. Tomás and his mother agree that it would be a good plan. He asks if his mom and brother can come, and when I respond that they can't, he lingers in the house distracting himself from getting his jacket by playing with his hamster, telling me that he needs to eat first, and using the restroom. When he is finally ready, I clearly explain the plan of walking around the same block twice and then being able to go back and play in his kitchen. Once we are out the door, I ask him if he has walked around his block before and what he had noticed in the past. Tomás is suddenly a different person; he is confident and expresses his purpose for today's exploration—he will collect rocks and leaves to bring back home. He finds an L-shaped stick that he says he will use to dig for rocks, reminding me of Eleggua's *garabato*. Outside, he is able to talk about the flowers he likes and he hears me when I talk to him about the plants we see, like the rosemary or citrus leaves that I like to pick and smell. The second week, we explore a different walk in his neighborhood, doing a scavenger hunt, and Tomás points out everything on the list before I can spot them. We conclude our hour-long exploration with him asking if we can go to the park next time and agreeing to get in my car. It's small steps of progress with Tomás. I continue looking forward to his confronting his anxieties and fears and challenging himself while I continue to support his achievements in taking small risks.

Conclusion

In treating people within the field of mental health, the baseline of "normal" or "healthy" is continuously shifting. The intersectionality of "normal" behavioral assessment now includes the inclusion of a variety of factors, such as culture, exposure to trauma, socioeconomic status, and so on. Although it is a common understanding that unless a certain behavior is affecting the functioning of a person's life, we try not to impose a shift in that particular behavior, the exceptions can be that the client may not see the negative effects of their behavior. It is our job as therapists to direct the client's attention to the negative outcomes of certain choices or actions and integrate a solution. The work that is done in diagnosing a specific behavioral issue and deciding on the best interventions happens within the context of our own experiences, our own beliefs, and our own proven examples. There are as many possible interventions for one behavior as there are theoretical frameworks. If we can provide an intervention that is theoretically not proven by any specific psychology framework but is therapeutically successful, we begin expanding on what is possible for treatment.

As a somatic psychotherapy-based clinician and a dancer, studies of movement and gesturing call my attention. As a priestess in the Lukumi faith, symbolism and repetition stand out in behavior. As a Reiki practitioner, felt senses and specific chakral deficiencies or excesses activate my curiosities. As a former Catholic schoolgirl, a client's structuring, organization, or lack thereof in presentation of themselves or their environment will be most obvious to me and will initiate further investigations. These personal experiences, I feel, fall parallel to the way I view and practice psychotherapy from all my different foundations of long-held traditions. I continue to accept that one tends to always have something to do with the other.

Mo'dupue y mo'juba gbogbo eggun eleri mi y mis guias espirituales;
Maferefun Shango y Oya, a mis padres Allier and Noemi (ibae), a mis hermanos, James and Allier;
Kinkamache Obinde Omollessa and Oloyu Oba Bi, my elders y abure,
Gracias, Mo'dupue, Tlazokamati, Mahalo, and Thank You a Grupo Xiuhcoatl y familia Martinez, to Halau 'o Keikiali'i and Kumu Hula Kawike Alfiche, to Reiki teacher Malia Okin; to Chango Dina, and Kym Warner

Chapter 3

thank god i'm fat: gifts from the underbelly

Jules Pashall

The body as home, but only if it is understood that bodies are never singular, but rather haunted, strengthened, underscored by countless other bodies.

—ELI CLAIRE

I was taught to distrust my fat body. Starting from a time before my memories begin, the most important thing for me to do was become less fat. When I felt hungry, people told me I was not *actually* hungry, so I was not allowed to eat. When I wanted to rest, people told me I should not be tired, so I was shamed into movement. These external controls convinced me that what I felt was wrong, so I learned how to deny my feelings and to live outside of my body.

Since the pathologizing and shaming of my fat were the poison that pushed me out from my body, removing the toxicity and turning fat into medicine are how I recover myself. This takes work. I was nineteen when I had my first framework shift: fat people are not bad; how we treat fat people is bad.[1] It shook my whole being. Now I am writing to you after a decade of this initial undoing, asking myself: What have I learned from being fat? What are the gifts of my fat body?

When I began writing this piece, I resisted. My chest constricted and heat flashed my cheeks pink. My fingers didn't want to type. Instead, they budded into fists. I felt like anything I said that was not a direct response to bigoted understandings of fatness would become ammunition that could be used against my body and bodies like mine. We have a "War on Obesity" and an "obesity epidemic": my body—a threat to battle. A contagion.

No wonder I was ready to fight.

This is the work so often thrust upon oppressed people: needing to defend our right just to be. But luckily, this writing is a process of coming to my fat body for wisdom. And she[2] has a lot to say. My fat body teaches me that my energy can be spent in better ways than convincing people I have a right to exist as I do, because my fat body is here, existing, regardless of how anyone (including me) feels about her.

In a culture that fears and vilifies fat so profoundly, it feels vital for all of us who work with and care about bodies to wonder what fat offers

---

1 The first moment I ever had this shift was during my first semester of college in 2008 when I was assigned *The Cult of Thinness* by Sharlene Nagy Hesse-Biber. From there I read Marilyn Wann, Nomy Lamm, Bevin Branlandingham, jessie dress, "Fat Girl" zines, and many, many fat-positive Tumblrs. At the time, almost all of my exposure to fat-positive frameworks and body positivity was coming through the bodies and voices of white women and femmes.

2 Sometimes I refer to my body as her and she. It feels like it goes against foundational somatics beliefs to separate body and self, to speak of my body in the third person. But I think there is value in naming that my body gets treated as an object, that all bodies get treated like objects and that treatment shapes the body and the people. I need some way to distinguish between my body as an object in the world assigned meaning by others and me in my body. Maybe this is a semantic strategy to put a little distance between myself and how my body has been treated so that it is easier to separate the narratives I have been given from the narratives I want to authentically cultivate from within. I use they/them pronouns when I am myself, but the ways in which my body has been treated and perceived as a thing in the world have been very much through the experience of being a "she."

us. I want to be part of building a world in which we look to all bodies as having wisdom to share, unique to the ways that their bodies are bodies.

Instead of relating to my fat body as a problem that needs fixing, my fat body is now my greatest resource, my wisest teacher, and the love of my life. This does not mean I always feel good or safe in my body. This does not mean that I bypass suffering or pain. But I do not blame my fat. I release the fantasy that I would be a better self, a better body, if I were not fat.

The soundtrack to my writing this piece has been whale song. I listen to the whales' deep transcendent echoes that move through space and time, reverberating through fat and water. It opens up a longing and heartbreak in me, a hope for something far beyond the reaches of my own imagination. Never have I doubted the vitality, necessity, and gift of whales' fatness. Their song keeps me company and reminds me that my fat too is vital, necessary, and a gift.

My mother would often describe her late-pregnancy body (she was having twins) with the phrase "as big as a whale" and the only place she wanted to be was in the water. Her words left such an imprint that my baby origin story of how I and my brother came to be was that we were born on top of a whale: we rode on her back as she swam us across the ocean to dry land. This familial folklore is born from my mother brilliantly naming the comfort that her big whale Mother body felt in water, her knowing of how to give her body what she needed. To trust her fat pregnant body.

I want us to trust fat bodies. Fat gives us life. It grows as we grow in wombs; it supports us as we come into being. There is no life without fat. I write this piece to breathe life from my fat.

tikkun ha-nefesh / tikkun ha-olam

It's not about self-care—it's about collective care.

—Leah Lakshmi Piepzna-Samarasinha

The first time I saw a picture of a fat family member, I was twenty-six.

My Lithuanian Jewish great-grandmother, Lizzie, was my father's father's mother. When I saw her face, something cracked in me. It helped me feel deeply that this was not my "before" body on the way to an "after" body; this was my right here, right now body. Here was this round face, double chin with my very Jewish nose looking back at me. I did not know how much I needed to see Lizzie until I saw her.

Lizzie reminds me that my fat body is gifted to me from my Ashkenazi Jewish ancestors, an inheritance, a sacred heirloom passed down to me. A body that knew to leave a place before she would be forced to leave in more violent, more permanent ways. When I touch my fat, I can feel Lizzie. In my fat I am connected to my Jewish ancestors. I feel their survival and their resistance. I feel my belief in God.

In my relationship to Judaism, I look to Kabbalistic teachings to offer me spiritual resources that come to me through my ancestry.[3] Kabbalah offers a framework of connectivity, "that whatever happens anywhere in the universe reverberates throughout the totality of creation. Thus our lives are affected by what is happening everywhere."

---

[3] As a white person, it feels important for me to base my spirituality and mysticism within my own lineage so as not to co-opt from people of color. There is so much intense spiritual appropriation I see by fellow white people in somatics. I am curious about how we shift this and feel a good place to start is by exploring my own people's connection to spirituality.

Kabbalah also gives us the responsibility of *tikkun ha-nefesh* (mending the soul) and *tikkun ha-olam* (mending the world) and tells us that "they cannot be separated; we cannot raise sparks in ourselves without raising those in the world, and vice versa."[4]

My spiritual healing and liberation are not separate from working for collective healing and liberation, as my ancestors knew "the individual cannot be separated from the integrated whole."[5] I cannot tend to my body without tending to the collective body, without tending to the ways in which the world is broken, in which something divine has been shattered. Social justice movements give us action and tools to do this type of collective healing. Social justice work is divine work.

I learn the most about how to work toward *tikkun ha-olam* from Disability Justice activists, Black feminists, and the healing justice movement. I look to them for their leadership because they offer us ways to tangibly work toward a better world, a world with less suffering and more connection. They were all started by and continue to be led by Black, Indigenous, people of color, trans people, gender nonconforming people, poor people, femmes, disabled people, people living rurally, women, and all combinations and intersections of those identities. It is not a coincidence that the brilliance and genius of how to transform this world, to create what Sonya Renee Taylor describes as a radical self love world—"a world free from the systems of oppression that make it difficult and sometimes deadly to live in our bodies"[6]—is potently being born every moment from the people and communities most directly targeted by these current systems of violence and oppression.

---

4 David A. Cooper, *God Is a Verb: Kabbalah and the Practice of Mystical Judaism* (New York: Riverhead Books, 1998), 179.

5 Cooper, 181.

6 Sonya Renee Taylor, "Making Self Love Radical," in *The Body Is Not an Apology* (Oakland, CA: Berrett-Koehler Publishers, Inc., 2018), 4.

These lineages hold that all bodies have a place in shaping new ways to be, while always centering queer, trans, disabled, poor, Black, and brown bodies. I am holding the tension of centering my own white, wealthy body in this writing, while knowing my body should never be at the center of the collective liberation I put my reflection in service of. I am learning from my body, as it is the place I feel I can learn most intimately from, so that I can offer what I learn to be in solidarity with movements not led by me. I am learning from my own body to be a better student and a better accomplice. I am a guest, taking my hat and shoes off before entering, always open to feedback about how I am engaging with these frameworks, to make my body and being in alignment with the world these movements are building.

I am never just for me. The healing I am in pursuit of is never just mine. My fat body reminds me that I do not end at the edges of where my body was told it was supposed to end—I pour out and create stretch marks to fit all that needs to fit. I look for what the gifts are teaching me about collective liberation, "toward a world where all bodies and minds are recognized and treated as valuable and beautiful."[7]

the gifts

It is through our own transformed relationship with our bodies that we become champions for other bodies on our planet. As we awaken our indoctrinated body shame, we feel inspired to awaken others and to interrupt the systems that perpetuate body shame and oppression against all bodies. There is a whisper we keep hearing; it is saying we must build in us what we want to build in the world.

—SONYA RENEE TAYLOR

[7] Sins Invalid, *Disability Justice Primer (self-published material),* 51.

to be big enough to hold the pain of hurting others.

Being fat has made me deeply aware of how much hurt people cause without any intention to do so. It is rare that I go a day without experiencing some kind of hatred or animosity directed toward fatness, my body's or someone else's, often without any awareness that what was done or said causes harm.[8] Being on the painful receiving end of these good intentions has made me deeply curious about the potential I have to cause harm without knowing. I had the great privilege to hear Dr. Joy DeGruy speak about her work, and in her lecture, she asked the amazing question of white people in the audience and the rest of the world: "What are you going to do about the bias that you do not believe you have?" I hold that question in a big way.

It is an inaccurate oversimplification to isolate my fat identity from the other politicized traits that construct my experience in the world. I come from a long line of rich, white women trying to make themselves as thin as possible. My mother was the first person to teach me my body was not what it was supposed to be. And her mother taught her. And her mother's mother, and so on, on and on. This is an intimate type of violence and heartbreak.

But there is a bigger, more expansive hurt. When I pull the thread of this part of my ancestry that vilifies fat, it is not a coincidence that it comes from the white, British, Puritan part of my body's lineage. The way I inherited how to feel about my fat body is connected to values that were based in my people's white supremacy, Christian hegemony, colonial violence, and enslaving and genocide of Black, Brown, and Indigenous people. There is no escaping that the way I was taught by my family to feel about my fat body is inextricably linked to this excruciating legacy.

Caleb Luna tells us that "by recognizing the white origins of the worshiping of thinness, we can begin to think about where, exactly, our personal and cultural distaste for fatness comes from ... an inclination (of any kind) to thinness, no matter on whose body it is on, cannot be separated

---

[8] There are also of course things that are said and done that are meant to cause harm. But I believe most people reading this are people committed to not harming others and so I am focused on harm that happens through ignorance and good intention.

from an attraction to whiteness in the current context and history of race and body size."[9] Doing healing work around how I was treated for being fat by my family and how I feel about my fat body is not just an exercise in soothing how I have experienced fat oppression—but it is an exercise in holding the ugly roots of this lineage that connects my body to the ways in which my ancestors and I oppressed and continue to oppress others. In undoing my own poisonous feelings around fatness, I also need to undo toxic internalizations of all of the systemic oppression that is compounded into our culture's body ideals. I need to be actively working to dismantle all of the systems of oppression that are wrapped up in how I have learned to relate to my body. In this writing, I am not attempting to claim the space of only the oppressed, but to write from a place of how I learn through how I experience all of my identities.

The very smallest thing I can do to be part of dismantling these systems is listen to people when they tell me I have caused them harm. It is a small thing and yet is something I know I am not alone in struggling to learn how to do. The only way to stop causing harm we do not intend is to become aware of when we are doing it. In order to become aware, we need to listen to people who are telling us we are hurting them; we have to stay present and receive what they are saying; we have to believe them.

When someone tells me I have caused harm, I can feel defensive and make myself small and rigid in an attempt to protect myself from the pain of shame. It is difficult to let my body feel into the truth that I have the ability to hurt others and that I do hurt others. That just by being myself, I can hurt people. But that is the truth of being a person living within oppressive systems we internalize. And I have to grow my ability to tolerate the sensations that come with knowing this, so that I can be accountable for my impact.

As people drawn to healing work, we want to support others and we are (hopefully) trying to do the opposite of causing harm. Because of

---

[9] Caleb Luna, "Your Fat Stigma is Racist—Here are 6 Ways to Shift That" published Jan 22, 2017 on Everyday Feminism retrieved from https://everydayfeminism.com/2017/01/how-to-shift-racist-fat-stigma/

that desire, it is perhaps even more painful when we hurt others without meaning to, because our intentions feel so clear to us. But it is inevitable that through our differences in experience and understanding that we will cause harm. It is vital that we lean into learning from this, that we develop our somatic ability to be big enough to stay present in our bodies when we cause harm. Especially when we did not mean to.

I find it far more unbearable to sit with the shame and guilt of having caused pain, than it is to sit with the feeling of having been harmed. When it happens, I feel pressure in my throat, pushing up into my head. This is my body working hard to expunge the feeling to a cerebral place, expel it from the sensory. I am working hard to not have to feel it.

The feeling tends to be centered in one part of my body, usually my solar plexus or chest. As I work with increasing my ability to survive and tolerate the sensations that are generated by guilt and shame, I have come into a practice of visualizing the center of the sensation bleeding out to the rest of my body, like a drop of ink into water. Sometimes I place my hand on the center, massaging it gently like you would a clenched muscle. The goal is to disperse the sensation so that my whole body can be used to digest and metabolize it, so it does not just become an acute burden for a small part of me to manage.[10] Because I am fat, I am bigger than if I were not fat. Which means I have more body to support these intense feelings. If I am afraid of my fatness, of parts of my body, I will not have access to all of it to help me hold this. And I need my whole body. The pain of causing harm, of the history of violence my body carries in me is immense. I need my whole body to digest it.

I have often witnessed that the responsibility for getting big enough to hold complexity and digest emotions is a burden placed on the person or people who have been harmed, and in many cases they are people who are being oppressed or silenced. The people who are being dehumanized

---

[10] "How to Improve Outcomes in All Therapies through Embodiment of Emotions?" by Raja Pavel, PhD, offers great explanations of how to work with and digest emotions through his Integral Somatic Counseling framework.

are asked to share their pain in a way that is gentle, patient, and non-threatening to those who have caused the harm. I have been told this a lot—to calm down, to try and be kind after someone expresses a painful lack of understanding or bias. We are not supposed to blame or be angry, because then we won't be heard. While I value finding ways to communicate with generosity, the responsibility of staying soft and grounded while in conversations about harm, power, and bias cannot be a burden placed on the person or people who are being hurt. This is a way in which power dynamics perpetuate, by continuously focusing on how the marginalized or oppressed can better communicate to get those with more power or privilege to listen. We know that is not real. We know that if people are not willing to believe that they are causing harm or invested in being accountable for their behavior, it does not matter how someone says, "You're hurting me."

In her brilliant book *Emergent Strategy*, adrienne maree brown offers us the wisdom that, "Where shame makes us freeze and try to get really small and invisible, pleasure invites us to move, to open, to grow."[11] Since so often these experiences of being told we have hurt someone elicit feelings of shame, I would invite us to shift to orienting to these moments as moments of pleasure and growth. When I offer someone feedback about the ways in which they have hurt me, it is because part of me is invested in them and our relationship. Even when I am full of rage, screaming at someone, I express what hurts because I believe in their capacity to change. I need them to hear me to maintain the relationship, the connection. It is a way I invest my love for them, by believing in their ability to grow.[12] It is when I do not express the hurt that tells me I do not desire deeper connection and intimacy with this person, that I am not invested in them, in our relationship. How can we orient to getting feedback about our impact as a pleasure? Especially when it is delivered to us in ways that are

---

11 adrienne maree, brown, *Emergent Strategy* (Chico, CA: AK Press, 2017), 21.

12 The notion that love is connected to supporting someone's growth is taken from bell hooks, *All About Love* (New York: Harper Perennial, 2000).

highly emotional and "unregulated." To show someone that you have hurt them, to express your pain and anger openly is vulnerable, and witnessing someone's vulnerability should be a gift.

How we listen to the impact and stay present to grow from those moments can offer small versions of a shifting world in which the feelings and experiences of those being harmed are the voices we lift up and center. To do that, we are all going to need our whole entire big bodies, the fat parts too, to hold those intense feelings. Undoing fat hatred in me has been such a valuable tool in expanding my ability to process these difficult emotions, like shame and guilt. When there are parts of my body that feel untouchable because of internalized fat hatred, I cannot utilize them to fully support me. There is a constriction, a block. When I instead turn to my fat with love and curiosity, I get my body back, to hold me in processing this pain. Giving myself access to my whole body as a resource offers me the ability to be so much more able to receive feedback and stay present so that I can be accountable to people I care about. Thank you, fat, for giving me more body to hold all of these feelings.

to expand and contract in relationship to your environment.

Swim tests in my childhood included 60 seconds of treading water. Thin kids around me would thrash, pant, and splash, while I bobbed up and down with ease, gently swirling my arms and legs. It is one of the only early memories I have in which there is a feeling of pride in my body. A sweet salve to the shame of being a fat girl at the pool.

This (and being a Scorpio-centric person) has nurtured my lifetime love affair with water. I would stay in for hours. The first one in, and often the only one in. After everyone else has gone to dry land, find me still floating.

To maintain a good float, I need to be both hard and soft, tense and relaxed. People sometimes confuse floating as a complete release, but it's not. To float, I need to hold some amount of rigidity by engaging my spine and back muscles to keep me above water, to keep my mouth and nose accessing air. Simultaneously, there also needs to be some release and surrender, giving over my arms and legs, fingers and feet to the movement and tempo of the water. My abdomen needs to relax to make my breath big and easy. There is always some constriction and some release; my whole body is always communicating with the water, with micro-adjustments and movement happening at all times.

What I learn from floating is that in order to be in harmony with my environment, I need to be in both contraction and release, a deep lesson of my fat body's buoyancy.

Having a fat body means the world is asking me to contract more often than release. There are clothes not meant to fit, so I am sucking my belly in; chairs not meant to bear my weight, so I am clenching into a squat; medical gowns leaving me naked and exposed, coaxing me to shrink and turn inward. I feel the ways the world tries to make me atone for my fat body most acutely in the privilege of airplane travel. The looks of disdain from fellow passengers as I walk down the aisle toward my row, their exacerbated sighs when seated next to me. This hostility pushes my body into a constant apology of constriction. It is all tension, no release. There is shame, embarrassment, and anger here. What my body knows from floating alerts me that being in this much constriction is not letting me be in right relationship with my environment.

The more I breathe, the more I soften, the more I release, I can notice all of the other people around me. The person with the very long legs. The person who is more fat than I am. The parent anxiously trying to soothe their crying baby. All of the struggles I cannot know. I think of all the people who could not even get on the plane, who are priced out of air travel, whose bodies are in too much pain, people who are kept where they are by borders, bigotry, and capitalism. When I can bring in release to these moments when all I feel I can do is constrict, when all I feel is shame from the world trying to make me apologize for how much space my body needs, I am reminded that I am never struggling alone. I feel how our struggles are connected. I feel how we need each other.

I spent the first year of studying somatics at the California Institute of Integral Studies (CIIS) in constant constriction. Body-based practice spaces have not historically made me feel like I could have any release. Recently, I went to a workshop that was taught by someone very respected in our field, and she literally rolled her eyes at my body. There is an intense bias against fat people present in this work and it is felt, even when it is not explicitly stated. As people attuned to bodies, we know how much is communicated without words. I reacted to this by being in a constant state of tension and defense. Often entering somatic spaces felt like getting on an airplane.

But luckily I have all that fat body float wisdom, so that I can bring release and awareness in times of deep contraction. When I let myself release, I can feel into how, like when I am on airplanes, I am far from the only person suffering. Fatness is one of many aspects of identity that makes it hard to be in this field. When I release enough to notice all of the other people struggling along with me, I feel strong and present. I feel grateful to be in solidarity and connection with others (writers of this book in particular) who are putting their bodies into places that are not always environments that let them have release, when often they need to be in a lot of constriction.

This spaciousness I can access when feeling in connection with others gives me a wider awareness to consider who is not even in the room in which I am struggling to stay present. Who was not invited? Who was deliberately kept out?

I believe our work is learning about healing from the wisdom of bodies. How does our learning suffer if we are getting a very limited array of bodies as our teachers? How much richer would our work be if our understanding and questions about bodily wisdom were coming from many different sources? There is work for us to do, to change our practices so more types of bodies feel invited to this work.

A place of beginning might be deepening our awareness to how much release or constriction we need in any given moment. While it hurts and angers me when I think about all the ways I navigate whether or not my body can physically fit somewhere, there is also a deep learning. It has made me very aware of how my body interacts with my environment and the people around me. It has offered me the chance to explore in deep ways the physical and energetic space I take up. I do not take for granted that I am impacting those around me, and that I need to be paying attention to how my behavior and presence do that.

I come back to my fat buoyant floating body and what I learn there about how to be a better member of the collective and the environment around me. Like floating, in order to be in harmony with the environment, there is an always-shifting relationship to how much expanding or contracting I need to be doing. I can never be still. There will never be a position I can keep forever that will keep me afloat. Adrienne maree brown writes in *Emergent Strategy* about how we can learn about being in better relationship with each other by looking to water for its wisdom:

Together we must move like waves. Have you observed the ocean? The waves are not the same over and over—each one is unique and responsive. The goal is not to repeat each other's motion, but to respond in whatever way feels right in *your* body. The waves we create are both continuous and a one-time occurrence. We must notice what it takes to respond well. How it feels to be in a body, in a whole—separate, aligned, cohesive. Critically connected.[13]

When does there need to be more release to make myself a little bit bigger, in order to protect myself or advocate for others? When do I need to have more contraction to make myself smaller, to let others take the lead? Constriction and release are always happening together, but there is a difference in the amount of each depending on the circumstance. I want us to be like waves, separate but together; sometimes we are big, sometimes we are small, always shifting. I want more of us to be able to find their float in this work.

fat vitality

I take my belly in my hands. It's warm. My fingers feel cool, but quickly warm, too. It has a good weight, is soft. I sit very still, and feel the pulse in my thumbs, then find the pulse in the place of my thickest fat. It's delicate and regular, there, yes, there, yes, there.... This is not dead lard. It's my body. It's my living fat.[14]

---

13 brown, *Emergent Strategy*, 21.

14 *Belly Songs: In Celebration of Fat Women* (Northampton, MA: Orogeny Press, 1993), 4.

I'm worried, dear reader, that I am trying to paint you a different kind of before and after narrative. In mine, there's no torso jutting out of a single pant leg, but there is perhaps a big bright smile replacing the formerly sad, dejected expression. It is a fantasy I want to tell you, but mostly, I really just want to believe it for myself: a story about how the poison has now been replaced completely with medicine. But that's not real. Because no matter how much medicine I put in and poison I flush out, the world is still dosing out a hell of a lot of poison. It is unfair to expect myself to be healed or to place any healing on some sort of linear path. This is forever work for me. It transforms but it does not end.

The week I turned in the final draft of this piece, Weight Watchers put out a press release stating that they would offer free memberships to people ages 13–17, promoting "the development of healthy habits at a critical life stage."[15] I started going to Weight Watchers when I was fourteen. It did not help me suffer less. It perpetuated some very painful ways of relating to my body, the ones I have spent the past ten years trying to undo. It did not help me develop healthy habits at a truly critical life stage.

What has been good for my health is witnessing other fat people loving their bodies. Letting myself eat delicious food without feeling like I need an excuse or a bargaining chip. Finding ways to move my body that bring me joy and energy, not resentment and exhaustion. Wearing clothes that make me feel powerful and embrace all of the ways my body loves to express gender. Learning the pleasure of touching my fat body, reveling in my own sensuality and in the sensuality of other fat people. Taking lots and lots of selfies. This has been what supports my health.

In the same week that Weight Watchers put out its press release to seduce teens to become lifelong dieters, a junior in high school posted in a radical fat Facebook group of which I am a member, saying she was a fat activist and was wondering if anyone knew of colleges where she

[15] From http://www.weightwatchersinternational.com/file/Index?KeyFile=392090462.

could major in Fat Studies.[16] When I saw her post, my heart swelled up and my stomach was so warm with love that I cried. I clicked on her profile picture—in it she is smiling big, her belly poking out from a crop top. Her public posts were about ending the occupation of Palestine and calling out feminism that did not include and center trans women. I told all of my fat friends, all of us in generations before hers, about the crop-top-wearing-intersectional-feminism-and-anti-colonization-posting sixteen-year-old, who is growing up in a time when she has access to resources letting her know her body is not wrong for how it is a body. I hope she has so much less undoing to do to be in her body. I responded to her post with multiple exclamation marks, telling her I did not know an answer to her question, but that it gave me a piece of my vitality back. Her question was such good medicine.

The process of writing this has been a physically strenuous one. Sitting in pain, feeling the poison and wounding to tell a story is draining. Every time I struggled, I have turned to my body in love and asked, "What can you teach me about how to handle this? Where is the medicine?" And she always had an answer: Be soft and gentle. Be big and strong. Expand and reach toward others.

Reframing my body as a resource and teacher, particularly the part I was taught should be desecrated and torn down, has given me profound healing. I wish that for all of us that we meet our bodies where they are and trust them to give us information about what we need.[17]

It hurts to sit with how much effort it took to relate to my body in this way. My jaw tightens in an effort to dull the sensation. This pain is excruciating and about more than just my own body's journey—it is touching an edge of all the ways the world takes so many of us from our bodies, and how much fight it takes for us to claim them back. And how many of us never get to. How many bodies are stolen and killed. How many of us choose to leave our bodies.

---

[16] Fat Studies is an academic offshoot of Fat Activism.

[17] A concept and teaching from Disability Justice and is explained in depth in Sins Invalid's *Skin Tooth and Bone: The Basis of Movement Is Our People,*

There are so many wise reasons why we, we whose bodies have been unsafe, we whose bodies are in pain, we whose bodies have been taken, choose to live somewhere else other than our bodies. It feels important to remember when doing somatics work that there can be no moral superiority to being "embodied." There can be no value judgment, when there are so many systems at play working to take bodies from some of us more than others.

And I still believe in the power of embodiment. I work to bring myself back into my body so that I can be more in connection with other bodies. So that I can be present to fight for myself and for other people. When I am in my body, I learn what I need for my own healing. When I can tend to my own healing, I can be more present for others. When I can be present for others, I can support them in their healing. There can be no individual healing without collective healing. *Tikkun ha-nefesh* and *tikkun ha-olam*—inextricably entwined.

Bibliography

brown, adrienne maree. *Emergent Strategy*. Chico, CA: AK Press, 2017.

Cooper, David A. *God Is a Verb: Kabbalah and the Practice of Mystical Judaism*. New York: Riverhead Books, 1998.

DeGruy, Joy. "On Post Traumatic Slave Syndrome: Joy DeGruy in Conversation with Denise Boston." Speech, First Unitarian Universalist Society of San Francisco, San Francisco, January 19, 2018.

Hesse-Biber, Sharlene Nagy. *The Cult of Thinness*. Oxford: Oxford University Press, 2006.

hooks, bell. *All about Love: New Visions*. New York: Harper Perennial, 2000.

Selvam, Raja, PhD. "How to Improve Outcomes in All Therapies through Embodiment of Emotions?" Integral Somatic Psychology. January 08, 2018. https://www.integralsomaticpsychology.com/improve-outcomes-therapies-embodiment-emotions.

Sins Invalid, *Skin, Tooth, and Bone: The Basis of Movement Is Our People: A Disability Justice Primer*. Self published. 2016.

Stinson, Susan. *Belly Songs: In Celebration of Fat Women*. Northampton, MA: Orogeny Press, 1993.

Taylor, Sonya Renee. "Making Self Love Radical." In *The Body Is Not an Apology*, 1–24. Oakland, CA: Berrett-Koehler Publishers, Inc., 2018.

Chapter 4

Somatics and Autistic Embodiment

Nick Walker

One thing I love about the field of somatics is that, whether or not they state it outright, all the best teachers and facilitators of somatic work I've had the pleasure to encounter are clearly motivated by a desire to see their fellow human beings blossom and thrive. This has always seemed to me to be the implicit mission at the heart of good somatic praxis in all its myriad forms. If there's one thing that unites the vast diversity of practices encompassed by the term *somatics*—and the vast diversity of individuals and communities that engage in those practices—it's that we all work with human embodiment, in one way or another, toward the goal of human thriving.

One topic that merits further exploration in the field of somatics is the question of how best to work with autistic embodiment, toward the goal of autistic thriving. This has been a topic of particular interest to me, since I occupy the dual position of being both a longtime practitioner and teacher of aikido and other forms of somatic work, and an autistic person deeply involved in autistic culture.

In the pages that follow, I'll share a bit about my own journey, and some lessons I've learned about autistic embodiment and about the application of somatic practices toward meeting the specific needs of the autistic community.

Autism and Human Neurodiversity

Unfortunately, the society in which we live is rife with ignorance, prejudice, and harmful misinformation concerning autism and autistic people. The prejudice and misinformation pervade not only the mass media and the beliefs of the general public, but also the academic and professional spheres; some of the most pernicious nonsense I've heard on the topic has come from the mouths of highly credentialed professionals. In light of this sad state of affairs, it seems best to begin with some basic facts about autism before discussing the particulars of my own story.

Let's start with the simple fact that just as different people have different genders or sizes or skin colors, different people also have different styles of perception and thought. These differences have their basis not only in differing individual and cultural experiences but also in innate biological variation in neurocognitive functioning. This neurocognitive diversity, or *neurodiversity,* is one of the numerous forms of diversity—along with ethnic diversity, gender diversity, diversity of sexual orientation, diversity of body size and shape, etcetera—that intersect and combine to create the vast and vibrant spectrum of humanity.

One manifestation of human neurodiversity is autism, a name for a particular cluster of neurobiological characteristics and associated cognitive traits that occur in somewhere between one and two percent of the population. The distinctive characteristics of autistic neurobiology give autistic persons our own distinctive styles of perception and cognition, our own ways of experiencing the world.

The Nature of Autistic Experience

All of us—autistic or otherwise—experience the world through our senses, as an ever-changing field of sensory information. Our brains are continually engaged in filtering and sorting this information: selecting what gets consciously noticed, and organizing the field into a perceived world of discrete and coherent objects and sensations, through a highly complex system of ingrained schemata that are developed beginning in early infancy. Until they develop at least some basic organizing schemata, a newborn infant's experience of the field of sensory information is, in the words of William James, "one great blooming, buzzing confusion."

Neurons in the cortex of the autistic brain are more numerous, closer together, and less insulated than the cortical neurons in a non-autistic brain. As a result, cortical neurons in the autistic brain tend to fire more readily and connect with each other more readily, and signals being transmitted along a given neural pathway tend to activate other nearby neural pathways in a sort of "ripple" effect. This creates a condition in which less of the field of sensory information is filtered out of consciousness, and in which any given signal in that field of information is likely to have an effect that's both stronger and less predictable than the effect it would have in a non-autistic brain.

What this all adds up to is that an autistic person's subjective sensory experience of the world is quite different from that of any non-autistic person, and far more intense and chaotic. The field of sensory information is much *more* of a great blooming, buzzing confusion for the autistic individual, and thus the process of organizing that field into a coherent world of discrete objects and sensations is more challenging.

Most non-autistic people, fairly early in their development, reach a point where parsing the sensory field into a stable perceptual experience of discrete objects and discrete sensations becomes automatic and effectively instantaneous. For the autistic, however, this process rarely becomes quite as automatic, instantaneous, or complete. Autistic perceptual experience remains to some extent (to exactly what extent varies considerably from person to person) an experience of a buzzing, blooming field of information from which ordered coherence must be continually created and brought into resolution.

In addition to the overall challenge of integrating the sensory field into a coherent and navigable sense of the world, autistic persons often experience other interesting perceptual and cognitive phenomena as a result of our distinctive neurology. Examples include synesthesia (signals in one sensory or cognitive channel manifesting in other channels as well, such as when sounds are experienced as having colors or textures) and strong idiosyncratic sensory responses (finding particular sensations intensely pleasurable or unpleasant, even if most people would find them innocuous).

The intense and chaotic nature of the autistic experience of the sensory field is at the root of the various distinctive traits and patterns of behavior associated with autism. Much of the myth and misunderstanding around autism has its genesis in attempts by non-autistic professionals and laypersons to draw conclusions from the outward, embodied behavior of autistic persons without adequately understanding the subjective internal experiences behind it.

Most notably, autism has been widely misconstrued as being primarily a set of deficits in the capacity for social interaction. Autistics do in fact face substantial challenges when it comes to social interaction, but this is just a side effect of our sensory experience. In infancy and childhood, because so much of our attention is occupied by the complicated process of learning to parse and navigate our sensory world, we don't internalize all the myriad cultural norms and subtleties of social interaction that non-autistic children pick up. Then, because we can't perform non-autistic norms of social interaction well enough to blend in, we tend to be rejected socially by non-autistic people from an early age—which deprives us of opportunities for positive social interaction, which in turn compounds the initial challenges to social development.

The resulting difficulties in social interaction—often lifelong—are incorrectly assumed to be the core defining feature of autism, when in fact they're merely a by-product of having to devote more mental "bandwidth" to processing sensory experience, combined with the effects of a long-term social alienation that stems less from autistic deficits in social potential and more from non-autistic deficits in tolerating difference.

Stimming

From birth—or at least as far back into my early childhood as I can remember—I instinctively responded to the great blooming, buzzing confusion of the world by dancing with it, exploring it with all my senses and allowing myself to move in whatever ways best enabled me to find coherence in it, to modulate its uncomfortable aspects, and to delight in its sensory wonders.

There's one surviving photo of me in my toddler years, taken during an outing to a park: I'm kneeling on the ground beside a flattish, roundish rock about the same size as me, engrossed in exploring its texture with my hands. My happiest fragments of early childhood memory are all of such moments: moments in which I could devote my full presence and attention to some specific sensory pleasure, whether it was feeling certain textures against my skin, being absorbed by the sight and sound of a column of living water in a fountain, or running at top speed across an open field. Whenever I had the chance to fully indulge in such pleasures—especially the ones with a strong kinesthetic or tactile component, like vigorously rocking back and forth or running the palms of my hands along the cool smooth surface of a wall—doing so invariably helped me to integrate the whole of my sensory experience, temporarily lending my perceptual world an increased coherence and navigability.

Many years later, when I became involved in the emergent autistic culture that began to take shape in the early 1990s and continues to develop and grow to this day, I discovered that some of my fellow autistics had coined a term for these various forms of bodily engagement with sensory experience: *stimming*.

To stim is to engage in any physical activity that stimulates one's senses, for the purpose—whether intentional or purely instinctive—of regulating one's experience and consciousness. Stimming can be proprioceptive or kinesthetic (rocking, pacing, waving one's hands, seeking physical pressure or impact), tactile (touching objects and surfaces with appealing textures, stroking one's own skin), vestibular (spinning or swinging), visual (gazing at running water or rising smoke), auditory (loud music), olfactory or gustatory (sniffing or tasting things), verbal (repetition of interesting words or phrases, like "blooming buzzing"), or any combination of these (drumming, for instance, is both kinesthetic and auditory). The list of possible stims is infinite;

every autistic person I've encountered has their own favorites. Stimming can serve many functions, including (but not limited to) helping to modulate, process, integrate, and bring greater coherence to sensory experience; facilitating emotional and cognitive processing and regulation; inducing or enhancing states of sensory pleasure; and enabling access to specific cognitive capacities or states of consciousness.

Stimming isn't something that only autistic people do. How many non-autistic people occasionally pace back and forth because it helps them think? Drum their fingers on a desk or table? Pause to deeply inhale a pleasing scent? Let themselves be soothed and entranced by the sound of rain on the roof or the sight of flickering flames in a fireplace? Spend time stroking a pet, or the hair or skin of a lover, because it feels good? Spontaneously move their bodies as they get into the groove of a piece of music? All these activities qualify as stimming. Everybody stims.

But autistics stim a lot more than everybody else, because to stim more or less constantly is essential for processing, regulating, and navigating the chaotic complexity of autistic sensory and cognitive experience. And because autistic sensory preferences are idiosyncratic and diverge from common non-autistic sensory preferences, autistic stimming stands out more to the judgmental eyes of the non-autistic because it tends to violate non-autistic cultural norms.

For instance: once, in kindergarten, I got in a great deal of trouble for stroking the skin of my left forearm with my right index finger. The teacher punished me much more harshly than other kids got punished for hitting their classmates. I suppose that's because while hitting is merely wrong, stroking the skin of one's own arm is (gasp!) *not normal.* And as every autistic kid learns early and repeatedly, there's no worse crime than not being normal.

Sensory Needs vs. Social Norms

I've mentioned that autistics tend to have less attentional bandwidth available to focus on childhood social development or the subtleties of face-to-face social interactions, because navigating autistic sensory experience consumes so much attention. A closely related dynamic occurs in regard to autistic embodiment. (When I speak of embodiment, I refer to all aspects of how we use our bodies, consciously or otherwise—including tension and relaxation, movement, body shape, carriage, breath, gaze, expression, gesture, and vocalization—and the ways in which these various aspects of bodily usage combine to create the overall gestalt of how we perform our presence in the world.) It boils down to this: the more one's use of the body has to be geared toward regulating sensory and cognitive experience, the less it can be geared toward social purposes like following cultural norms of embodiment and nonverbal communication. Everyone uses their embodiment to regulate their experience, and everyone uses their embodiment to convey social meaning in accordance with learned cultural norms. But relative to non-autistic embodiment, autistic embodiment involves more of the former at the expense of the latter.

For example: like most (but not all) autistic children, I avoided eye contact whenever possible. Why? Because to my relatively unfiltered autistic perceptions, eye contact was so loaded with information that it was too intense to process while I was also trying to process anything else (like other sensory input, or language). Making eye contact in a social situation dysregulated me to the point where it was impossible to deal with any other aspect of the situation, like remembering how to use or comprehend words. And like most autistic children, I'd avoided eye contact so much since infancy that I'd never internalized any of the non-autistic cultural norms around how to use it (and like most autistic adults, I still don't make much eye contact—and when I do make eye contact, my timing and style still don't follow non-autistic cultural norms).

Now, I was a white kid growing up in a mostly Black neighborhood, and going to a school with mostly white teachers. According to the cultural norms of the Black adults in my neighborhood, it was a sign of disrespect if children looked their elders straight in the eye. But according to the cultural norms of my white teachers and most of the other white adults I encountered, *lack* of eye contact was a sign of inattention and dishonesty (an absurd myth that persists in white non-autistic culture despite the accumulation of scientific studies demonstrating that liars tend to make more eye contact than truth-tellers). The result was that I was constantly targeted by white adults for being disrespectful, inattentive, and "obviously hiding something," while Black adults tended to be much nicer to me than white adults (I once overheard one of them remark to another that I was unusually well mannered for a white kid).

Since I rarely said much, the snap judgments these various adults made about my character were formed, to a large degree, on the basis of how they interpreted my lack of eye contact (on numerous occasions, the white adults even said as much). And their interpretations were based on what their cultural norms said about the meaning of eye contact or lack thereof.

What none of them understood was that my avoidance of eye contact, like my stimming and most other aspects of my embodiment, had no social meaning behind it at all. It wasn't in any way about them or about my attitude toward my interactions with them; it was about regulating sensory input in a way that was necessary if I was going to be able to interact at all.

That's the sort of thing I'm referring to when I say that relative to non-autistic embodiment, autistic embodiment tends to be more shaped by the need to interact in specific ways with the overall sensory field, and consequently less shaped by cultural norms or by any social agenda.

Dyspraxia

There's one other significant factor that contributes to the distinctive nature of autistic embodiment: the same cortical hyperconnectivity that causes incoming signals to ripple across neural pathways, producing the chaotic intensity of autistic sensory experience, also affects the outgoing signals that the brain sends to the rest of the body when one performs any physical action. This creates interference with the smooth execution of intended actions, a phenomenon known as *dyspraxia.*

Like sensory sensitivity, synesthesia, or any other autistic trait, dyspraxia manifests differently and to differing (and often fluctuating) degrees in each autistic individual. In some, it's noticeable only as a certain physical awkwardness, an odd gait, a slowness at picking up new motor skills. In others, there's extreme impairment of motor skills, sometimes including speech. (One of the more damaging non-autistic social prejudices impacting the autistic community is the unfortunately commonplace tendency to equate oral speech with intelligence. Autistics who are unable to speak due to dyspraxia are frequently dismissed as lacking in basic intelligence and self-awareness, and denied respect and self-determination, despite the fact that a growing number of non-speaking autistics who spent their early lives being similarly dismissed have proven to be eloquent and insightful when given the opportunity to learn to communicate through typing or other assistive technologies.)

Autistic Embodiment

The motor effects of dyspraxia, the heavy use of stimming, and the need to orient the use of the body toward the goal of sensory and cognitive regulation at the expense of orienting toward nonverbal communication, all interact and combine to inform autistic styles of embodiment. Individual embodiment is shaped by many factors, of course—including genetics, culture, and personal experiences—and individual embodiment varies as much among autistic individuals as among non-autistic individuals. And yet, I've met a great many autistic people over the years, hailing from many different backgrounds and cultures and possessing widely disparate personalities, and in each and every one of them I've observed certain distinctive qualities of embodiment—certain shared movement signatures, subtle and nigh-impossible to describe yet readily recognizable to the attuned and experienced eye—that transcend cultural differences and mark them unmistakably as members of my scattered tribe.

A World That Didn't Want Me

When left alone, as a child, I would contentedly follow my natural impulses toward movement, learning, exploration, and creative engagement with the world, in whatever ways and at whatever pace best suited my particular developmental needs and inclinations. But I was never left alone as much as I would have liked. Instead, every day was an extended series of baffling, stressful, and traumatic situations in which nearly everyone I encountered—other kids, my parents, my teachers, and other employees of the school system—rejected and psychologically and physically abused me for being different, for being not-normal, for needing more time to process and understand things than the other kids needed, and for failing to follow non-autistic norms of embodiment, cognition, speech, and interaction.

Conforming to all those norms, while simultaneously trying to navigate the incessant demands of the non-autistic world at the sort of pace that was required of me, would have been impossible for me even if I'd understood what the norms to which I was supposed to conform actually were (which I didn't—because, as most autistic children learn, the first rule of non-autistic social interaction is that no one explains the rules, and the second rule is that anyone who asks for a clear explanation of the rules gets abused instead of being given helpful answers). So my daily childhood experience, except when I was alone, was one of bewildered floundering under an overwhelming bombardment of confusing noise, incomprehensible demands, implacable hostility, and seemingly random eruptions of verbal or physical abuse that could come from anyone around me at any moment.

What I learned later, reading the stories of countless others in online autistic communities, was that the hostility, abuse, and trauma I experienced as a child were more or less standard fare for an autistic childhood in the modern world. If anything, my childhood seems to have been on the pleasant side compared to that of many of my fellow autistics. To grow up autistic is to grow up in a world that doesn't want you—a world where the mass media, politicians across the political spectrum, giant money-grubbing "autism charities" run by non-autistics, and often our own families speak of our very existence as a "tragedy," a "burden," and an "epidemic." I've found that most non-autistics, including non-autistic professionals who work with autistic clients, have very little understanding of just how much traumatic abuse the vast majority of autistics experience in childhood, adolescence, and beyond.

Losing Myself

A shard of memory: I'm in kindergarten, walking around the playground. Just walking and walking, a favorite activity throughout my life. Feels good, helps me integrate. I'm letting my hands move around as they are wont to do, letting them hover in the air around me, now flapping like butterflies, now floating like seaweed. No language spoken by non-autistic people has words for what this does for me. I'm jolted by the sudden sound of boys laughing. I look and see a group of bigger boys horsing around nearby. I think they're the same boys who taunted me and hit me at recess a couple of days ago, calling me "freak" and "retard." This time it's not me they're laughing at, but they might turn their attention to me at any moment. I remember that other kids have mocked and sometimes assaulted me for the way I move my hands. It occurs to me that if these boys spot my hands moving it will draw their attention. I quickly jam my hands into my pockets and walk on, pretending to be going somewhere. The boys ignore me. It worked! Next time I walk around the playground, I keep my hands in my pockets. It makes me a little bit safer, and I barely notice that I feel a little bit less alive.

I hardly think that was the very last time in my childhood I moved my hands like that; it's just one moment I happen to remember, one representative glimpse of the story of my childhood. The suppression of my visible stimming habits was a long and gradual process, and even the stifling of any one specific form of stimming, like those particular hand movements, can't be boiled down to any single decisive moment. To repress the embodiment of one's truest and most vital self, to extinguish the unique dance by which that self intuitively seeks to engage with the world, takes countless tiny decisions, most of which end up lost to conscious memory if they were even consciously made in the first place. A slow accumulation of moments in which the spontaneous dance of stimming is put on lockdown for the sake of the partial safety of briefly passing for semi-normal, until the lockdown becomes habit and the dance is buried and forgotten under layers of rigid armor.

It's never a price worth paying. For autistics, especially, stimming is essential to our well-being in every way—essential to ever attaining any measure of ease in navigating our world, essential to self-regulation and stability, essential to accessing our best gifts and highest potentials.

In the long run, suppressing our visible stimming and other aspects of our natural autistic embodiment doesn't even buy us the safety from abuse it appears to offer. We can never truly pass. An autistic person can't thrive and find social acceptance as an imitation of a non-autistic person just by forcing themselves not to move like an autistic person, any more than an eagle can live comfortably as an ostrich by forcing itself not to use its wings.

Locking the beauty of our autistic dance away under layers of chronic tension warps our embodiment into a perpetual state of awkward rigidity, a clumsy stiffness and dissociation, lacking in vitality and physical confidence. In the eyes of non-autistics this sorry condition, combined with our inability to convincingly perform the subtleties of non-autistic social norms, marks us as Other and as targets just as surely as our stimming ever did. And without access to the dance, without the integrative and restorative power of stimming, it's impossible to cultivate the sort of resilience we need in order to thrive in this world.

By the time I turned twelve, the years of accumulated stress and trauma, compounded by the loss of resilience and vitality from repressing my stimming, had taken a severe psychological and physical toll on me. I was depressed, wracked with tension, often dissociated. Pale, anemic, and skeletally thin, I was often unable to eat due to ulcers and other stress-induced digestive problems. My posture was hunched, shoulders up and head down, always curling inward as if to shield myself from the unrelenting rain of abuse. I was plagued with headaches, illnesses, obsessive-compulsive symptoms, and an assortment of nervous tics and twitches. Most of the time, all that kept me alive was sheer stubborn defiance: the world didn't want me, so as long as I stayed alive the world didn't get to win.

Finding Aikido

I was twelve when I made the decision to start fighting back physically against bullies. This improved my life a bit: it scared off some of the more cowardly bullies, partially alleviated my digestive problems because less of my tension was turned inward, got me thrown out of the public school system and put in a school for "socially maladjusted" youth where I finally made friends, and gave me some much-needed self-respect. All this came just from *trying* to fight; I was too weak and sickly, and too clumsy from dyspraxia, to actually win any of the fights I got into. And while the consequences of fighting back and losing were better for me than the consequences of not fighting back at all, it was clear that I wasn't going to survive long if I didn't get some sort of martial arts training.

I chose aikido because it was mentioned in the science fiction novella *Babel-17,* by Samuel Delany, which back then was one of the few books I'd found in which weird misfits like me were portrayed in a positive light. Aikido was less widespread in the USA back when I started. The only local aikido teachers, a married couple, had just moved to town. I was the youngest and only autistic member in a cohort of beginning students, mostly adults.

Like so many autistic kids, I'd spent my whole childhood being abused for not meeting mysterious rules of conduct that everyone else apparently knew but that no one would clearly spell out for me. The traditional aikido dojo (school) observes a code of formal etiquette that governs nearly every aspect of conduct and interaction. The rules of dojo etiquette were as foreign to the non-autistic students as they were to me, so no one was expected to start out knowing them and they got clearly spelled out for everyone. As soon as I walked in the door, one of the teachers came up and gave me explicit instructions on the proper etiquette for walking in the door. If anyone forgot to follow a rule, they were reminded in a simple and direct way. Unlike all my previous experience of social interaction, interpersonal interactions in the dojo weren't a treacherous minefield of unspoken rules and opportunities for failure and rejection. The rules were clear: no nonessential talking during practice, here's when you bow, here are the exact phrases you use and the precise actions you perform in these particular types of interaction. To me, this seemed nothing short of miraculous. It was the first social environment I'd ever encountered that was accessible to me, my first time interacting with non-autistics on a level social playing field.

The Alienation of the Autistic Body

Aikido was also my first experience of receiving intensive training in mindful embodiment. Which was exactly what I needed, because I came to aikido profoundly alienated and dissociated from my own physicality—a condition I've since found to be tragically commonplace among my fellow autistics. The chaotic nature of autistic sensory experience makes it exceptionally challenging for an autistic person to learn to tune into and process the flow of kinesthetic and proprioceptive sensory information that provides much of the basis of bodily awareness. I am convinced that this challenge could be surmounted with relative ease—and turned into a positive opportunity for joyful exploration, learning, and development—if autistic children were provided from an early age with the sort of supportive, engaging, and vigorous training in mindful physical play that I found in the aikido dojo. Instead, the way most autistic children are raised, educated, and socialized not only fails to address this difficulty with bodily awareness, but compounds it.

The traumatic abuse and bullying to which most autistic children are subjected promotes a state of dissociation, a common trauma symptom. Constant pressure to conform to non-autistic developmental norms, and the relentless regimen of "therapies" and "treatments" to which many parents subject their autistic children, can also produce a state of perpetual overwhelm that also fosters dissociation.

On top of this, the pressure to suppress stimming and other natural autistic bodily needs and mannerisms, the chronic physical tension necessary to effect such suppression and to armor the child against the onslaughts of an overwhelming and often hostile world, and the tendency of non-autistic adults to treat autism as an undesirable pathology rather than as integral to the child's selfhood, all serve to engender in the autistic child a sense of alienation from their own natural physicality—a sense of the body as other rather than self, and as a site of failure and discomfort.

And finally, because the combination of sensory confusion and dyspraxia tends to make autistics significantly slower than non-autistics when it comes to acquiring competence at new physical skills, the competition-obsessed culture we live in shames young autistics for their lack of physical aptitude and teaches them that they have no place in the worlds of athletics, dance, or other such physically oriented pursuits. A sad state of affairs, because these are precisely the sort of activities that, if presented in a supportive and accessible way, could help young autistics to develop much-needed bodily awareness, coordination, and joyful physicality. Writing off young autistics as having no potential for physical prowess becomes a message they internalize and a self-fulfilling prophecy. That was certainly the case for me, until I began my aikido training.

Under Pressure, in a Good Way

In aikido, I soon discovered, training in the use of the body went far beyond the expected "this is what to do when someone tries to punch you" sort of instruction. Integral to the practice was a rigorously mindful approach to the most fundamental aspects of embodiment: how one sat, stood, walked, breathed, found one's balance, focused one's gaze, carried one's shoulders, gripped with one's hands, engaged the body in any physical action.

This mindful embodiment was taught in the aikido dojo primarily through nonverbal feedback in the form of direct physical pressure. For instance, we would kneel or stand or move, attempting to simultaneously maintain stability and keep our breathing and our muscles relaxed, while fellow students pushed on us from various angles with gradually increasing force. The instructors might test our stability in this way at any time, pushing on us just as we finished a pivoting move or returned to upright after rolling over our shoulders. We would extend our arms and try to keep them straight yet free of excess muscular tension, while fellow students tried to bend them. Our training partners would tightly grab us and try to hold us in place while we tried to move and take their balance without straining. From practices like these we learned over time to stay calm, stable, poised, and centered under pressure; to cultivate full-body awareness and a sense of connection to the ground and the space around us; to notice and release excess tensions as they arose; to develop well-aligned postures and harmonious ways of moving that deployed the body's power with fluid ease.

This approach to teaching through physical pressure worked for me where no previous attempt to teach me any sort of body awareness or physical aptitude had worked. Attempts to use verbal instruction and visual demonstration to get me to stand with better posture, or to perform some feat of coordination like kicking a ball, had failed for the simple reason that between the dissociation and the difficulty processing kinesthetic and proprioceptive sensory input, I couldn't tell what I was doing. How could I change the way I held my spine or moved my feet, when I couldn't *find* my spine or my feet? Intrusive physical interventions, like when teachers at school would grab me and force my body into some semblance of the posture they wanted me to hold, hadn't worked either—as soon as hands were no longer touching me, I would again lose track of myself and within seconds I'd shrink back into my habitual hunched and twisted pose without even noticing.

But the physical pressures and resistances that were continually provided in aikido training worked for me. Instead of trying to impose changes on my body from the outside, these pressures gave me the feedback I needed to adjust and refine my own embodiment from within. The sustained pressure of a push helped me to feel my body, to locate myself, and provided moment-to-moment information on the efficacy of each adjustment I made.

For instance, when I sat in the traditional Japanese kneeling position called *seiza* with someone pushing steadily on the front of my shoulder, the push would cause me to tip over unless I maintained a well-aligned upright posture, dropped excess muscular tension without going limp, and grounded myself through focus on the *hara* (the energetic center in the lower abdomen). If the quality of my posture lapsed, I knew it instantly because I'd start to tip over. If I tensed my shoulders, I knew it instantly because I'd start to tip over. Allow my breath to become shallow, tight, or uneven? Muscular tensions would start to arise, and I'd tip over. Hunch forward and strain against the push, and I'd tip over. Go limp, and I'd tip over. Couldn't ask for clearer feedback than that! The only way to keep from tipping over was to remain impeccably mindful in my embodiment.

Through these practices of mindful embodiment under pressure, I got gradually better at staying tuned into my body, gradually better at noticing incipient tensions or other lapses in the quality of my form and correcting them *before* I started to tip over. And over time I gradually gained the ability to locate myself, to stay grounded, centered, relaxed, and well aligned in my postures and movements, *without* any external push or pressure to help orient me.

Persistence and Plasticity

The chaos of my sensory experience interfered not only with my ability to keep track of my own body, but also my ability to process the instructions and demonstrations from the teachers. And even when I could manage to figure out where all my limbs were and what I was supposed to do with them, my dyspraxia meant that sometimes my body just wouldn't do what I intended. All in all, I was about as unpromising a novice aikido student as one could imagine.

But in a transformative practice like aikido, what ultimately matters most is persistence. Nothing in aikido came easy for me—but then, I hadn't expected easy. Nothing had ever been easy. Aikido was beautiful, and one thing at which we autistics famously excel is sustained, intensive focus on those things—whatever they may be and however odd they may seem to others—in which we find an often inexplicable beauty. Who knows what peculiar dynamics of neurology and spirit cause some autistics to perceive a compelling and transcendent beauty in plumbing fixtures or railroad trains, while others find similar beauty in urban architecture or baseball statistics, in Disney animation or higher mathematics, in the sensory experience of running water or the music of Bach? We find beauty where we find it. Aikido did help me achieve my original objective of getting better at fighting; by the time I was seventeen there wasn't a bully in town who'd risk tangling with me anymore. But by that time I'd nearly forgotten that that was why I'd started training. I was in it for the beauty, and I still am. I knew from my very first aikido class that to be able to participate in the beauty I saw in the art, I'd work as long and hard as I had to. So I persisted.

And with persistence came transformation. With persistence, bodyminds learn—including autistic bodyminds, even if they learn differently from non-autistic bodyminds. Autistic brains may be different from non-autistic brains in some ways, but neuroplasticity—the brain's wondrous capacity to form new neural pathways, to continually modify itself in response to experience—appears to be a universal human trait. Over time, like the waters of a river slowly carving a path through solid rock, dedicated practice built new pathways in my brain, new capacities for mindful embodiment that countered and gradually came to supplant the dyspraxia, the disorientation of sensory and cognitive overload, and the effects of trauma.

Mindful Presence

In aikido, one practices dealing gracefully with physical attacks by working in harmony with the attacker's movement and power, redirecting the force of their attack in order to take their balance. In order to do this well, one must remain mindful in one's own embodiment: centered and grounded so as not to be overwhelmed by the attack, well aligned in order to make efficient use of one's own power, and relaxed so that one's tensions don't interfere with the flow of one's movements. At the same time, one must attend deeply to the person who is delivering the attack; the only way to truly work in harmony with them is to remain present and attuned to their embodiment as it shifts from moment to moment.

This type of dual attention, in which one stays centered, relaxed, and able to continually regulate one's own embodied state while simultaneously attuning to and interacting mindfully with others, is perhaps the most important and transformative capacity that aikido helps its practitioners to develop. A significant part of the value of aikido training lies in the fact that with dedicated practice one can cultivate this dual attention in every area of one's life, bringing a centered, mindful presence to one's interactions with the world and everyone in it. After all, if one can learn to remain mindfully present while under direct physical attack, one can learn to remain mindfully present for just about anything.

What I discovered early on in my own aikido training was that the qualities of presence we practiced embodying in aikido also had the power to transform my relationship with my sensory experience. Once I began learning the somatic skill of making subtle moment-to-moment adjustments in my embodiment in order to remain centered while my training partners pushed on me or attacked me, it wasn't too big a leap from there to finding similar ways to work with my embodiment in order to remain centered when dealing with those chaotic floods of sensory input that we autistics so often find ourselves overwhelmed by.

The fundamental nature of my sensory experience didn't change; it remained as intense and chaotic as ever, blooming and buzzing with vibrant synesthesia. But the qualities of embodied presence I was cultivating in my aikido practice enabled me to navigate the blooming, buzzing confusion gracefully, to work in harmony with it without being destabilized or overwhelmed by it, just as I'd learned to meet the power of my aikido training partners with serene stability and to work in harmony with the incoming force of their attacks. Through this approach I was able to gradually free myself from the stressful and debilitating effects of sensory overload, while still retaining the benefits of my intense sensory and cognitive experience. (And there are indeed benefits, which I in no way mean to downplay when I write about navigating autism's challenges. Autism has persisted in the gene pool for good reasons. Autistic perspectives hold the potential to produce novel contributions to human cultures and communities; the richness of autistic sensory and cognitive experience provides a built-in access to transcendent states and "outside-the-box" modes of creative thinking that most non-autistic people tap into only through psychedelic drugs or moments of profound psychospiritual awakening. I wouldn't trade this for anything.)

Expansiveness

Autistic children overwhelmed by the intensity of their sensory experience often seek to shut out the blooming, buzzing confusion as best they can—curling up, shrinking away from intrusive and overstimulating contact. For as long as the existence of autism has been recognized, these perfectly natural responses to sensory overload have been misinterpreted by non-autistics as "withdrawal from reality," or "retreating into a world of their own." Imagine if you were seated too near the speakers at a concert, and you covered your ears because of the painful volume levels, and got accused of "withdrawing from reality"!

Though they generally find strategies for coping to some degree with the overwhelming clamor and sensory assaults of the modern world as they grow up, autistics often remain in an ongoing struggle to defend against overload—a struggle that curtails their activities and social lives, and consumes a great deal of their mental and physical energy. I see this struggle, this experience of being continually under sensory attack, manifest in the embodiment of many fellow autistics as a constant tension, a pulling inward. I know just how it feels to go through life pulling oneself inward like that; my own embodiment was similarly pulled inward, until it was transformed by my aikido training.

The style of embodiment cultivated in aikido has a distinctly *expansive* quality to it. The dual attention that's integral to aikido is attained in part through the practice of maintaining a centered and grounded state while expanding one's sphere of attention and sense of presence outward to include the space around one. This expansiveness isn't about puffing oneself up in a macho, blustering way. Rather, it involves a softening, a radiant receptivity, an opening to connection with the surrounding space and anyone in it. It's very much the opposite of pulling one's energy inward or tensing against the world. In the early years of my aikido training, I diligently practiced finding this quality of expansiveness. I would walk around just imagining the field of my presence blossoming outward. This practice gradually reshaped my embodiment—opening up my breathing and posture, dissolving long-held tensions—until my habit of defensively pulling inward was a thing of the past. I didn't need to shrink from the world or tense against it anymore; it turned out the world was far less overwhelming when I could greet it with centered expansiveness.

The Missing Piece

By the time I was in my mid-twenties, I'd been practicing aikido more than a dozen years. I was centered and expansive, strong and agile, physically confident, unruffled by the intensity of my sensory world.

And I was miserable.

I felt good during aikido classes, immersed in training. I had other good moments, sometimes, when I was absorbed in some physically engaging sensory pleasure like dancing to loud music. But much of the time, underneath the confident physical presence, I lived in a bleak haze of depression. Being centered enough that the world couldn't rattle me somehow didn't help me feel at home or at ease in the world, or able to thrive in it. Luck, plus the ability to be expansive instead of overwhelmed in social situations, had brought me more friends and lovers than many of my fellow autistics find in their lives—yet I still felt perpetually lonely and disconnected.

I hated the life I was living—the poverty, the string of meaningless and degrading minimum-wage jobs on which I had to waste most of my time and energy just to barely scrape by, the desperate periods of unemployment and homelessness—but I couldn't seem to organize myself well enough to follow any plan of action that might improve things. When I so much as thought about trying to enroll in a college course or some such step, I would quickly become baffled by the details and end up paralyzed by despair. I wanted to make art, to write, to engage creatively with the world, but I couldn't make it happen; I could sense a smoldering creative fire somewhere inside me, but I felt like I was separated from it by thick walls of gray mud.

Plainly, something was missing, but I didn't know what. I just struggled through life, day after empty day, my centered and confident bearing hiding a nigh-unbearable sense of alienation and loss.

What was missing, it turned out, was me. More specifically, what was missing were the essential aspects of my being that I'd learned to repress and banish from my embodiment in childhood: the unique and ever-emerging dance of stimming that is each autistic individual's natural way of connecting with the world and with the full spectrum of our cognitive capacities, the dance of distinctively autistic movement and embodiment that is the physical expression of each autistic individual's authentic self.

Aikido had done a great deal for me: transformed me, enabled me to discover and embody potentials for grace and power beyond what anyone (myself included) would have expected I had in me back when

I first began my training. But without stimming, without including in my embodiment the authentic and distinctively autistic dance of *me,* I couldn't be complete.

Of *course* I felt alienated and disconnected, unable to engage fully in my life. In order to make true connections—with the world, with others, or with the sources of one's own creativity, vitality, and joy—it's necessary to actually be there to connect, as one's true self. How could I be anything other than disconnected, when instead of embodying my true self I had locked it away behind an ill-fitting, less-visibly-autistic mask?

But back then, in my twenties (half a lifetime ago, as I write these words) I didn't understand any of this yet. It took a brush with death to get me pointed in the right direction.

Paratheatrical Research

I was twenty-one when I stumbled across a book called *Angel Tech,* by someone named Antero Alli. The book had a sort of do-it-yourself punk aesthetic that set it apart from the other books on spiritual work I'd seen. It was clear the author possessed some hard-won wisdom, but that much of this wisdom—like much of what I was learning in aikido—didn't translate readily into writing. If nothing else, it was a unique enough book to be memorable.

I was twenty-six when I got *E. coli* poisoning. Having no access to medical care, I almost died before I was miraculously able to fight off the sickness on my own. When my raging fever finally broke, I emerged from my delirium determined to embark on a new path of psychospiritual exploration and transformation. Next time I found myself face-to-face with death, I wanted to be someone who knew his own soul, someone who could die well because he'd been fully alive.

The very next day, while I was still in bed recuperating, my housemate brought home a photocopied flyer announcing that Antero Alli, author of *Angel Tech,* had just moved to our town and was looking for people with experience in movement-based work to be part of a group he was forming called Paratheatrical Research. I set up a meeting with him, and ten minutes into our conversation I already knew this Paratheatrical Research project was the path I was looking for.

Antero had developed a unique form of transformative movement work with roots in physical theatre and Jungian psychology. Paratheatrical Research became an ongoing project in which small groups of participants met in a dance studio or similar space on a regular basis to experiment with this work in group rituals—not rituals in any religious sense, but in the sense of structured activities that facilitated access to levels of psychospiritual experience beyond the everyday conscious ego. The aim of these rituals was to explore and give embodied expression to various aspects of the personal unconscious and the collective unconscious, in a process Antero described as "an archeology of the soul."

Each session of paratheatrical ritual work began with a sequence of vigorous warm-up exercises and meditation practices intended to produce a state of heightened receptivity. Then we would invoke whatever archetypal force or aspect of the unconscious we'd be exploring (for instance, the Shadow or the Anima), by naming it and inviting it into the space and into our bodies to move us. It's remarkable how effective this sort of simple invitation can be once the bodymind is sufficiently primed and receptive. The biggest challenge was to maintain that receptivity and allow ourselves to be moved from within by the unconscious forces we'd accessed, relaxing the tendency of the conscious ego to second-guess or over-control.

When we could accomplish this, the results were extraordinary. We would move around the room in strange new dances, intricate yet unplanned, alien choreographies spontaneously emerging from the unconscious. Sometimes it was dreamlike and unearthly, sometimes wildly cathartic: we'd writhe on the floor, wracked by violent tremors or paroxysms of sobbing and laughter, as deep tensions broke down to make way for the energies moving through us; minutes later we might find ourselves pacing serenely in winding spirals, like monks walking an invisible labyrinth, voices lifted in ecstatic wordless song.

The experiences I had in my nineteen years as a core member of Paratheatrical Research could fill a book. But as far as our present narrative goes, what matters is that as the paratheatre work broke down layers of deep chronic tension that had been held in my body since childhood, layers deeper than those my aikido practice had been able to undo. And as the work brought buried aspects of my being to the surface and into embodiment, I spontaneously began to stim again.

Recovering Myself

It took about three years of the paratheatre work before my natural autistic stimminess, repressed since childhood, began to reassert itself here and there in small ways: an impulse to run the palm of my hand repeatedly over a pleasingly textured surface; my arms rising now and then to wave in the air in front of me, fingers twisting, as I spoke. Gradually and subtly, over the next few years, my impulses to stim increased.

I didn't fully understand what was happening yet; this was before I'd ever heard the term *stimming*. I just noticed I was having these impulses toward odd movements, these sudden hungers for specific sensations, with increasing frequency. I had the sense that it was part of how the paratheatrical work was transforming me, so I figured I'd embrace it. Let the movements happen, follow the impulses. And when I did, it just felt *right*. Natural and familiar, even if I couldn't yet put my finger on why.

Stimming was intrinsically satisfying and rewarding; I did it for its own sake. For those first few years I didn't even make the connection between the "new" ways in which I was spontaneously moving and engaging with the sensory world, and the changes in my psychological state. My long depression was fading. My focus and mental acuity were improving. I had more energy, felt more alive.

I was in my early thirties when I first got involved in online autistic communities and finally learned what stimming was. Then the pieces started falling into place. Up to that point, the reemergence of my stimming had merely been a fortuitous side effect of the paratheatre work. Now, though, I began to actively focus my work in the paratheatrical ritual sessions on the goal of fully recovering my capacity for stimming, fully recovering every aspect of the dance of autistic embodiment—the dance of my true self that I'd suppressed and lost so long ago. The working methods of Paratheatrical Research were perfectly suited to such a task.

Sure enough, with every breakthrough in the recovery of my dance came a corresponding breakthrough in the healing of my psyche and the blossoming of my cognitive capacities. My creativity sparked and blazed to life; I wrote, I made art. My ability to think clearly, to make and follow through on a plan of action, improved so dramatically that I was able to start attending college for the first time in my life, and to excel at my studies, which led me in time to a quite unexpected career in academia. The sense of alienation that had haunted me began to melt away as I became able to more fully embody my authentic autistic self in my engagement with others and with the world.

Recovering the dance of my autistic self also transformed my aikido. I'd benefited enormously from my aikido practice over the years: it had taught me how to be centered, mindful, and expansive; it had been a rare source of stability and pleasure in my life. Until I began recovering my dance, though, the way I did aikido was an imitation of the way my various non-autistic teachers had done aikido—and trying to do aikido like a non-autistic person meant I wasn't bringing my full authentic self to it. I hadn't realized this, because unlike the rest of my life, my aikido practice had still felt good. But as I learned to allow the dance of my autistic self to come into embodiment in my practice, a whole new level of aikido began opening up to me—a depth, flow, and grace beyond anything I'd previously known. Aikido, after all, is ultimately about connection—to other people, to the world, to life—and the quality of one's connections, in aikido as in all else, depends very much on one's capacity to show up as one's true self.

Flamingly Autistic and Thriving

Everything I do these days—aikido, teaching and learning, writing and public speaking, loving and parenting, being in the world and in community—I do as my authentic self, autistically. My embodiment is flamingly autistic. If you know how to recognize it, you can see it in the movements of my hands, the rhythmic rocking of my body as I sit, my walk, the tilt of my head, how and where I direct my gaze, the way certain things in my environment draw my attention, the small and seemingly random stops and starts and moments of silence in the pacing of my conversation, the endless small stims that are a constant part of my engagement with the world.

To those who don't know how to recognize autistic embodiment, I suppose I just come across as weird. Which is accurate, if we consider *weird* as the opposite of *normal.* To thrive as an autistic person, one must allow one's embodiment to be autistic, and this puts one in constant violation of non-autistic conceptions of "normal" embodiment.

Many non-autistic people, even some who've spent time with other adult autistics, don't recognize me as autistic these days. Sometimes this is just because I don't fit whatever popular stereotypes about autism they've encountered (very few real autistic people actually fit the popular stereotypes). But most of the time, I've come to understand, it's because severe trauma is so widespread in the autistic population that most people (including most autistic people, sadly) can't even imagine what we might be like without it.

So when people say I don't seem like other autistics, what they usually mean is that I don't have the pulled-inward quality or the overwhelming anxiety, nor the awkward rigidity that comes from deeply ingrained chronic tensions—tensions established as defenses against constant overstimulation and abuse, and as a means of repressing any stimming or other characteristically autistic movements that might attract further abuse. But none of these things—the pulling inward, the anxiety, the rigidity and tension—are traits innate to autism; what they are is symptoms of trauma. And I don't have those trauma symptoms anymore because I've overcome them through many years of actively working at it via somatic practices like aikido and paratheatre.

Being autistic is neither innately traumatic nor incompatible with thriving; our trauma is the result of living in cultural environments in which our fundamental way of being is regarded as wrong and undesirable, in which our developmental needs are not well met, and in which we are subjected to all manner of traumatic abuses (often in the name of "therapy" or "treatment"). Like most humans, we're born with the capacity to thrive if our needs are properly met—and one of those needs is the need to be accepted as autistic people with autistic styles of embodiment, rather than being pressured to conform to non-autistic norms of embodiment or abused for diverging from those norms. We can only thrive to the extent that we're free to live and move autistically.

Working with Autistic Students and Clients

I've been teaching aikido and facilitating other forms of somatic work for many years now. Although the majority of my aikido students, coaching clients, and workshop participants are non-autistic, I do get plenty of autistics as well (especially these days, as my published work and public speaking on autism have become known to an increasingly large audience). The lessons I've learned from my own journey have proven to be quite applicable, and invaluable, when it comes to working with my autistic students and clients.

Based on my own transformative experiences of somatic practice and my experiences facilitating somatic work for autistic students and clients, here's a quick summary of the key elements that a regimen of somatic work should incorporate in order to have maximum benefit for autistic participants:

Body awareness. Practices to improve the processing of proprioceptive, vestibular, and tactile sensory information. Many autistics instinctively seek to do this through highly physical stims like jumping on trampolines. In autistic children, this sort of vigorous stimming should be encouraged. Every aspect of aikido training fulfills this function in some way or another; the practices of trying to stay grounded while being steadily pushed on, and of frequent falling and tumbling on a padded floor, were particularly valuable for awakening my body awareness in the early days of my training.

Centering. Practices for remaining centered, grounded, and relaxed. Such techniques—for instance, focusing on the center or *hara* in the lower abdomen, or deep and steady mindful breathing—have many benefits, but for autistics they're particularly helpful in preventing sensory overwhelm.

Expansiveness. Practices for expanding one's sphere of attention and sense of presence beyond the boundaries of the skin and into the space around one, while still maintaining body awareness and centeredness.

Dual attention. Practices to build the skill of interacting mindfully with others while still maintaining one's own body awareness and centeredness. Autistics are often pressured to interact with non-autistics on non-autistic social terms even when they're not feeling up to doing so, prioritizing the social preferences of non-autistics over the autistic person's well-being. So especially when it's autistic children I'm working with, I emphasize that maintaining their own center comes first, and should be prioritized even if it means needing to temporarily withdraw from engagement with others.

De-armoring. Breaking down layers of chronic tension that may have accumulated as defenses against overwhelm or abuse, or as a means of repressing stimming in order to avoid rejection and abuse. Note that because breaking down these tensions can be destabilizing, it should only be attempted *after* a person has developed good centering skills.

Freedom to stim. For adult autistics, cultivating the freedom to stim may entail a process similar to the one I went through: an active effort to recover the capacity to stim, to tune into long-repressed stimming instincts, and to break down any chronic tensions that may have built up as part of the process of repressing stims. For children who are still in touch with the stimming instinct, it's mostly a matter of keeping them out of the clutches of toxic adults who will try to force them to conform to non-autistic norms of embodiment, and sometimes also a matter of helping them to replace potentially harmful stims with less problematic stimming options (for instance, kids who slam themselves into walls to satisfy their need for impact can be redirected to trampolines or taking flying leaps onto tumbling mats; kids who loudly drum their hands on their desks at school can be given a rubber ball to squeeze or some similarly non-noisy hand-held stim toy).

I hope these guidelines will be of benefit to my fellow autistics, and to my fellow practitioners, teachers, and facilitators of somatic work. And of course, one doesn't have to be autistic to benefit from incorporating all of the above elements into one's somatic practices.

Liberation for Every Body

When I first started doing college lectures and public speaking engagements about autism and somatics, I talked about stimming only in terms of how it was a somatic need for autistics. I talked about the harm that results from the suppression of stimming, and about the importance of recovering the capacity to stim and defending the right to stim, only as issues facing the autistic community.

And then people started reaching out to me after my college classes and public speaking gigs. It didn't surprise me when people sought me out to tell me their own stories of having been forced or shamed into suppressing their own childhood stimming, and to thank me for inspiring me to reclaim their stims. It didn't surprise me when people contacted me months after hearing me speak, to tell me that recovering and following their long-suppressed stimming impulses had helped to restore their joy and vitality, had reduced their anxiety and boosted their creativity, or had given them a sense of engagement with the sensory world that they hadn't felt since childhood. What did surprise me was that a lot of the people who were telling me these things weren't autistic.

So whether you're autistic or not, I hope reading about my journey will inspire you to stim. I hope it will inspire you to experiment with being a little more expansive, a little more engaged with the sensory world, a little more free in how you move your body, and a little more weird.

And I hope it will inspire you to more fully embody the unique beauty of your own authentic self.

Bibliography

Alli, Antero. *Angel Tech: A Modern Shaman's Guide to Reality Selection.* Boulder, CO: Vigilantero Press, 1985.

———*Towards an Archeology of the Soul: A Paratheatrical Workbook.* Berkeley, CA: Vertical Pool, 2003.

Delany, Samuel R. *Babel-17.* New York, NY: Ace Books, 1966.

Holiday, Linda. *Journey to the Heart of Aikido: The Teachings of Motomichi Anno Sensei.* Berkeley, CA: Blue Snake Books, 2013.

Leary, Martha, and Anne M. Donnellan. *Autism: Sensory-Movement Differences and Diversity.* Cambridge, WI: Cambridge Book Review Press, 2012.

Leonard, George. *The Way of Aikido: Life Lessons from an American Sensei.* New York, NY: Dutton, 1985.

Manning, Erin. *Always More Than One: Individuation's Dance.* Durham, NC: Duke University Press, 2013.

Mukhopadhyay, Tito Rajarshi. *Plankton Dreams: What I Learned in Special-Ed.* London, UK: Open Humanities Press, 2015.

Sequenzia, Amy, and Elizabeth J. Grace, eds. *Typed Words, Loud Voices.* Fort Worth, TX: Autonomous Press, 2015.

Silberman, Steve. *NeuroTribes: The Legacy of Autism and the Future of Neurodiversity.* New York, NY: Avery, 2015.

Sutton, Michelle, ed. *The Real Experts: Readings for Parents of Autistic Children.* Fort Worth, TX: Autonomous Press, 2015.

Yergeau, Melanie. *Authoring Autism: On Rhetoric and Neurological Queerness.* Durham, NC: Duke University Press, 2018.

Chapter 5

The Gap: Social Wounds and Personal Transformation

tayla ealom

Welcome

I want to welcome you here with me, in this moment highlighted in words scrawled across a page. As I sit, fingers to the keyboard, I take a few deep breaths and call upon the life that I have lived that has led me to this very moment. I consider the weight of what it means to be asked to speak to the world of somatics from the place I occupy, and there is a welling of energy across my chest and into my shoulders. To be invited to share through such a platform as this book requires that I come into my body to get a sense of what it is that this body has to say about the world and the many ways we express life within it. To do any justice with this space and the words I have to share, I must come back to my body and inquire from within, for if I have learned anything, I only know things if my body knows them … if they have *made sense* (or been sensed) in tissue, in flesh. What is it about living in this world, as a human being, that I know because of the skin I have, the muscles that manifest my movement, the breath that reflects every impact of every moment? In order to speak honestly, I must get quiet. I must listen. What follows is a practice of listening, and a sharing of what I have heard, that is based on my lived experience in my multiracial cisgendered woman's body. It is an invitation into an understanding of what it means to live a life embodied, an offering from my tissue and felt sense of the world.

This body of mine is the result of the many lives that have traveled through the length and depth of history so I may be here in this moment as a breathing human being with thoughts and imaginings. I was born into this body, and ever since have been building my capacity to hold all the sides of a story that manifested into a single human. My DNA can be traced to four of the seven continents on the planet, excluding Asia, Australia, and South America, resulting in a personhood that stands as the culmination of people who have survived, who have struggled, and who have made their way into connection against all the odds. My heritage links the story of Ashkenazi Jews with Black Americans (West Africans) with Europeans with Native Americans in such a way that my body relates this history before the forming of words. As a multiracial woman, I am standing alive in a time when the multiplicity of races in a single person is slowly becoming a new normal.[1] This multifacetedness has shaped me to be the carrier of not only ancient forms of grief, but also the various forms of medicine that come from each of these lineages.

I come here, through this winding spiral of time and people, to offer you the medicine I carry. As you take in these words, know that they are here for you. May you learn to hold them gingerly and carry them forward. By doing so, you assume responsibility for the medicine they carry and have the opportunity to bring them forward into your own life in a good way. Taking in these words, I invite you to highlight, to question, to share, to engage in conversations which perhaps

---

[1] In 2013, *National Geographic* released an article with images of multiracial people in the United States, highlighting that the number of interracial marriages had hit an all-time high of 4.8 million, a number that continues to grow.

you've never had, and continue to try on ways of knowing that open you to the world that has created your body.

What follows is an exploration of what I call "the Gap"—the space created between us and our healing that makes something like change seem so impossible and daunting. By sharing the story of my never-ending dance with the Gap, I hope to illuminate another way of considering healing, or at the very least offer words to one kind of shared experience. Looking at my experiences as an individual, as an activist and as a woman of color, I will weave a web of experience with which the Gap has taken form in my life. As I give language to my own experience, maybe you will track your own, and find the words needed to help situate you in the larger context of your life.

There are many things this exploration is not. It is not a how-to manual of engaging the healing process. It is not a step-by-step set of instructions on how to embody transformation. It is not a quick fix. It is a set of questions and a way of thinking about these things that will perhaps open the door for us to imagine engaging with the Gap. These are my revelations, and I hold them with an open palm in offering. Thank you for being here with me. Welcome.

Shapes of the Gap

Part I: The Gap and I

I call it the Gap. That space between healing and me that I have been learning to swim across, every time I seek myself anew. The Gap is not unique to me, for I am coming to understand that the space between the wounding and healing processes tends to be vast throughout the world. This Gap, between the moments of impact that create pain and suffering and the moments of connection that allow for relief and healing, exists in such a way that I wonder if it can only be cultivated in idealizing an individualized culture, which leads to the striving for "my" healing as a component of "my" existence that lives somehow out of time, space, and sync with the pressures and demands of "my" modern life. Even now, as I attempt to give language to this experience, I find myself in a fumble, as if standing at the edge of an abyss: wary of looking down, warier of looking away.

The Gap between moving into a space of healing and out of a space of wounding is a place of unknowns, where we go from knowing where we are and having a concrete story of who we are, to completely disoriented and confused, and hopefully then reoriented with more space for clarity and perspective in wholeness. This experience of wounding, be they trespasses of the physical, emotional, psychological, spiritual self, or any combination thereof, is what has kept me from moving into the full process of healing for much of my life. The Gap, the space between, is what I face every time a wound arises, every time I find my body in a new position to the world where I can see an opportunity for healing. By seeing the Gap, I can contextualize my experience as I move from one moment in life to another as a body incarnated on this holy Earth.

As I envision this space between wounding and healing, I recognize that the Gap can take many forms. For me, it is shaped as depression. I've struggled with bouts of depression since I was a tween. To say that now, aloud, offers relief to my system. Knowing it is written to be held in posterity is at once horrifying and humbling, as I strive to invite others into my story of healing. Depression can take many shapes and forms for many people, linking a sense of hopelessness to life, creating a misery that seems to suddenly be the only thing that gives life meaning. My flavor of depression takes on many forms, shape shifting throughout my growth into adulthood—though for all appearances, I seem to be rather high functioning. Even so, my internal world has many dark places that have guided me toward coping styles that have resulted in self-harm. With a history of cutting, eating disorders, binge drinking … I've danced with many coping mechanisms in my life. Whatever place or state I could get my body into to staunch the pain of feeling insignificant, ineffectual, unimportant, and unwanted.

At the tender age of twenty-six, I was diagnosed with a condition that deformed my femur bones in the hip socket, resulting in a need for urgent hip surgery. As a twenty-six year old, I suddenly felt old and fragile as I entered into a major surgery without much space for processing this change, lest I wait and require a full hip replacement by the time I turn thirty-five. I suddenly had to address my body and the way that I was making my way through the world; understanding the impact of my life choices in a new way as I lost my ability to actually walk or do the basic things that we take for granted when we have two functioning legs. Having lived my life as a fully able-bodied person, I was suddenly stopped in my tracks. Being able-bodied was among the only things that had made life tolerable in my states of depression; it was one of the only ways I had learned to trust myself and my identity. The exploration of how to create beauty with my body through gymnastics, dance, and yoga *asana* has been a life-long journey. All of these practices have developed a sense of self that allows me to feel a flavor of self-trust and self-knowledge that has otherwise remained elusive in other aspects of my life. And then, rather suddenly, my only sense of trust in my being was in limbo as I faced the potential that I would never move the same way again.[2]

This physical wounding manifested after years of fighting myself for a sense of worth. In that moment of diagnosis, I settled into the deep exhaustion I had been carrying that stemmed from years of self-sabotage and foiled attempts to find worth in my life. I had long before settled into patterns of self-destruction, incorporating them into normal daily doings. And now, unable to walk, all I could do was sit in my own company. In that slow recovery period of self-with-self, it became crystal clear that something *inside* needed changing: I needed changing and my patterns needed changing. And yet, there I remained, confused and unsure how to move forward at the edge of the Gap. I was busy "knowing" (AKA thinking) that healing was needed, yet I stood frozen, unable to move myself into the space between the wounds I carried into a place of healing. Standing up for the first time

---

[2] I'm very lucky to say that I have achieved a successful recovery with near complete pre-injury hip function, though my injured joint remains a teacher and can now sense weather changes.

by myself after surgery awoke the seeker in me, a symbol shared by many cultures, as the one who embarks on a journey while looking for a thing, a feeling, and experience that elevates the knowing closer to a truth—something not always tangible but known nonetheless about what it means to be a human, incarnated.

Since this moment, every day has been a choice of how to dance with the Gap as a partner. What I have unearthed myself are the impacts of the collective wounds caused by a shared history of racism, colonialism, patriarchy, and domination as one seeking healing. My life has aligned me with this conversation in a unique way. The wounds I carry, which are both mine and not mine, have directed me straight to this moment, to these words on this page. Pulling from my lived experience, my work as a justice shield-maiden,[3] and my research on racism and trauma, I hope to shine light on the Gap and offer into our world just one way of navigating it. In doing so, my prayer is that we may find ourselves *as* the healing we so deeply seek, dancing our way across the Gap.

What wound did ever heal but by degrees?

—William Shakespeare

I once met a fallen Redwood in the traditional lands of the Tolowa, Karuk, and Yurok peoples in the so-called Siskiyou Wilderness in Northern California. Her large body rested open on the ground, her massive root system exposing the inner workings of a giant. Taken by her form, I crawled onto her long side and walked some forty feet closer to her center. She was a nurse log covered in the next phase of her life; mushrooms, ferns, mosses, and small saplings all sprouted from her body. I laid my belly upon hers and whispered, "When I grow up, I'd like to be a Redwood," and she whispered back, "Then live your life so that in your return to soil, you leave fertile ground for more growth to arise from." From that moment, I've been trying to live that

[3] Pulling from my Scandinavian lineage, "shield-maiden" is a Norse term referring to a female warrior.

lesson to the best of my ability. It's been the moment that has ushered me toward the Gap and healing.

There are countless options for healing experiences available today that promise not just symptom relief, but *healing*. As someone in this field of study and inquiry, hearing a term with as profound implications as healing tossed around as frequently and abstractly as it is, I find myself in a large pause, asking myself what *I mean* when I use this term. The word has swarmed our collective consciousness as we experience another iteration of the New Age movement, ushered in through yoga, mindfulness, and meditation, psychedelics research, and most certainly somatics and somatic psychology.

According to the definitions in the *Merriam-Webster Dictionary* in 2017, to heal is

> to make free from injury or disease
>
> to make sound or whole to make well again; to restore to health
>
> to cause (an undesirable condition) to be overcome
>
> to patch up or correct (a breach or division)
>
> to restore to original purity or integrity.[4]

Many of these definitions highlight notions of *removing* or *restoring*, which points me to the basic understanding that the true state of a person/place/organism is in a healed (static) position, and to heal is to correct or remove that which is incorrect, undesirable, or a function of disease. Yet, something feels vacant, if not downright inaccurate, about these definitions that we work with. Though they seem to give much validity to the current medical model of treatment for any "disorder" or "disease," they seem to direct us toward a way of being that is not inclusive of the *process* of healing. Put another way, these definitions imply a beginning point (disease) and end point (healed), with being healed being the end goal, without space for exploring *how* one goes about it.

---

[4] I chose to use contemporary dictionary definitions here to focus on our most basic understandings in U.S. society.

If we look at incorporating the concept of process into the definition of healing, with process being understood as something going on, a natural phenomenon marked by gradual changes that lead toward a particular result, and a continuing natural or biological activity or function, something more inclusive becomes available. These three definitions ground the understanding of process as a phenomenological experience in the living world. To focus on them, especially when referring to healing, is to call into awareness the basic, natural qualities of movement from one way to another.

By understanding that healing is a phenomenon, part of a natural process, there is the opportunity to become interested in the *how* of *healing,* not to be confused with *being healed.* Anchoring the healing process into phenomena that are gradual and a continual manifestation of change begs for an understanding of how to manifest, participate in, engage with, and shape *healing*. In this way, this interest in process moves the inquiry away from a static line with two end points into the dynamic and living *process* of the act of moving from one place to another.

What feels incredibly important about this definition in relationship to healing as a process is the inclusion of an organism's biological activity and function, as it is but one way to include the human body. The impacts of this are wide-ranging and touch on much of the research and understanding that has come out of the somatics and somatic psychology fields. A clear example of the process of healing comes from the extensive trauma research conducted in the somatics fields. The physiological effects of trauma and its impacts on the nervous system direct us straight to my current definition of healing. Stephen Porges's research on the vagus nerve and its role in nervous system and affect regulation is but one of the leaps and bounds that have been made in contemporary trauma research. His study of the vagus nerve and development of polyvagal theory breaks down the autonomic nervous system into subsystems to better understand how the body develops behavioral adaptations to traumatic events through the fight, flight, and freeze responses. The work of Peter Levine, Bessel van der Kolk, and Pat Ogden further show that these responses can then become "stuck" in the body as it continues to protect against further injury long after the initial threat has diminished. These basic anatomical and physiological understandings of trauma aid in further understanding the role of biological functioning in the healing of the large emotional/psychological/spiritual wounds that people experience.

To move across the Gap into healing, there is a wound to be attended to. These wounds can have devastating impacts on the nervous system, even if they are largely psychological/emotional or emerge well after the most apparent physical wounds have turned to scars. Our current understandings of trauma lead to definitions of healing that automatically include the notions of process and the small, gradual changes that occur as we move away from our traumatization. Further, research on working with trauma highlights the slow process of coming in contact with and integrating fragmented parts of ourselves, to allow for more response-ability and flexibility in lived experience. The work of Peter Levine and *Somatic Experiencing* presents a way of working with this wounding that follows the process of the body, allowing for the fight/flight/freeze response to complete its cycle, thus moving people out of the trauma cycle and into the healing process—into the Gap. Levine's work shows the necessity of slowness and patience to allow for the natural unfolding of healing to occur in its own time, at its own rhythm. The movement away from fragmentation toward a sense of wholeness becomes another central intention of the healing process. This wholeness, born of the integration of parts, is a way of being that does not attempt to abandon that which has wounded us, but instead attempts to include the wounded parts of self into the whole.

Healing then becomes a process to engage, allowing the Gap to become the teacher that instructs the wounded in *how* to move across it. Considering all of these explorations, perhaps a working definition of healing could look something like: a natural phenomenon going on, marked by gradual and continuous changes as a part of an organism's biological activity and total functioning toward wholeness.

This definition resonates in my system in a specific way, though I'm not convinced myself that it contains the whole story. In the moment with the Redwood, I came to realize that even in death, there is so much occurring. The act of decomposition, of becoming that fertile soil, is not an inactive static transition from life to death, but a continuous going on where the tree gradually goes through endless states of being. It is not just the standing grove of trees that makes this forest teem with life, but in its falling, this tree provides the foundation of life itself. The ants that stroll along the soft bark, the mosses that cling to Her sides, and the soil that welcomes Her body back into the cycle all require this process of death.[5] There is a reverence for the entirety of experience felt in the growth that continues taking place long after the fall of a giant. This moment with the Redwood provided me with a window into a new understanding of process. I started to understand that to heal also requires the direct engagement and relationship with all that surrounds a single expression of life. That in the exploration of the biological functioning of a body moving toward wholeness, a key element of that wholeness comes through relationship to other, through our relationships to death and that which we turn into rich soil.

In this profound moment of witnessing, I began the process of wondering how this cycle plays out in my own being. How can I, in my waking life, give myself over to the living process of death to be in service to growth and more life? I often call upon this moment when the darkness of depression begins to fill my world more actively. How can these dances with death of Self actually lead me into the process of becoming? How are the processes of death, letting go, or surrender into new stages of life acts of connection that makes space for that continuous movement toward wholeness?

This depression of mine has guided me into toying with death on many levels. From suicidal ideation to isolation, I have encountered my own process of death in my living. In the fear of living, death became an option for relieving my pain as an absolute end, but the Redwood showed me that there is no end, just a transition from one way of being toward another. In resting my body on Hers, there came the exhale. The settling into knowing that my ideas about death were forever reshaped

---

[5] I refer to Redwoods as grandmothers of the forest, and capitalize the use of Her in respect to that being as a teacher. That is not to apply standard gender norms to a tree, but to acknowledge my direct experience of these trees as sentient beings.

by witnessing the actuality of death. In this pause, there was a movement toward the edge of the Gap; movement toward healing that was at once simple and profound. I began the first line of inquiry, the humble acknowledgment that perhaps I have had it wrong the whole time: that perhaps I could indeed develop toward something new. That wholeness is a process of learning to be in right relationship to that urging toward death and how it shapes the whole of life.

Unsatisfied with the definitions I've given so far, the journey starts again.

Getting into the *how* of engaging the Gap, engaging the healing process, I need to situate the body as an ongoing process. As I have started into the process of healing, I have become curious about the experience, the felt sense of this new way of moving. A favorite thinker of mine on this topic, Eugene Gendlin, speaks beautifully to the understanding of human experiences as an ongoing process between a living body and the rest of the world. In his speech to the American Psychological Association, he stated that the experience of any given moment is "an interaction, not a thing. It breathes; it lives itself forward through the interaction with the environment. It's a process. Tissue process already has its own sense making, its own intricate way of creating its next moment, its next step, its next event."[6] In reading Gendlin, I immediately envision this profound Redwood teacher. I find the truth of his statement in the ways Her body is living itself forward through multiple interactions with the environment that both aids in and benefits from Her death process. As I take a moment to reflect, I sense in my belly the memory of the pressure from the Redwood and Her interaction with my own body. I recall that as I rested on Her, there was a distinct deepening of my breath and a soft focus in my eyes that allowed me to receive the truth of Her death as a teaching to me in my life. Together, we were in process, in direct interaction, through my living body.

---

6 Eugene T. Gendlin, "On the New Epistemology" (excerpts from Gene Gendlin's awards talk at the American Psychological Association, August 6, 2000). *Staying in Focus: The Focusing Institute Newsletter,* 1, no. 2 (2001): 5-6, http://www.focusing .org /gendlin/docs/gol_2173.html.

In thinking about the human body as a process of constant interaction with other beings, Gendlin points the process of life as an embodied being. He offers a way of understanding how we come to shape ourselves and are shaped by our relationships with the "other;" especially that which causes dis-ease. Greg Madison summarizes this point well:

> In addition, for Gendlin the body is not a passive derivative of culture—Gendlin's conception of the body is always more than these models of the body: the living body is interaction. We feel our life events because our bodies are a continuous experiencing of the whole situation that we are living. We are not only taking in information through five senses and then computing that information in the mainframe of the brain. The whole body is interaction with its environment in an intricate way. This back and forth being-world interaction is so radically characteristic of "body" that to talk of a separate "body"' and "environment" leads us into familiar but mistaken assumptions about living.[7]

Understanding that the human body is not passively computing stimuli also accepts that our bodies are, as Rosemarie Anderson claims, *"utterly embedded in the world"* where there seems to be a "miracle of flesh and bones through which we live—call it what you will, spirit or awareness or consciousness."[8] Just like the fallen Redwood, the body is not just embedded in the web of life, but is also a delicate web in and of itself that plays in interactions with the entirety of the larger environment. It is not just our material form that is in this process, either. As we move, speak, cry, scream, and laugh into the world, the world responds to our impact with a chorus of animal responses, silence, wind, or stillness. As we live, we both are touched by and touching the

---

7 Greg Madison and Eugene Gendlin, "Palpable Existentialism: An Interview with Eugene Gendlin," in *Existential Therapy: Legacy, Vibrancy and Dialogue* , eds. L. Barnett and G. Madison (New York, NY: Routledge/Taylor & Francis Group, 2012), 81–96.

8 Rosemarie Anderson, "Embodied Writing and Reflections on Embodiment," *Journal of Transpersonal Psychology*,33, no. 2 (2001): 83-98.

air, the earth, the waters. This delicate dance of interaction keeps us in an ever-changing relationship to the world, allowing us to take shape as individuals only within the context of the whole.

This constant dance between the body and the world can give way to an entirely new way of relating to those that make up a life. In our engagement with the larger world, we become not just aware of the "world outside" but also how that world lives and breathes within us as we move from one moment and interaction to another. In contrast to many Western ways of thinking about individuals as distinct entities separate from each other, with a dualism of internal and external, this notion of embodiment highlights a way of being that is intricately and intimately tied to the rest of life.

In my accepting the notion of body as process, I was opened to the opportunity to step away from the conceptual notion being healed and witness myself as an embodied healing process. Through this moment of connection with the Redwood, I found an opportunity to intentionally engage with the felt sense of life as it surrounds my single expression of it. In that felt sense of interconnection with all life, something of the mystic is born, an interaction with spirit in a compelling and embodied way. This is beautifully articulated by one of my favorite passages from Alice Walker's novel *The Color Purple,* in which the character Shug speaks to the move away from conceptual interconnectedness into embodied connection. In her letter to Nettie, Celie explains how Shug moved away from the "old white man" of God first by coming into relationship with the trees, "Then air. Then birds. Then other people," until one day, she had the "feeling of being a part of everything, not separate at all." Shug states, "I knew that if I cut a tree, my arm would bleed" and that she simply knew it to be true.[9] Shug gives language to this complex sense of being so simply and beautifully. She reminds me that an essential element to finding a sense of wholeness is not something

[9] Alice Walker, "God Is Inside You and Everybody Else," in *Weaving Visions: Patterns in Feminist Spirituality,* eds. Judith Plaskow and Carol Christ (New York: HarperCollins, 1989), 103.

to be completed in a vacuum, but something that becomes available when, and only when, we are consciously participating with the world that is at once shaping and being shaped by us. When there is a felt understanding of the inseparability of Self and the world, it is easily known "that I harm myself by harming another, even non-human, creature."[10]

In this opportunity for connection to the rest of life, the notion of healing once again has been enlarged to incorporate interconnection, relationship, and the planet on the whole. Remaining with the process of differentiation, a new definition of healing could be: a natural phenomenon going on, marked by gradual and continuous changes as a part of an organism's biological activity and total functioning toward wholeness through relationship and a felt-sense of interconnectedness.

That definition has given me a large exhale. There is something inside my system saying "yes" to this way of conceiving healing.

In the Redwood's return to soil, the interconnection of life became apparent and clear. Not only was Her return interconnected with all the other life that was made possible in Her death, but Her death also became connected to my own life and the ways in which I am learning to navigate my wounding. Forever connected through this lesson of death, my body could soften into a sense of being held by the larger world. That direct and intimate relationship to this tree, with my belly to Hers, allowed me to see my own relationship to the forest, the trees, the mosses, and the life-giving process of death and return to the soil. By relating to Her body with my own in this way, I was and am able to acknowledge myself as process, in direct and felt relationship to that which is outside of my skin, but forever a part of my being. Her life in process reflected back to me my life in process, through our bodies in relationship to one another.

---

[10] Catherine Keller, "Feminism and the Ethic of Inseparability," in *Weaving Visions: Patterns in Feminist Spirituality*, eds. Judith Plaskow and Carol Christ (New York: HarperCollins, 1989), 263.

Part II: The Collective Gap

I've taken many breaks in writing this chapter. I've been in my own tumultuous living experience. I've been immersed in study on equity and the dynamics of racism. I have been coming into a brand-new relationship with myself, my childhood, my body. I have been pausing, stalling, and waiting. I think about this body of mine now, as I write out a notion that I've been carrying around inside me. The notion of *the process of healing* being really all there is, as we move from one wound to another, into ever-changing bodies in an ever-changing world. That learning to be in relationship to the healing is the point—if I can claim such a thing. The process is the end point. I know this because I as a body know this.

From this point, holding in mind my working definitions of the body and healing *as process*, I begin to look again at the experiences in my life that have led me to this moment of inquiry. Learning to navigate the Gap, to understand how to initiate movement away from the sticky nature of wounding and into the process is no small task. As I continue to step into my various identities and the intersections they occupy, I am continually finding that I am not alone in the midst of the Gap or at its edge. The more I speak to this process and unpack my own understanding, the more I am coming into contact with the ways that other people are in their own dance with the Gap. As the destruction of both our social and ecological fabric seems to be progressing at a maniacal rate, learning how to engage with the process of healing feels ever more urgent and necessary on the margins. Even so, there is that ever-familiar freeze at that edge that longs for healing and yet stays entrenched in the patterns of the wounding.

In my dance with the Gap and the experience of being a body as an interconnected process, "my" healing has expanded beyond my individual needs to include the collective that is both human and nonhuman in form. The further I go into the Gap, the more I am motivated to be surrounded and supported by those made vulnerable by a capitalist, patriarchal, extractive, and hyper-individualized society—women, indigenous and First Nations peoples, people of color,

LGBTQI, differently abled bodied people, working-class and poor people, youth, the elderly, and the Redwoods. I'm certain men, especially cisgendered white males, are in this place as well, but the awareness of the edge, of the Gap, of asking *how* we heal seems to be most alive in communities on the margins. In these spaces of solidarity, call them activist spaces, there is a conscious collective desire for healing in such a way that it leads to balance and harmony for all life. And yet, the more I am in these spaces, the more I see the strength of the Gap and its power to keep us wounded.

Activist spaces are some of the most profound teachers for me about the Gap. Taking the advice of the Redwood, I have been showing up in gatherings, protests, and conversations out of my commitment to living in a world that can be different than the way it all unfolds today. These spaces take many different shapes and contain a multiplicity of intersectional identities that know so much about various levels of wounding, the Gap, and therefore healing. Though it is beyond the scope of this chapter to go into detail about each gathering, suffice it to say that all of them are focused on deepening connection to place, protecting endangered parts of the planet, building functional community, deconstructing patriarchy, capitalism, and white supremacy, though in very distinct ways.

In all of these gatherings, there was such beautiful desire to cultivate a community that practices a reverence for the earth, that works cooperatively to create that community, and that is willing to be in deep connection to all parts of that community—human and more-than-human alike. Conversations range from learning to listen to the language of the birds to social justice solidarity, from new economic structures to direct action focused on stopping destructive forces. As a cisgendered woman of color, my movement toward healing has had me coming into contact with all of the ways these identities are supported and how they are oppressed in that larger web. As a living process, I have surrounded myself with radical thinkers that strive to make the world as I do: equitable, just, and following the guiding principles of life. Yet, as I continue to show up to each of these communities, the Gap continues to show itself, both in observation and experience.

These communities, dedicated to so much good, end up sacrificing the space and time needed for deep healing processes to unfold. Though conversations about the roles of healing, trauma, and connection take place, they seem to remain anchored in the realm of concept, with no space made for the work of healing. For example, in one Earth connection–based gathering, there was an entire day dedicated to telling an indigenous tale about the importance of the role of the healer in creating a healthy village. At the same time, the storytellers were not attending to the fact that the gathering itself was composed of a largely white and middle-class community adapting indigenous skills to build this village. As one of the only women of color in the gathering, I could feel a tension growing in me that the clear lack of accessibility and welcoming to brown and black people was not being addressed in a gathering dedicated to building diversity and creating village. The longer it went unaddressed, the more psychosomatic and emotional pain I began to experience. It was so clearly problematic that some facilitators took it upon themselves to speak to the people of color present and address the cultural appropriation that had been taking place all week. But these conversations remained one-on-one and outside of consciousness of the larger collective, and so it was not held by the community. Once again, I found myself and many of the other folks from the margins together, at the edge of the Gap. This tenuous teetering of being at once aware of the need to address the inequities present in order to heal the wounds of injustice and unable to step past the edge into the process of healing.

In this space, where there is much talk about healing, there comes the illusion that a clear cognitive understanding of the role of healing will do the healing itself. With little or no time to simply be with the wound and allow for the natural phenomenon of healing to occur, the process once again goes missing, unconsciously reinforcing the mind-body dualism that we are seeking to deconstruct. The collective then remains at that edge, in the wound and seeking the healing without engaging the *how,* without engaging the process. Given the state of the world, there is an understandable urgency to change course, and yet, without space and time given to the states we strive to move between—that of being wounding and that of being healing—the transformation struggles to occur.

In sharing the ways cooperatives focused on reforming and transforming society struggle to move into the Gap, there is an acknowledgment that it is not just an individual learning process, but a cultural norm established around how we believe and engage the process of healing. Even in spaces dedicated to healing and transformation, the systems that structure our world, especially those of us located in the USA, have helped to establish a way of engaging with our wounding that attempts to bypass the Gap completely, refocusing efforts on those two single moments of wounded and healed, the Western medical model being our biggest teacher. With the wounded turned patient and the doctor turned expert, the Gap begins to widen as we allow healing to transform from a natural phenomenon that we are forever a part of to a mysterious act of medicine bestowed upon us by those with the right credentials. The human process, the human being, the organism that is striving to move toward wholeness becomes inconsequential to the movement toward *healed*. With a pop-a-pill culture to soothe all that ails us, we as a society have removed the process from the healing, leaving us with two static points and the prayer for a quick way between the two. This way of thinking remains so embedded in the collective psyche that even groups dedicated to a radically different way of living struggle to find themselves as a process.

In my experience of these groups, for I can truly only speak to my own experience, I witness a deep longing that I have felt in my own body for years. A longing for things to move, to be different, to be connected and woven into the fabric of all that is. I sense that I am able to witness this in the groups I circle in because it is my own experience.

How can we take these moments of wounding and have them guide us toward what needs to be attended to? How can all of this death and destruction teach us the invaluable lessons of interconnectedness and the glory of the process of changing states? How can we collectively embrace the death that surrounds us as our main entry point into the Gap? What is needed for us to engage in *the how* of death; *the how* of transforming from one state of being toward another? What's more, how can we come to understand that it is our individual healing processes that can teach us the invaluable lessons we need to also engage our collective healing process? What is needed for the slowing down of our urgency, so we can place our bellies on the earth and learn from the more-than-human community what is needed from us? Big questions were born at these various gatherings seeking healing but stopped at the edge of the Gap.

Part II: Structuring the Gap

How I occupy the world as a person of color has also been deeply shaped by the impacts of the unique racism that has manifested in my birth country of the USA, though I do not think the responses are uniquely a part of life as a U.S. American. What I deem to be appropriate ways of engaging the world, how I have learned to take up very little space, and my practices of invisibility, though certainly informed by direct experience of many violations of my personal safety, were also formed from the society I was born into. This social fabric has created survival strategies in all people, myself included, that often create larger wounds. Depression, invisibility, and isolation are both familial habits as well as a common experience of marginalized people as a consequence of internalized oppression. The relief that comes to me now as I put this experience to paper is strange. There is an experience of grief in my chest, a welling of tears in my body that says, "Oh my ... what a sad story has had to be told for me to be here." I am opened to the truth of the size and shape of the actual wound, not just the wound that I have been busy attempting to get away from. I can sit still knowing that there is a wound that has been passed down through the generations of people that have had to live in a certain way to allow my life to take shape at all. The isolation lifts, the illusion of aloneness gives way to the truth of interconnectedness, and suddenly something new is able to happen. There is more to the story, a wholeness to the depression that was missing for so much of my life. In that wholeness, I find myself once again moving toward the Gap. There is suddenly an option for healing.

In order to better situate my lived experience in a wider context, I turn to the research of the people doing the hard work of uncovering the seemingly endless implications of racism as it manifests in the USA. By settling into the findings of others, I can know I am deeply held by this knowledge. I am reflected by it. I can be *in process* with it—picking it apart to find myself a bit more whole. And this is just one aspect of the process. As with the many groups that are working to make the world a more just and equitable place, there is a need to see how these larger stories not only impact our ability to create the world we want externally, but how they have also taken shape within us. This is the painful work of seeing the true depths of interconnectedness we experience, to acknowledge all the anguish and pain that have to occur for us to simply exist in order to move beyond it.

Acknowledging this need for healing has required that I come into a deeper understanding of the ways in which trauma has shaped the society I am born of. The culture of the United States (not as an exception) is steeped in trauma; it is born from it and continues to perpetuate this trauma in many ways. From the first contact of Europeans on this land, the traumatic process of the "American dream" has taken hold and shaped our relationships with one another. From the genocide of indigenous peoples to the stealing and enslavement of African peoples, to the gender divisions between men and women (not to mention gender nonconforming and transgender people), to the extractive economy that forced subsistence-based cultures into the capitalist structure, the flow of trauma has deeply informed how we as a nation function. I only speak to the experience here in the United States because that is where I was born and raised. For my line of inquiry, based on the multiracially brown body I am, I have had to return to one of the major wounds of our collective world to further understand the Gap. In looking at larger issues, there is a clarity available for the depth and breadth of healing that needs to occur and a situating of my individual experience within the culture that has shaped it, because of the body I am. As a multiracial woman of color, investigating the impacts of the social structure of racism has helped to reorient me to the Gap experienced by and through the collective.

Intersectionality, a term coined by Kimberlé Crenshaw, has been defined by Leslie McCall as "the relationships among multiple dimensions and modalities of social relations and subject formations"[11] and exists as a feminist term that seeks to understand the interdependent elements of identity formation. Within this umbrella, feminist theorists strive to understand interlocking and interconnected systems of race, ethnicity, class, gender, power, and sexuality and ways in which those various identities shape a sense of self.[12] Further, these interlocking elements create power dynamics both within the cultural fabric as well as within individuals as they strive to make space for themselves in the world. Intersectionality highlights the differences of the body and relationship that reflect these identities and situates people within a culture. Like the Redwood, it is through our bodies that we recognize that we are embedded in, and emerge from, a web of social relationships organized by varying accessibility to power and privilege.[13]

For me, I have had to start the painful process of attempting to understand the implications of these intersections as they relate to my own experience of trauma. So, I started to explore the phenomenological experience of a given position. By looking at the "lived experience" of how members of a culture navigate differences of body, I started to better understand the larger web that I have emerged from to find more understanding of myself and the Gap. In understanding elements of my difference, I hope to have a starting point for my

---

[11] Leslie McCall, "The Complexity of Intersectionality" *Journal of Women in Culture and Society*, (2005): 1171–800.

[12] Dondxaio Qin, "Toward a Critical Feminist Perspective of Culture and Self," *Feminism and Psychology*, (2004): 297–312.

[13] Qin, quoting M.B. Lykes. Here, Lykes has completed empirical research looking at the power differential among black and white U.S. women as well as poor women in South America in social movements. This research moved *power* to the center of feminist theories, critically examining that power is not just an element of gender, but a dynamic energy that changes and multiplies based on a person's various intersecting identities.

particular humanity in order to find more mutual interdependence with others who are different from me but still reflect back the shared similarities in various ways.[14]

There has been much research done to situate racism along a spectrum of trauma. In her 2009 study of embodied oppression, Rae Johnson concluded that hypervigilance and somatic tension were also a shared phenomenon among those faced with various oppressive circumstances based on race, gender, ability, or sexual orientation.[15] Racism is not just a conceptual framework, but a lived and embodied wound that shapes how we move through the world. It creates certain tensions that manifest into certain realities. This study gave voice to an experience I had long known but was not yet clear on how to articulate. Hypervigilance became a part of my experience at the earthy-connection gathering named above, where over the course of my time there, I began experiencing a form of somatic pain in the shape of muscle tension in my body as the collective wounds continued to remain unaddressed.

So, if this is my experience in a brown body, I began to wonder what the experience is of a white body. "Whiteness" as a distinct settler-colonial concept has a certain intersection as well, and therefore occupies the world in a specific way. When I speak of whiteness as a phenomenon, I am attempting to look at what whiteness DOES, without assuming whiteness as a given truth of race, but rather as a construct of a racialized society. In other words, I am referring to "whiteness" not as a fact of race, but more looking at how whiteness has developed a lived experience and shaped a culture. In studying this phenomenon, Sara Ahmed claims "whiteness could be described as an ongoing and unfinished history, which orientates bodies in specific directions, affecting how they 'take up' space, and what they 'can do.'"[16] Put another way,

---

14 Qin, 300. Qin points to Audre Lorde and bell hooks as authors who have crafted a theory of understanding that from particularity comes access to similarities.

15 Rae Johnson, "Oppression Embodied: The Intersecting Dimensions of Trauma, Oppression, and Somatic Psychology." *USA Body Psychotherapy Journal*8, no. 1 (2009).

the concept of whiteness leads to the lived experience of the ways in which bodies are permitted to behave, or not behave, in a given culture. Understanding U.S. American racism requires defining the normalcy of whiteness in order to move beyond it as a conception of race and see it as a function of American racist culture, to better understand what whiteness is doing in a multiracial society.

In my experience of U.S. culture, the divisiveness of race is not inherent to any given body, but structures how that body is experienced and thus how it is permitted to operate. The experience at the gathering was a perfect example of this. For many (not all) of the white-identified and passing people at the gathering, the dynamic of race at play was not at the forefront of their minds and the need for healing in order to create village. They were able to carry themselves through the gathering without giving so much thought to the reality that they are a white body in a space dedicated to building community. Though they may be aware of their gender, sexual orientation, age, size, or ability, their race is permitted to stay in the background of experience. However, as a person of color in this same space, I became increasingly aware first and foremost I was a body of color in this very white space. In this way, my race remained at the foreground of my experience, before other intersections of identity. Therefore, the phenomenon of whiteness dictates that white bodies do not have to consider their whiteness in most contemporary contexts, while bodies of color generally do, especially in many spaces dedicated to remembering earth-based skills and practices.

Part III: Inside and Outside

For much of my life, I have thought that my depression is mine alone and that there was something that "just went wrong" somewhere to cause the endless well of misery that seems to live inside my being. Convinced of my isolation, I have become quite a master isolationist,

---

[16] Johnson, 150.

attempting to tend to my problems in a vacuum, forever imagining I am somehow able to remain unentangled with the larger world. And then, I learned the tragic news of a familial pattern of suicide ideation and self-hatred on the black side of my family that goes far, far back—way beyond my thirty-something years. Histories of abuse, of isolation, of suicidal tendencies, and of drug abuse have surfaced in times of my own grief and pain. In learning that this pain runs so deep and is so old, I suddenly came to understand the direct impact of living and surviving in a racist society as it has manifested in my own life. For some in my family line, especially those whose bodies have made them the recipients of racist social treatment, oppression has taken the shape of internalized self-hatred and a deep desire to either vacate the life process or isolate from the world as a whole. The impacts of racism can take endless forms, and for the bodies of my family, it has manifested as depression and a desperate desire to eradicate misery through violent self-erasure.

In my ignorance, I had long imagined that racism was a series of violations from the outside: a sequencing of history that has resulted in a split between persons and society. I have watched numerous films on the Civil Rights Movement and witnessed the abuses of slavery through imagery and story, and though they always impacted me in such a way that moved me to tears, for many years I was unable to feel myself as an active part of that living story. The experience of depression has, in some ways, increased a sense of individualism that comes from extreme isolation and disconnection. That disconnection is not just from the sources of trust and healing in the larger whole, but also the collective wounding as it is alive and well in our bodies right now. I had long thought that my tears from witnessing these histories were a reflection of flawed oversensitivity that came along with the depression … that they were yet another reflection of what is wrong with *me*. Now, in learning the lineage of depression that has existed in the many processes of family and relationship that have resulted in my body, it has become clear to me that this depression is both mine *and* not mine. It is both individual and collective. It is an intergenerational manifestation of the socialization of racism and collective wounding.

In learning this, I found myself in a circle of people who were willing to listen to my story, and I allowed myself the pain of that truth. I allowed myself to be physically shaped by the grief in the form of tears, wailing, pounding fists, and a shaking belly—all bodily expressions of the Gap as I attended to the wounds of my story. In that slow space, I was witnessed in the death process of who I thought I was, given time and connection to shake through the denial of the truth and find myself held and witnessed in the experience. I allowed myself to be held because it was clear that my story is *our story*.

I invite us both to take a moment to allow that to sink in. Take a breath with me. Then another.

Closing the Gap

I have experienced *a* truth of the matter, which is that healing is a much slower, and often painful, process than we would perhaps like it to be. When attending to the issues of trauma, somatic psychology invites a leaning into the pain, into the wound, in order to learn new options. It is only by facing these issues that we can learn that there are other ways of being. To lean in is not just to give lip service to this wound. It is to feel it, allow it to take shape in our bodies, and move it through. It is hard, slow, and messy work. Further, if we accept that we as bodies exist as a process of relating to the larger whole, we must come to understand and accept that healing is not something to be done alone.

I take a pause here to catch my breath. I feel my feet on the ground, the cold air wrapping around my calves in my mountain home where snow glistens in the early winter night. There is a pain at the back of my heart that I give my attention to. I give it a big breath and notice. It's a familiar pain that comes from trying to articulate something as complicated as the Gap. From trying to find words for the things I know in my body that don't easily translate into written language, from attempting to weave the web I see, allowing it to be visible to others. I let my head hang and listen to the back of my heart as I give it another breath, then another. It tells me something wise ... "healing is not the seeking of relief; it is the slow and gentle process of learning a new way of relating to that which causes us pain, fear and suffering." Certainly, there will be relief that comes in waves, and that relief is just as precious and temporary as the pain can be. When we slow down, attend, and surrender to the process, something will always change. The impermanence is where healing resides.

I remember the adage "slow is smooth and smooth is fast." There is no doubt an urgency to unraveling the collective madness that is leading us further and further away from one another and ourselves. As water levels rise, as desertification accelerates, and othering continues to wreak havoc on communities, we are most certainly at the tipping point. The Great Turning, as referred to by Joanna Macy, awaits us. Yet, in order for anything to transform, in order for us to become a global community of healing, we must advocate for slowing down. We must advocate for the time, space, and attention required to tend to wounds. Just as hip surgery has required me to learn how to be still and allow the process of healing to occur in flesh and bone, so too must we all learn to slow down enough to witness the pain we carry and allow it to heal. In this time, we are attempting to unite over our collective wounds without taking the much-needed time to get to truly know one another.

If I have learned anything through my dance with the Gap, it is that this healing process is not to be done in imagined isolation, for the turning toward the wounds requires reflection so we can be truly held in our interconnectedness. In that turning toward, there will be grief. There will be anger and rage. And, if we are able to stay slow enough to be with that grief and anger, we will find ourselves entering the Gap, because in truly allowing those experiences to occur, something new becomes available. We will stop trying to "fix" the wound, and instead tend to it gently to allow it to heal as it best knows how ... at the speed of nature. At the speed of a Redwood returning to soil. The slowness invites us into a way of living that is an act of reciprocity for all that has come before us that has allowed us to be in such questions about healing. In my engaging the Gap, in my moving toward the wounds I carry, I am doing honor to all those bodies that had to carry the wounds through life and death in order for me to come into being. Lastly, if we are able to see one another, not as actors of the wounds, but as sensitive bodies attempting life through the wounds, perhaps we will find that what divides us is also the way toward our coming together.

This dance I have been in with the Gap is nowhere near a complete thought, and I hope that in the future, when I come back to read my own words, I will have encountered many new things that help me learn the steps to the dance that much better. What is here is an offering into just one way to think about healing as the process that it is. These words I've offered here have been a gesture to the greater collective that we may learn to engage in this process together, side-by-side, taking plenty of slow time to get to truly see one another and the stories that have shaped the body before us. This has been a prayer for collective healing through each person's brave engagement with the Gap as it has manifested in their lives and larger communities. It has been an attempt at offering backward to my ancestors the healing that they themselves could not engage as they battled to navigate the continuous wounding. It has been a practice of speaking the truth of my body as I have come to know and engage the world. It has been a reflection of the whole back to the parts so we may all be held in the forever connected tangle of life and being. It has been an articulated engagement with the unending process of healing. It has been a sacred act of attempting to honor that everything in life is holy and, when seen clearly, forever in service to more life. It has been a step with the Gap.

Thank you to all those that have come before me.

Thank you to all of those that will come long after me.

May this exploration of the Gap bring healing to my body—

To your body—

To our collective body.

Thank you for joining me here, in the Gap.

Recommended Reading

For further reading on trauma.

Levine, Peter. *In an Unspoken Voice.* Berkeley: North Atlantic Books, 2010.

Ogden, Pat et al. *Trauma and the Body: A Sensorimotor Approach to Psychotherapy.* New York City, NY: W. W. Norton & Company, 2006.

van der Kolk, Bessel. "Developmental Trauma Disorder: Toward a Rational Diagnosis for Children with Complex Trauma Histories." *Psychiatric Annals* 25, no. 5 (2005): 401–8.

For more information on the way intergenerational trauma is currently understood, I highly recommend looking at the work of Joy DeGruy Leary.

Leary, Joy DeGruy. *Post Traumatic Slave Syndrome America's Legacy of Enduring Injury and Healing.* Milwaukie, OR: Uptone Press, 2005.

Bibliography

Anderson, Rosemarie. "Embodied Writing and Reflections on Embodiment." *The Journal of Transpersonal Psychology* 33, no. 2 (2001): 83–98.

Behnke, E. A. "Embodiment Work for the Victims of Violation: In Solidarity with the Community of the Shaken." n.d.

Gendlin, Eugene. "On the New Epistemology (excerpts from Gene Gendlin's awards talk at the American Psychological Association)." *Staying in Focus. The Focusing Institute Newsletter* 1, no. 2 (2001): 5–6.

Johnson, Rae. "Grasping and Transforming the Embodied Experience of Oppression." *International Body Psychotherapy Journal* 14, no. 1 (2015): 80–95.

——— "Oppression Embodied: The Intersecting Dimensions of Trauma, Oppression, and Somatic Psychology." *Journal of the Association of Body Psychotherapy* 8, no. 1 (2009): 19–32.

Keller, Catherine. "Feminism and the Ethic of Inseparability." In *The Weaving Vision: Patterns in Feminist Spirituality*, eds. Judith Plaskow and Carol Christ, 256–65. New York: HarperCollins, 1989.

Leary, Joy DeGruy. *Post Traumatic Slave Syndrome America's Legacy of Enduring Injury and Healing.* Milwaukie, OR: Uptone Press, 2005.

Levine, Peter. *In an Unspoken Voice.* Berkeley, CA: North Atlantic Books, 2010.

Macy, Joanna. *Work That Reconnects.* Accessed October 8, 2017. https://workthatreconnects.org.

Madison, Greg. "Chapter 6 Palpable Existentialism: An Interview with Eugene Gendlin." In *Existential Therapy: Legacy, Vibrancy and Dialogue*, eds. Laura

Barnett and Greg Madison, 81–96. New York, NY: Routledge/Taylor & Francis Group, 2012.

McCall, Leslie. "The Complexity of Intersectionality." *Signs: Journal of Women in Culture and Society* 30, no. 3 (2005): 1771–1800.

Ogden, Pat et al. *Trauma and the Body: A Sensorimotor Approach to Psychotherapy.* New York, NY: W. W. Norton & Company, 2006.

Plaskow, Judith, and Carol P. Christ. *Weaving the Visions: New Patterns in Feminist Spirituality.* New York, NY: HarperOne, 1989.

Qin, Dongxiao. "Toward a Critical Feminist Perspective of Culture and Self." *Feminism and Psychology* (SAGE) 14, no. 2 (2004): 297–312.

Staudigl, Michael. "Racism: On the Phenomenology of Embodied Desocialization." *Springer* (2011): 23–39.

van der Kolk, Bessel. "Developmental Trauma Disorder: Toward a Rational Diagnosis for Children with Complex Trauma Histories." *Psychiatric Annals* 35, no. 5 (2005): 401–8.

Walker, Alice. "God Is inside You and Everybody Else." In *The Weaving Visions: Patterns in Feminist Spirituality*, eds. Judith Plaskow and Carol Christ, 101–4. New York, NY: HarperCollins, 1989.

Chapter 6

Black and White: Biracial in America, Reflections on My Embodied Experience

Stephanie Francis-Ecoffey

I often feel I am trapped inside someone else's imagination, and I must engage my own imagination in order to break free.

—ADRIENNE MAREE BROWN

Where do I land, as a person whose lineage is both African and European? Both of the colonized and colonizer. How am I to rectify that? My body was created from two of the most racially polarized groups in America. Black (father) and white (mother). As far back as I'm able to trace my paternal ancestry, we are Southern Black from Louisiana. My maternal ancestry composed of English immigrants who were Mormon and settled in around the middle states. How do I integrate these parts of myself? I am a contradiction. A neither. A displaced floating human looking for some place to land and ground. What I also am is here. Something like a miracle, standing on the shoulders of every one of my ancestors. I'm here and there are many more like me, biracial. Not ready to be categorized or put into boxes. Continuously finding ways to love ourselves today, as we are. Embracing the fullness of our identities.

This work is complex. The exploration of my inner workings specifically as it relates to my embodiment as an individual both of African and European ethnic origins is rich with emotion. There is something especially heavy about contemplating my own experience in the larger framework of how we move toward collective healing. Much of my personal release in this work has been accepting my limitations. I don't have all of the answers. I'm okay with that. I can hold myself as an individual who still has something to offer even in my woundedness. Even in my unknowing, it's my belief that the healing begins with the commitment to honest reflection and, in this case, deeply vulnerable sharing. That's where I find the love and that's what I hope to share.

As I'm in the process of this transformational work, the writing, I recognize my need both for the spaciousness of solitude and the connectedness of community. For warmth and rest. I am emotionally and physically stretching. This is a raw and honest exploration of how my biracial identity shapes and moves me. It's pieces of my story. It does not attempt to generalize the experience of any other black and white biracial individual. It's a reflection of where I am right now with my many curiosities. The transformation hurts and includes a lot of tears, of shrinking and expanding. It's my hope in sharing these vulnerabilities that others who have been marginalized due to the restrictions of this culture will see themselves reflected in some way. It is also my hope that other mixed and biracial individuals with similar thoughts or experiences will feel heard and seen. And that those who do not resonate with my experience will have just one more way of understanding the complexities of existing in the world for someone different than themselves.

This piece, as do others in this volume, includes implications for the ways in which early experiences, the felt sense of nonbelonging, and the burden of healing in the face of adversity have shaped me.

Transference

During my first year of graduate school, I had a striking realization at the conclusion of one of my courses. Towards the end of the semester, we were assigned to read the article "White Fragility" by Robin DiAngelo.[1] The piece begins like this: "White people in North America live in a social environment that protects and insulates them from race-based stress. This insulated environment of racial protection builds white expectations for racial comfort while at the same time lowering the ability to tolerate racial stress, leading to what I refer to as White Fragility." Boom! I was eager to engage with my classmates about the piece. I read the article with gratitude for the content, excited that someone was naming these things. It would have been entertaining to record myself reading this article. I found myself saying, "Yesssssss!" shaking my head either in agreement or as an expression of frustration, making sounds like "mmm," and so on very often throughout the reading. I all but kissed the pages, highlighting key points and filling the margins with notes including some of my own experiences with white fragility.

Simultaneously, I experienced the anxiety of broaching this topic in a classroom where I was the only person of color. I anticipated silence, variations of anger, fear, discomfort, and claims of feeling unsafe. In short, I anticipated the embodiment of white fragility. During class, I sat waiting for the reading discussion. As the opportunity was presented by the instructor to converse about the piece, there was a stale silence in the room. A defensive move directly addressed in DiAngelo's piece. After a few moments of waiting for someone to speak up, I realized by reading nonverbal cues and sensing from the energetic atmosphere that nobody was going to. So, I did. I felt my heart beating fast. My mouth opened to speak before I knew what I would share. While I don't remember the exact words I spoke, I recall stating my appreciation for this reading being brought into the course,

---

1 "White Fragility, "*International Journal of Critical Pedagogy*, 3, no. 3 (2011): 54–70.

sharing also how much I enjoyed this perspective. At some point, I named that as the only person of color in the room, it was frustrating to be the only one speaking. I even heard it slip from my lips that this led me to feel unsupported by the cohort. While I'm not a stranger to being vulnerable as a way of inviting others in an opportunity to do the same, I was surprised by this part of my share. In an attempt to move away from it quickly, I asked to hear what others thought. A handful of my classmates expressed their appreciation for my voice as well as their desire to discuss the piece. Yet the conversation never really started.

In the final moments of class, another perspective was shared. It came from a white female classmate who expressed hating the article, referring to it as dangerous. This felt like a shot to my heart. Like a personal attack. As she continued to speak, it felt as if my heart was pounding against the inside of my throat and I would soon throw it up. I was red with anger. I had to cry. I had to cry from a deep place but I wouldn't shed tears there in front of them. In front of her. I held my tears for as long as it took to remove myself from the campus. We were to revisit the reading the following week.

I spent the days leading to the next class meeting rereading "White Fragility," looking up critiques, processing my own experiences in which I'd witnessed white fragility. It's as if I were collecting ammo to defend the work, to point to the necessity of this perspective. It was deeply personal. I felt a certain responsibility to educate others from my point of view. Really, it was an attempt to be seen, by asking my classmates to hold a mirror up to themselves. See my humanity. See your white privilege. Acknowledge it. Take a critical look at whether or not you are demonstrating white fragility. See me. The following week, I walked into our last class meeting with mixed emotions and low expectations. I tried to be present, but it was challenging. I found myself between not caring, as a defense, and caring so much, a reality. There was a guardedness about me and it lived on my face. My eyes carried a sad fierceness, both longing and sharp. I participated as much as I could in the experiential work but kept my eye on the clock and the door. I thought to myself, *this is your work to do, not mine.* I was partly present and partly gone. Both hopeful and discouraged. Nothing shifted for me in the final class. I walked away feeling validated in my sentiments of being unsupported and was left with another example of white fragility. There was a hardening of my heart and a sort of validation of my lacking trust to be vulnerable there. This experience would simply be added to the list of things that made me wonder what I was doing at this institution and in this field.

As I processed what happened through my individual therapy, contemplation, and writing, I became aware of just how familiar this experience was for me. It strongly resembled experiences within my own family. As a young girl, I was made aware of my *otherness* by white family members. The earliest memory I have of being *othered* by family occurred around the age of about ten or eleven years old, though I'm sure I felt it prior to this particular memory.

My first cousin who would have been around the age of eight or nine years old replied to a playful and juvenilely ignorant inquiry posed by his stepsister and myself about what kinds of girls he liked, to which he passionately yelled, *"I would never date a nigger!"* Similar to the way I described feeling earlier in that classroom, I felt personally attacked by this statement. In that moment, I became aware that he harbored some sort of hatred for people like me. Strangely, I don't think he recognized that his speech included me as an object of that hatred; a scenario I would see played out time and again throughout my life due to my racially ambiguous appearance. In retrospect, I see he was a child and this was a reflection of his racial socialization. He learned these white supremacist ideologies from somewhere. In this moment, he was mirroring the type of behavior he witnessed somewhere in his own life. Perhaps even repeating an exact phrase. Which meant that whoever taught him this, directly or indirectly, was likely someone who had access to me. This may be the origin of my self-protective disposition toward a lacking or slow-to-develop trust toward white people. Other experiences only seemed to encourage this self-protective defense. When I think about my racial identity, I remember the white individuals who communicated to me through words and through gestures that I was less than them.

Who was there to protect me from these psychologically harmful situations? After recovering from my momentary shock at my cousin's words, I ran out of the room, tears welling up behind my face until I found his mother. With tears now streaming down my face, my ears hot and red with anger, I told my aunt what her son had said. I don't know how she responded. I cannot remember. So, earlier this year while attempting to find some sort of healing from this old wound, I reached out. I called my aunt to ask for guidance and support. In an attempt to better understand what happened that day, I retold her the story and inquired whether or not she remembered how she responded. I anticipated hearing her full recollection of that day. To hear how she had seen it impacted me, the conversation she had had with my cousin, and how the rest of my visit had been. But she could not recall the memory at all. This hurts. And my stomach is sour with the thought of my younger self, there in my brown skin, my psychological suffering due to evidence of racial prejudice within my own family as just another day.

Even as I write these words, I find myself wondering how to curb them to protect the emotional well-being of family members. My maternal aunt was instrumental in my upbringing, yet I largely exclude her from my narrative. I guess she came to represent white fragility at a time when I was finally deciding to choose myself. A time when I came to believe that my pain deserved space and a platform for healing. We both chose to take care of ourselves in the way we each saw fit. I didn't get to share my pain because it was too much for her and would somehow mean that I did not love her. That I did not see all she had done for me. That I looked down on her. So, the conversation ended and I walked away feeling poorly for having ever broached it. It left me feeling like I was too much. Which was all too familiar to the ways in which I learned to understand myself when fraught with emotion due to familial disagreements.

I wonder how may this experience parallel with earlier ones when I was expressing hurt at the insensitivities around me? Because somewhere I learned that I was too much and my hurt was for me to figure out alone. I really just wonder where people were to protect my heart before I myself knew how to protect myself? It feels important to make clear that I'm not blaming any one individual for any one thing. I am going toward the healing power of written word to name some of the things that have impacted me. Yet, there's still an anticipation of being further rejected by speaking my truths. What I seek is real conversation and deep healing. I get to be hurt. I get to feel upset. Where do I find my healing without them? I know that forgiveness is a part of that story but if I speak forgiveness to myself, will it stick? Or will the ways I have felt unloved within my own family continue to transfer onto the ways I see the world around me? A place to be weary. To take everyday slights as cuts that run deep? Where do I find my peace?

When I reflect on my experience growing up around white family members, there is a sense of being on the outside. I am there but I am not like my family and I have an idea that they will never really understand me. Never see me in my fullness, because they don't care to. I am, however, fortunate enough to say that my mom is an exception to this piece of my experience. While she was a mere fifteen years old when she brought me into this world, I believe she cared for me to the fullest of her abilities. I could sob as I write this down on the page because while our relationship has been imperfect, as is any mother-daughter relationship, she is awake to many of the realities of social injustice. She recognizes her privilege resulting from whiteness, names white fragility, and sees the way racism and prejudice operate. Namely through the eyes of her children. Such as the way my youngest brother, with his locks, is profiled. Or the ways she recalls being looked upon with judgment by strangers when carrying her second-born child, my middle brother, around as a child. Consciously aware of being received so vastly different as a single white female and as a white female with brown babies. She sees it through my eyes, in the pain and frustration I have for feeling objectified as a mysterious creature to be figured out. There's peace in being able to speak to her honestly and know that she will open her heart. There's peace in witnessing her continuously evolve her understanding. And so important to me as her daughter is feeling seen by her.

Stephanie and her mother after taking part in a day-long grief ritual at Spirit Rock facilitated by the late Sobonfu Somé. Photo taken in September of 2016.

On the other side of this came subtle slights from the comments, jokes, and debate challenges made by my uncle, one of the most prominent male figures of my childhood and adolescent life. In this case there's a disposition toward remembering more of the negative aspects of my experience, including their lasting impacts. However, I will share that I was very drawn to my uncle. He was the funny, storytelling, adventurous uncle that I wanted to be around as much as I was able. Yet, his various displays of racial prejudice left with me a lasting ambivalence. This is a confusing predicament to be in as a child looking for love from close family members, especially from male familial figures in a situation where my father was not present. Even more confusing were the times when my experiences were brushed off as my being too sensitive or when his jokes were directed toward any and every one. That was never complete for me. I did not and do not accept those explanations. I don't believe that language that is harsh or abusive in nature should be normalized or considered harmful only as the result of a child's sensitive temperament.

It's challenging to recall the various comments that were made, a feature that for some time led me to question the validity of my pain.

I found great release in learning that I needn't recall their nuances to remember the negative connotations.

> Depending on his or her family's attitudes, the child will learn that there are positive or negative connotations to black or white, to dark skin or light skin. Though they may not be able to understand these differences, children do feel them. A child will be able to sense from subtle messages that being lighter or darker is better or worse.[2]

As a young girl, I lacked the necessary tools or education to understand why such comments led me to feel isolated and upset. These comments that carried negative racial undertones occurred regularly and led me to internalize anger toward myself for wanting to be loved by someone like him.

My educational pursuits were driven by the desire to understand my own experience and history as well as to learn how I could impact social change, specifically related to race. From my middle school years forward, I took tremendous interest in learning all that I could about black history, going on to later earn my bachelor's degree in Africana Studies with a minor in psychology. I utilized my expanding knowledge base to directly challenge my uncle's prejudice. Challenging him activated my nervous system and was draining. Yet, nobody else was doing it so I took it on as my responsibility. I became the outspoken person in the family. I thought I could beat him over the head with my knowledge until he saw me. Saw the impact of his prejudice. Through some enlistment of hope or naivety, I thought I could change his views. I was wrong.

What I experienced in this course was real. To reduce it to a transference alone would be false. Yet, the situation had striking similarities to experiences within my own family. In becoming aware of the transference, it seemed as though I was on the brink of a deeper understanding. Something in the knowing evoked a sense of freedom from the anger and helplessness it seemed to have caused. I experienced my cohort, composed of predominantly white individuals, as similar

---

[2] Marguerite A. Wright, *I'm Chocolate, You're Vanilla: Raising Healthy Black and Biracial Children in a Race-Conscious World* (San Francisco CA: Jossey-Bass, 1998).

to my white family members. Specifically, in the moments that I was pulling for engaged dialogue toward an honest look at white fragility, I experienced my classmates as family members who had left me with a lasting negative psychic imprint. In the situation with my classmates, I employed the same strategies as I had with family: education, voice, engagement, and sometimes self-care in the decision to walk away.

Realizing that I replayed a scenario from the wounding of my younger years provided me with information about the closure I was seeking. I thought that I could lead them to take that look in the mirror, see the privilege of their whiteness. I thought I could somehow lead them to see the reality and impact of white supremacy in this country while unpacking personal fragilities insulated by their whiteness. I also struggled with understanding whether or not it was my place. As I attempted to make more sense of what happened, I was reminded of a piece in Audre Lorde's essay, "Age, Race, Class, and Sex."[3] It reads, "Traditionally, in American society, it is the members of the oppressed, objectified groups who are expected to stretch out and bridge the gap between the actualities of our lives and the consciousness of our oppressor." She elaborates further, "Whenever the need for some pretense of communication arises, those who profit from our oppression call upon us to share our knowledge with them. In other words, it is the responsibility of the oppressed to teach the oppressors their mistakes." I was subconsciously expecting, hoping for a corrective experience in which I would be seen and the white people in the room would see themselves, within the construction of whiteness. The emotional labor required to orchestrate this is exhausting. Ultimately, I did not get this corrective experience from them, just as I did not get it from within my own biological family. I found it myself, in the realization and release. I find it in forgiveness and continuing to show up in these spaces. So while it is not my responsibility to teach, it's also one that I haven't been able to put down entirely. It's a choice that I'm making. It is one of the ways I employ my privilege toward social change.

---

3 Audre Lorde, *Sister Outsider: Essays and Speeches* (Berkeley CA: Crossing Press, 2007).

Who Am I? Questions of Lineage

While race is a social construct, it is so deeply entrenched into this country's existence that it cannot be ignored. Unless you're white and therefore *normal* and therefore have the choice to ignore the realities of injustice, oppression, prejudice, and microaggressions inherent to the lived experiences of people of color. This is a function of white privilege. Of course, privilege is complex and varies across the intersections of one's identity. So, my thoughts are only a piece of a larger conversation. Yet ignorance is a choice. For one to say that they don't see color means to say that they don't acknowledge the reality of this country's history of immeasurable violence against people of color. A history that includes atrocities such as genocide, human slavery, and internment camps, and continues systemic oppression through mass incarceration disproportionately imprisoning black and brown bodies.

Since the time I was in grade school, I was curious about my family origins. Really, I was curious about my paternal ancestry. My father, while present for many of my early childhood years, sort of disappeared. When attempting to recall when he stopped being present, my mind is blank. Aside from a few memories, all I have is a photograph of us to prove that we spent time together. In the photo, I'm about five years old and am sitting on his lap, his arms wrapped around me. We're sitting on the grass in what looks like an outdoor amphitheater, both leaning back looking at the camera. Our smiles are big with laughter. Very recently, I have reconnected with my dad and we're now building a relationship. Hearing him recall memories of me as a girl is helping me to integrate the way I understand my story, such as the first time he took me fishing and our collective surprise at my actually catching a fish! In fact, one of the themes I heard in listening to stories from each of my parents is how they showed up for me when I needed support. Like my dad taking me to school and setting straight a boy who was bothering me. Or my mom seeing me come home from school while in the first grade, upset because a kid told me that my mom was not my mom because I was brown and she was white. She walked me to the bus stop the following day and shared with him that she was in fact my mom and that she is white and my dad is black, so I am brown. Then looking on as the kid and I ran off and played together on the playground until the bus arrived.

Stephanie around five years old with her father

My dad's side of the family didn't talk much about where we came from and there seemed to be an unspoken rule communicating that it was off limits. In fact, I didn't ask my paternal grandmother questions about our family origins until I was in my late twenties. Even then, familiar with the reality of intergenerational trauma, I approached the conversation with a certain gentleness, unsure of what my questions might evoke.

My maternal ancestry was much more accessible. Alta, my maternal great-grandmother, was the family historian. Sometime between my middle school and early high school years, she made a family tree book tracing back from herself an additional two maternal generations and three paternal generations. One year, during our traditional Christmas Eve celebration at her home in Lodi, California, she gifted this to all of her children. This book, now in my possession, is forty-six pages of history. It's a simple book complete with a yellow cover and iron clamps holding it together. The pages hold photos, stories, letters, family trees, and marriage certificates. It also holds a map of the family migration trail from the island of Jersey in the Channel Islands of England to Utah and Idaho as well as a family coat of arms. I was unable to appreciate it then. I was suspicious of it even, unable to connect to it as a part of my own lineage. The first time I held the book in my hands, I raced through it searching for any indicators that my family owned slaves. I found nothing of the like. In the stories I found indicators of challenging farm life, commitment to their Mormon faith, and of their deep love for one another. Yet I was still disconnected from them. At that time, during my adolescence, I thought: I wonder if any of these people were racist. How would they feel about me and my brown skin? To me, they were not my family. They were my mom's family. They were my grandpa's family. They were my great-grandmother's family. But they weren't mine. I believed that they were people who would not love me if they were alive. These people were strangers to me, not because they had passed away or because I never met them. They were strangers, and not my ancestors, because they would reject me if they had the chance.

My third maternal great-grandmother and great-grandfather immigrated to the United States from Denmark. Rereading the story of their daughter Emma, my maternal second-great grandmother, written by one of her daughters, I'm overwhelmed with emotion. As I wipe away tears I'm with mixed feelings. Both with happiness at the opportunity to connect with my ancestor through this recollection of who she was and sadness for having so harshly disconnected myself from this heritage, a result of my own experience of feeling unloved within it. As I reflect on the aversion I felt to my maternal ancestry in my youth, I am left still with a hollow feeling. There is an ambivalence to which I wonder, if members of my living family could have such disdain toward people like me, then how could I expect my white Danish-American Mormon ancestors to love me in my brown skin? I will never know. Yet in reading Emma's story it's as if I can feel her through the love that was poured over and into me by my great-grandmother Alta. And I feel compelled to voice my apology to Alta and to Emma for having ever turned away from them as if they are not within me. As I take a break to open a fresh box of tissues, I walk around holding onto my own body. I speak aloud gratitude for feeling the presence of my great-grandmother Alta, and I hear myself say, "Your love is redeeming." That is it. The love that has held me continues to transform me.

I met my paternal grandfather for the first time when I was twenty-nine years old. He was ninety-two. My journey to him was unintentional. I didn't imagine I'd ever know who he was. I'd learned his name for the first time a year earlier when I began having conversations with my grandmother. As I sat across the kitchen table from my paternal grandmother, I shared with her, perhaps for the first time, my sentiments of displacement. A displacement rooted in the complexities of being biracial and in my lacking knowledge of our family history. In the recording of our conversation, my voice is a certain combination of soft and strong. It may even be a tone reserved specifically for communicating with her. In it is the resiliency she's fostered within me, the softness that is inherently me, and the reverence I hold for her. It's all of these things. In these moments, she shares more than I have ever known about her life, about our family's lineage. I hear my grandmother saying, *you are not alone* in the way she connects similarities of our experiences through her sharing. I learn, or am reminded rather, that she's from Natchitoches, Louisiana. I say it: "Natchitoches!" and hear her repeating it back. Then I realize she's correcting me because I'm mispronouncing it. I take away not only newfound knowledge about my family history but an even deeper connection with my grandmother. I also make connections to the ways in which the legacy of slavery has impacted generations of my family, including myself. Dr. DeGruy's work on Post Traumatic Slave Syndrome has been revolutionary in beginning to heal from this collective trauma, first by putting language to it. In Post Traumatic Slave Syndrome, I see reflections of myself, of my father, and in generations of so many of my family members. It's in the stories of separation, abuse, of lacking esteem and the triggering nature of disrespect, in the silencing of our stories. It's in my father's absence from my life and his father's absence from his. But I keep opening my heart and searching for ways to heal through connection.

So I take my newly attained information—my paternal grandfather's name—and plug it into my online family tree. The process of having my

DNA run and building out my family tree led me to a distant cousin from the South who grew up with my paternal great-grandfather, my dad's paternal grandfather. She shared that my grandfather was not only living but residing in the same town as me. She was able to get in touch with him and his wife and about a week later I was at their house. Meeting my grandfather for the first time was beautiful. I remember walking from the front of the house, a gardenia and bag of grapes in hand as a gift, to the back of the house where he sat in his walker chair next to the window. He remained seated, debilitated by several strokes that had taken place over the years. I walked up to him and he never took his eyes off of me as he held my hand in his, just smiling and looking up at me. I came prepared to ask him about his experience in the Jim Crow South and everything about his life, his parents, and what happened that caused his absence from my father's life. Unfortunately, I was never able to ask these questions. His speech was impacted by the strokes he had suffered and I was only able to make out some of what he said. His wife helped me understand when I was unable to. While it's unclear whether or not my grandfather knew of my existence before that day, the way he welcomed me was endearing. The way he looked at me and held my hand in his. From his disposition toward touch, his sentimental shares, and his smile, I saw a reflection of him in myself. This came to be the greatest gift in meeting him before he passed away less than two months later.

Stephanie and her paternal grandfather, Lucien. Photo taken in November of 2016.

Dolls

While I find it challenging to access many childhood memories, including objects such as toys or things I found myself interested in, I remember Cory. Cory was a dark brown Cabbage Patch Kids doll that I adored. He was my baby. Earlier this year while focused on doing work with my younger self, I got more curious about Cory. Going off of memory and a photograph, I took to the Internet in search of a doll like him. What I found was upsetting. From their website, I found that their dolls are no longer made as dark as Cory was.

But why not? Skin is still this color!

Cory was as close in skin tone as a plastic doll's face can get to the way I remember my own father's skin. Beautiful and rich and deep brown. I don't know why I loved that doll so much. Maybe Cory made me feel closer to my father, closer to my own blackness. An object that I could hold and feel, talk to, be with. An entity that would stay. Meanwhile, I continued searching various websites and came across a female version of my Cory on Pinterest. I ordered the doll. Prior to that I had found another Cabbage Patch doll, bigger and a bit lighter in color than Cory was. I ordered that doll too. When the second doll came, I was filled with a childlike excitement that was visible in my smile. I held the doll and felt like a girl. I also felt like a woman raising myself.

Stephanie around five years old with doll, Cory

In the process of all of this, I wondered who purchased my beloved Cabbage Patch doll. I asked my mom. I learned that she had. My white mom knew that it was important for me to have black dolls while I was growing up. I also learned that Cory was a Christmas gift when I was around the age of five years old. She recollected his being the first doll I ever connected with and one that I carried everywhere with me.

I also remember my collection of porcelain dolls, a tradition started by my maternal aunt. My relationship to these dolls was different, however. I can't recall toting them around or playing with them. They were just there. Some people find porcelain dolls eerie and they're often depicted as sinister in horror films. This was never my experience; I was not afraid of them. Given we didn't have a lot, I was appreciative to have a collection of anything. Yet, I wonder if my aunt took into consideration that the dolls she purchased for me, each of them white, appeared as if they were from the antebellum South. Fortunately, my granny joined in on this tradition and made sure I also had black dolls. One year, she gifted me a very intricate porcelain doll. Newborn "Charla" was number 475 of 2,000 dolls like her worldwide. She came in a large box, complete with a long white gown and even fitted with earrings and a gold necklace. My granny certainly gave me so much but the best gift in this was seeing myself reflected through the art of this doll.

Self-Loathing and Interacting with Other Mixed or Biracial Women

In the seventh grade, I was invited to the popular Mercedes's house. As I recall, it was sometime during the summer and she was throwing a pool party. Everyone who was someone was there so I was both nervous and surprised to be invited. By the end of the pool party, my friends and classmates were commenting on "how black" I was, or had gotten from being in the sun for so many hours. I wore this like a badge of honor. When one of my friends said this, I beamed with pride. It carried a sense of acceptance. I felt and received it as a compliment.

As an adolescent, I admired Mercedes. She was smart, outgoing, seemingly liked by everyone. She wore her hair in big curls and I felt connected to her because while we were in a school of racially diverse students, we were both "mixed" girls. I learned that she was Mexican and black. Her best friend was another mixed girl who was black and white. Though I was friends with them, I was never able to move beyond that and into their clique. We were separated by socioeconomic status. To my knowledge, each of them belonged to middle-class families who owned homes and whose parents were still together. On the other hand, I belonged to a working poor family run by my single mother. We moved homes often and I was raised by a village of people.

As I write this, I surprise myself with tears. As I allow myself to cry, I am reminded of the craving within myself. For sisterhood. For a place to be seen. To be loved by others with shared experiences. To see another and see myself, my humanity, my beauty. Yet when I see another biracial woman, I view her with competitive eyes. I believe the simple truth is that I feel threatened. The twelve-year-old girl inside of me longs for connection yet I look onward with distrust and coldness. If I slow it down and really reflect on what happens, it begins with something like a twinkle in my eye. For a moment, I'm excited at the possibility of connecting with another biracial woman. I attempt to make contact through a smile or closer proximity. Depending on the situation, maybe we'll have the opportunity to speak. The interactions that follow tend to include some sort of internal assessment in which I evaluate whether or not I can be myself with this person. Curiosities fill my mind and I wonder, what is their experience of racial identity? Are they more identified with their blackness or their whiteness? Or are they *colorblind?* Do they believe that they have transcended race altogether? Will they hear, like, really hear and understand my experiences or will they consider themselves above them? Will they have the rage that I do about the realities of the white supremacist culture we live in or do they attempt to avoid reality? If I want to talk about how painful it is, will they think it's too much? Will they think they are better than me? Are they?

Are they better than me?

It seems there is more information in this inquiry than whatever my answer may be. What am I insinuating with this inquiry? The answer is daunting and arouses shame that lives in the tension of my shoulders and jawline. There is hiding until I *figure it out.* Until I deem myself worthy of being seen. This inquiry is an inheritance of colonization and oppression. And I have internalized it. There is disgust and anger in my flared nostrils, frowning mouth, and turning stomach. I have internalized the oppressive narrative that insinuates, *as a WoC you are not good enough and you never will be.* I see it for what it is, false. At least I think I see it in its manipulative nature, designed to instill doubt. And I believe I am standing up against it, undoing years of oppression, and decolonizing my mind. Yet I see it all over the way I hide and the lies I tell myself about what I am capable or incapable of.

It's embodied in my own response to others seeing something valuable in me. When the founder of my program and a pioneer in the field of somatic psychotherapy approached me about being a part of this book, I was confused. I wondered and asked, *What makes you think I have something to contribute to this book? Why me, why do you think I am capable of doing this?* Surely, I am not. Surely, I have nothing to say. Right? In a room of colleagues discussing our intentions for each of our pieces, I was intimidated. I thought, what am I doing here with all of these brilliant thinkers and doers? I am not worthy of sitting at this table. When asked what I intended to write about, I stumbled over words that were so finely articulated in my mind but then confused in my throat. Communication throughout my body was like a game of telephone and my words came out shaky and less articulate than they were formed in my mind. But I stayed at the table. I continued to write.

Perhaps awareness of having internalized some of the lies given to me from years of oppression is the first step toward healing from their painful impacts. The knowledge that oppression is systemic serves as a reminder for gentleness in the process of shaking it from my body.

Rage and Grief

Earlier, I reflected on these questions as a part of my mental process when meeting another biracial individual: Will they have the rage that I do about the realities of this white supremacist culture we live in, or do they attempt to avoid reality with ignorance? If I want to talk about how painful it is, will they think it's too much? Writing and authentic movement served as a useful intersection of platforms to process some of this pain. In a prompt to inquire into an experience of my body moving, I wrote the following piece:

the micro movements in my face
the numbness
the clenching of my jaw
the shaking of my lower lips
the air coming in and out of my body like an accordion
my chest shaking in a way familiar
this is grief
accompanied by hard and long blinking eyes that struggle to process the tears fast enough

My entire face is turned downward
each cell allowing itself to get closer to another as if an attempt to feel some sort of nearness
deep scrunches to signal another release
each release signaling pain so familiar

this is a collection of grievances
add another of my brothers

I sob
My head aches,
my tears are thick like the blood of my ancestors' bodies when the slave ships split them open
rubbing them raw

Raw
not as a state of emotional being
but as a state of physical being
Perspective

I grace my ears with the sounds of the mbira
a sound that brings me peace
then I allow my body to move me

I walk around and come to a place on the floor where I attempt to lay on my side
to rest
I feel pulled
One leg stretches out followed by the other, propelling me into a state of action, of attention
This happens with a swiftness that informs me that rest is not fitting

Now on my knees I tilt my head back as far as I can, exposing my neck
My face is tight with angst but soft in breath, my mouth open
exhaling, allowing exit

With the movement of the sage smoke and sound of the mbira *I allow my head to fall*
and raise again
to be brought back again each time facing a different direction
as if to shake off the suffering

On the floor with my knees bent I allow myself to shake my head vertically several times
and then I begin to slowly pick my body off of the floor
first allowing the tips of my fingers to make contact with the floor
feet making small steps
then pushing myself back up

I reorient myself to my surroundings and decide to close

The bottom of the page I wrote on includes the context. It was written in response to the killing of Terence Crutcher who, while unarmed and with his hands in the air, was shot by Tulsa police officers on Friday, September 16, 2016.

When another black person's life is cut short by police brutality or a fearful citizen, I am with full body grief that aches. There's trembling inside of me and I want to scream and I could scream and cry and I fear I would find no end. I think of the one we just lost and their aching, grieving family members. I look at them and attempt to avoid imagining my own loved ones. It never works and I am left with the future grief that sits in my body. I look at photographs of the black men shot down by police and I can't help but think of my own brothers. With this grief, I find myself floating through the world trying to keep my eyes open and dry. To do the things I need to do to be okay. I go to work and I am not okay. I go to school and I am not okay. Sometimes I can't stay at work and I have to go home because the grief is too thick to be held there. I find some peace through crying and conversing with friends also hurting from this. Yet when I am out in the world with this hurting and I look up, I am floating, unaware of how I got from one place to the next. And with lacking discernable features communicating to other black folk around me that I am also black, I'm alone. So, I am eyes red with grief and alone in the world. I crave brief connections with strangers out in the world as a way of communicating our collective grief and offering one another some small gesture of peace and togetherness. But I don't look like my community so I am outside of it. It is lonely. And it hurts more.

Soul Sistah Circle

When I was searching for community and seeking a place to allow my emotions spaciousness, my individual therapist recommended a group for black individuals socialized as women called Soul Sistah Circle. I missed the first iteration and decided to apply for the next one when it came around. As part of the process for potentially joining Soul Sistah Circle, I went through two interviews with the therapist putting it together. First, we spoke on the phone. I took my lunch break from work and walked to a nearby park to take the call. The warmth of the sun was a source of comfort helpful to my unsurprising nervousness. During that call, I shared what I knew of the group and what interested me in participating. Mainly, I was in search of connection and community. A place to feel normal and reenergize from the challenges of navigating predominantly white spaces daily. In the time I was provided to ask questions, I inquired whether or not it would be okay for me to join the group.

In those moments, I sought comfort for my insecurity of non-belonging. I wanted to know: Will you accept me as a biracial person? She assured me of my belonging and we scheduled the next interview. Our conversation served as a beautiful reminder that I am an individual of the African diaspora. The black experience in America varies so widely across the intersections of each individual's identities. But why then did I feel the need to ask for permission to be there? The need to define blackness is rooted in racist white supremacist ideologies and to some extension I have internalized it in my belief of non-belonging.

For the in-person interview, I was invited to meet the therapist running the group at her private practice. So, I arrived early and sat on the sofa of the waiting area trying to look relaxed. I wondered why I'm nervous. There's something about the idea of selling myself that makes me uncomfortable. Especially granted the possibility of being declined from participating in the group. I thought to myself, *what if that happens . . . if I am declined from joining the group?* Would that then be a reflection of my non-belonging within the black community? But that didn't happen. She invited me to join the Soul Sistah Circle for a ten-week process group. I felt proud and accepted. In my feeling accepted there was a sense of, *I'm black enough to be a part of the group,* and the thought, *maybe I even have something to contribute.*

Prior to the group's first session I found myself ruminating over possible scenarios. My mind played out all of the ways I would be unwelcome, my presence protested. We were to meet at seven in the evening and already that morning I was sensing overwhelm. While in the process of group therapy, I took notes to document my experience. On October 6, after the group met for the first time, I wrote to myself:

This morning I was beginning to feel overwhelmed about my day ... sensing some anxiety about going into group therapy for black women, as a biracial woman.

I found myself with this internal dialogue loop in which one individual in the group would object my presence and I would have to decide how to be with that....

I imagined different scenarios. None of them came from a place of acceptance in my mind. They were all ones objecting my presence, my membership.

There's a hypervigilance.

An internalized story that I can never belong or be truly accepted.

That I am a woman of the African diaspora cannot be taken away from me.

Is it wrong for me to seek community in other black women?

Or rather, and on a deeper level, why do I need validation from black women? Or from the black community?

Where did this come from, this sentiment that I do not belong or am unworthy? I believe I have a glorification of the black woman. I think the black woman is god and I think about the black women in my life being ones that loved and took care of me. I think about my internalized biases toward my own whiteness ... and I think of glorifying the black woman as a way I have dismissed myself from ever being capable of being, or attaining ... being as worthy as.

This was not my experience. I was not met with resistance or disdain but with acceptance. I was simply another woman there looking for community in other women. In fact, from what I am able to recall, this rejection that I anticipate from other black people, namely women, has not been a part of my larger narrative. The black women in my life have always nurtured my existence. From my paternal grandmother and my nonbiological adoptive maternal grandmother to all of my closest female friends.

In the fourth session during our opening grounding exercise, I internally set an intention to go deep during check-in and process. As I sensed the woman next to me wrapping up her check-in share,

I noticed myself shifting in my back-jack in an attempt to feel more comfortable. But my lack of comfort was an internal experience that couldn't be fixed by moving my crossed legs into another position. I share that I'm in a contemplative space around identity, that I'm doing a lot of writing and processing around my embodiment especially as it relates to being biracial. That day I was holding a personal inquiry into whether or not self-loathing is a part of my experiencing my whiteness. This reminded me of a dream I had in which I was speaking to an older woman about navigating identity. I said to her, *I can hold myself as a black woman, I can hold myself as a biracial woman, but I can't hold myself as a white woman.* I shared my sense of displacement, feeling like I don't belong anywhere. And that I exist in the world with this question: *Is it okay for me to be here?* This question is accompanied by a shrinking and a hiding. I think it may be embodied in my challenge articulating myself. As I speak, my breath is much more shallow than usual. It's shaky as if I will run out of breath. I'm on the verge of tears but they're tucked neatly behind my throat. My throat is full and I'm unable to make eye contact. I pause for what feels like a long time when taking up space is uncomfortable. So I wrap up and conclude my check-in. When our therapist asks me what it was like to share what I did, I feel acknowledged. Throughout the session, I search for signs of validation or disapproval. I look for this in the eyes and gestures of my group members and our group leader. I find myself wondering if they feel toward me the way I feel toward white women: prove that you're trustworthy. And if they do, how much this hurts.

Who Decides Group Membership?

In my personal inquiry into where my anticipation of rejection from other black people comes from, I am reminded of something I saw online recently. For Harriet, founded by the brilliant Kimberly Foster, "is an online community for women of African ancestry" according to its website's "About" page. In a photo posted on the For Harriet Instagram profile was a photo of Prince Harry and his fiancée, Meghan

Markle. The caption read, "My princess is BLACK."[4] Something I've learned is to avoid the comments section online unless I'm prepared to be upset, but I thought, *1. I appreciate the content and messages that For Harriet shares in their posts, and 2. I'm curious what people are saying because they're likely going to be judgments about her blackness.* The comments ran along the lines of the following criticisms and questions as a way to grant or dismiss her membership: One is not black if they are mixed; How black is this person's black parent?; What does the individual claim she is?

Though I've interchanged identifying myself as black and white and black, I've spent most of my life identifying simply as black. While I am of African American and European American parentage, I have always identified more with my blackness. Meaning, I've felt more comfortable and connected to other black people, to the culture, and committed to learning about the history and issues impacting the black community. Sometimes people would challenge my blackness, saying things like, you can't be *just* Black, what are you mixed with? I did not lie. I shared that I am also white. Or sometimes, especially when questions about my mixed race included commentary about their perception of my beauty, I challenged their even asking what I am. *Why do you ask?* In other words, why are you concerned about it? Often these inquiries into my race, ethnicity, nationality, what I'm mixed with, where I'm from, made me angry for reasons challenging, delicate, and complex to articulate. I wondered, why does it matter to you? What are you going to do with that information? I thought, do you want to put me into a box so you can know how to treat me? Which always led to, *you don't deserve that power.* This type of experience, while intrusive and annoying, is also indicative of the unwarranted privilege granted by my lighter skin and more European features. My blackness is not always apparent to others, which means I can choose whether or not to claim it.

Once when I was nineteen years old and working at a major retail store, a black customer walked up to me with an amused look on his face and asked, "What are you?"

---

[4] @forharriet Instagram post

"I'm black and white."

"Oh no, you're black. You know about that one-drop rule!"

What he was referring to was the notion that one drop of "black blood" would *taint the purity of whiteness* therefore making one black. This was way before terms such as biracial or multiracial. I understood the racist historical context that led to the creation of this race-based classification. Yet at the time I received this comment as a strange expression of acceptance of my blackness by another black person. This would have been offensive and derogatory had it come from a non-black individual. Yet coming from a black man, I felt seen though in a conflicted, confusing way given the nature of the one-drop rule throughout history.

At times, I would interchange labeling myself as black with mixed or biracial or black and white, but for most of my life I have claimed myself simply as black. Yet something about it feels incomplete, untruthful even. In a way, it feels almost disrespectful. Disrespectful as if in referring to myself as black I am failing to acknowledge my privilege. My white privilege.

My choice to refer to myself as biracial came not as a dismissal of my blackness but as a way to be honest with myself about who I am. About my lineages, both of them. Whether or not I have rectified with their intersections.

These thoughts occur all within the context of still sitting with the comments about Prince Harry's fiancée, Meghan Markle; my heart beats fast so I take a break and come back to them. Not black, biracial. Not black, mixed. Reading through them, my breath shallows and I feel my body shrinking. There is physical pain at being misunderstood. If I identify as biracial, I am not rejecting my blackness. If I am biracial, I cannot be black? Who gets to decide? How may I empower myself to accept the intersections of my existence? How may I choose for myself that I belong in the face of opposition to my group membership? There's a hollowing throughout my midsection.

As a second-year graduate student, I am not yet working with clients, which leads me to believe that my thoughts about how we may, in the field of somatic psychotherapy, move toward a more inclusive somatics are in some ways limited. However, woven throughout this piece are the ways in which I have sought out healing specifically related to the challenges of being a black and white biracial woman in this country. The act of telling my story has alone been transformative. Throughout this piece are also themes of the human need for connection with others, the redeeming nature of love, the importance of knowing where we come from, and the beauty of giving voice to our younger selves. I believe that it's healing in nature to be honest about our pain, and to allow it a platform for expression. I also believe that when we advocate for ourselves and for others, we are doing the work of healing and moving toward a more inclusive somatics.

Much of my embodied experience as a biracial individual reflects spaces where I have felt loved or unloved. As I write my stories and often surprise myself with tears, I realize how much of what hurts is feeling, believing that I am unwelcome. My embodiment is a reflection of my wounding and resilience but this process has led me to question my relationship with viewing myself as a victim. It's a hard question to ask myself mostly because I fear any indications of its truth. I'm reminded that the nature of my studies encourages a rich knowing of oneself. So much of studying to become a psychotherapist has been working through my own unresolved issues. The process of digging into oneself requires a tremendous amount of honesty and commitment. It often feels worse before it feels better. Having the spaciousness to pursue this deep work is a privilege. I can be honest, say that I have been hurt and that some of that hurt is still with me. Sometimes I even notice that old hurt in new experiences and I'm able to recognize it as transference. These honest reflections are the way that I find the love again. Even in the uncomfortable experience of sitting at a table where I once believed I didn't belong, I stayed. I continued writing because being real about my pain is how I'm able to find forgiveness and deeper compassion for both myself and others. Being honest is how I find the strength to stand with dignity in the complexities of my identity. Bell hooks said that "getting in touch with the lovelessness within and letting that lovelessness speak its pain is one way to begin again on love's journey."[5] This has been my lovelessness speaking its pain.

---

[5] bell hooks, *All about Love, New Visions* (New York, NY: Harper Perennial, 2000).

Bibliography

"About." For Harriet. Accessed February 5, 2018. http://www.forharriet.com/p/about.html#axzz52bNCcBdf.

adrienne maree brown. *Emergent Strategy: Shaping Change, Changing Worlds*. Chico, CA: AK Press, 2017.

DiAngelo, Robin. "White Fragility." *International Journal of Critical Pedagogy*, 3, no. 3 (2011): 54–70.

@for.harriet Instagram Post. Accessed February 5, 2018. https://www.instagram.com/p/BcAYkGghaio/?taken-by=for.harriet.

hooks, bell. *All about Love, New Visions*. New York, NY: Harper Perennial, 2000.

Lorde, Audre. *Sister Outsider: Essays and Speeches*. Berkeley CA: Crossing Press, 2007.

Wright, Marguerite A. *I'm Chocolate, You're Vanilla: Raising Healthy Black and Biracial Children in a Race-Conscious World*. San Francisco, CA: Jossey-Bass, 1998.

Chapter 7

Dancing with Babaylan: A Somato-Spiritual Herstory of a Burgeoning Somatic Psychotherapist

Antoinette Santos Reyes

Introduction: The Noise of Empire

I struggle with the space between. As I sit with my clients' stories, the space between us fills with images and sensations—waves of unmet needs, longings yet to be acknowledged, somaticizations of rage and grief, paralyzing fears of uncertainty, scabs and scars that grow and peel on top of each other. We share joy, laughter, resilience, secret defiance. The rough terrain of finding ourselves, with each other. Battles for authenticity. Mistakes made, mistakes avoided. Confusion. Doubt. As we explore our individual and collective truths, the gravity of the room changes. My embodiments buckle, resist, surrender to the world tipping on its axis. The impact of their stories leads to abrupt changes in my breathing, visceral pangs, muscular tensions. I become porous, vulnerable.

I am constantly humbled by how little I know. The more I evoke this unknowable "therapist-body," the more I contain and control. I feel my body being pulled into different directions as if by marionette strings, shaping me into awkward positions. I feel fragmented. I become a cluttering frenzy of thoughts and I become a series of arbitrary boneless and bloodless sounds. I cannot feel myself. I am not myself.

Overwhelmed, I quake with self-doubt, anxiety, fear, worry. The marching industry of perfection finds itself in my neck and shoulders. Imposter syndrome creeps into my spine. I no longer feel the gentle and powerful flow of my intuition. My body is not enough. My wisdom is not enough. I shouldn't be surprised at how quickly this occurs; after all my body has been shaped, trained, socialized, forced, and collapsed into the many somatic manifestations of the disbelief in my knowledge and capacity. These noises perpetuate my inferiority. And it takes an incredible amount of fortitude to fight back. To fight internalized oppression. Being hypervigilant from the start makes finding my center, my equilibrium even harder.

However, I am constantly surprised at how much I know. As quickly as I lose, I find. My insurgence begins with a deep slow breath: an invitation to meet any one of the million sensations of my body. I notice the rise and fall of my chest. The expansion of my rib cage. I remain here and nurture this experience until something new emerges. I feel a small shift. A lazy undulating flow starts at the soles of my feet and slowly rises to my pelvis. It stops there and connects to the many tributaries of my torso, rising up and permeating the varied anatomical elements of my body.

This shifts my consciousness as my throat feels more lubrication, more spaciousness in between its tight muscles. In one united movement my chest and throat collect and gather what has been accessible all along—community, ancestors, guides. Cellular memory activates and calls the warriors inside me. New stories flow out and charge against this oppressed socialization. New choices, new actions present themselves and I take my body back from the intersecting and interlocking barbs of internalized oppression of white supremacy, patriarchy, and Judeo-Christianity.

How in the midst of all this noise and confusion can I create a body, a personhood, without the tar of shame and guilt? Where my slanted almond eyes don't distort the truth of my body? How do I reconcile my authentic identities with my colonized ones? How do I create a narrative that heals and supports the same in others? I realized these questions are not about carving out a "therapist self" but an investigation and excavation of what healing means to me, of forming a new self, a warrior-healer that trusts intuition, Nature, and authenticity.

As I delve into the practice of somatic psychotherapy, I feel deep gratitude for such valuable theories, tools, and interventions. The field has supported me in consciously accessing more of my body than ever before. Somatics demonstrated for me how my quality of life is dependent on how much body engagement I have in relationship to people and my environment. I have learned that accessing more of my body gives me the capacity to correct the many wrongs by bringing in more options and alternatives in my life. I get to re-pattern and re-shape how I see myself and the world, which brings in more vital options and responses. I am also honored to have learned about the anti-fascist origins of somatics and the people who have made somatic psychotherapy what it is today—individuals who transformed their pain into medicine for others.

However, Western somatics is still in the process of acknowledging and affirming that many of these practices have emerged from primal and ancestral knowing. Although Western somatic approaches emphasize subjective experience through the body, they do not extensively explore the body through a sociopolitical or geopolitical lens.[1] What *theories* reflect my flesh, history, and resistance? The potential of integrating the legacies of the oppression of empire[2] and colonialism into the understanding of somatics is manifold. These lenses facilitate the understanding that

---

1 Rae Johnson, "Oppression Embodied: The Intersecting Dimensions of Trauma, Oppression, and Somatic Psychology" *USA Body Psychotherapy Journal* Volume 8, no. 1 (2009): 6.

2 Empire is defined as the large-scale political organization that extends a country's power and influence through military and/or diplomatic force. These structures and symptoms are responsible for the colonization of countries over the last two millennia, and are currently seen in America's global expansion through military intervention. The systems of white supremacy, patriarchy, capitalism, and Judeo-Christianity all contribute to neocolonialism in "the Third World."

> reclaiming the body as self is a profound act of political resistance ... The body is the site for authoritative knowledge ... as personal and social power ... and resisting oppression. Johnson illuminates the power of body to "transform oppressive experience, not just enact and reproduce [it].[3]

By including an understanding of how the trauma of colonialism reproduces oppression in bodies, somatic practices can contribute to systemic change and social justice.

It is through this politicized lens that a new understanding of somatics begins. I seek to integrate a framework that is culturally relevant to my body. I believe the liberation of my body requires a historical exploration of how colonialism in the Philippines emerged and shaped generations of people into fractured, severed selves. This exploration will be the foundation of understanding the space between somatic theory, my ethnic/cultural identities, and the path of decolonization. I seek to contribute my medicine story to deepen the complexity of somatic theory and practice.

Part 1: (My) Somatics of Colonization

I am a second-generation Pinxy American,[4] shaped by a remarkable instinct to survive. My body holds generations upon generations of pain and struggle, joy, and resilience. My ancestors are alive in my embodiments, my choices, and in my work of healing the human heart. My body bears the scars of trauma, evidence of my family's fight of living in the United States.

Both of my parents endured traumatic events in their homeland: World War II, the Japanese Occupation of the Philippines, the death marches of Bataan, and the disappearances of dissidents during the

---

[3] Johnson, "Oppression Embodied," 10.

[4] Pinxy is the genderqueer/agender/gender nonconforming demonym referring to people who descend from the Philippines. Pilipina denotes the feminine version and pilipino is the masculine version.

Marcos regime. As violent as these events were, my parents were already recipients of the ongoing insidious context of Spanish and Catholic imperialism and colonization. From 1521 to 1946 the archipelago known as the Philippines experienced the devastation and death of indigenous culture and community. The Spanish were brutal in their level of violence. They had killed all of the spiritual and cultural bearers as a way to ensure that indigenous culture would not survive, and they completely replaced the tribal system with a feudal system with conquistadores and religious nobles in charge.

The indigenous way of life was decimated. Animism and polytheism were replaced by Catholicism, alibata[5] replaced with the Latin alphabet, native names with Spanish ones, interdependence with others and nature was replaced by individualism, isolation, and competition. The abundance of nature was destroyed by reckless disregard. Pride in the brown native body turned to shame. The native brown body became objectified and used, devalued at the hands of the Spanish.

Jose Rizal,[6] a Pinoy national hero who was executed for his beliefs in liberating the Pilipino people, asserts:

> Then began a new era for the Filipinos; little by little they lost their old traditions, the mementos of their past; they gave up their writing, their songs, their poems, their laws, in order to learn by rote other doctrines which they did not understand, another morality, another aesthetics different from those inspired by their climate and their manner of thinking. Then they declined, degrading themselves in their own eyes; they became ashamed of what was their own; they began to admire and praise whatever was foreign and incomprehensible; their spirit was dismayed and it surrendered [to] ... this disgust of themselves.[7]

---

5 Alibata is the indigenous alphabet of precolonial Philippines and Southeast Asia. The ancient language derived from Brahmic scripts of India.

6 Rizal was a Filipino nationalist whose writings advocated for political reform against Spain and subsequently contributed to the rebellion against the Spanish colonial government.

7 Maria P. P. Root, *Filipino Americans: Transformation and Identity* (Thousand Oaks, CA: Sage Publications, 1997), 58.

Several years later, black activist and scholar, W. E. B. Du Bois voiced the same sentiments in *The Souls of Black Folk*, that black people in the United States experience

> a double consciousness, [a] sense of always looking at one's self through the eyes of others, of measuring one's soul by the tape of a world that looks on in amused contempt and pity. One ever feels ... two-ness,—an American, a Negro; two souls, two thoughts, two unreconciled strivings; two warring ideals in one dark body, whose dogged strength alone keeps it from being torn asunder.[8]

Despite the fight for independence, Pilipinos were betrayed and once again overpowered. After the Philippine-American war, the Philippines became a U.S. Protectorate, a euphemism for colonial rule and once again victim to imperialist and colonial rule. Similar to the Spanish, the United States used insidious tactics to shape the country into their likeness. For the sake of American imperialism, they brought Thomasites to teach English and glorify American values to prevent indigenous insurrection. Even more devastating was the use of Freudian psychology to develop U.S. colonial rule. According to Ronald Tataki, Freudian psychology emphasized that only men/masculinity have the power of reason and rationality, and that patriarchy is the only model strong enough to subdue the instincts and impulses of the uncivilized Pilipino people.[9] The United States used this rationale of saving the Pilipino to plunder the land, avail themselves of trade with Asia, strengthen their military presence, and continue the colonial work that Spain had started long ago, replacing Spanish values with American ones.

---

8 W. E. B. Du Bois, *The Souls of Black Folk* (Mineola, NY: Dover Publications, 1994), 2–3. There have been many instances of allyship between Black and Pilipino communities, from the racial solidarity movements during the Filipino-American War in 1899, throughout Anti-Asian sentiment/labor organizing sleeping car porters in 1925 to the Black Power and Civil Rights era. I feel this solidarity most potently through Renato Constantino's "The Miseducation of the Filipino."

9 Leny Mendoza Strobel, *Coming Full Circle: The Process of Decolonization among Post-1965 Filipino Americans* (Santa Rosa, CA: Center for Babaylan Studies, 2015), 49–50.

After nearly five generations of colonial violence and intergenerational trauma, the indigenous brown body had successfully internalized their oppressors in the hopes of thriving under colonial rule. The cost was high and the body split in two, forming the double consciousness that Rizal and Du Bois poignantly describe. These embodiments would form into a potent self-hate and self-loathing as they come to realize they would never be seen as equals, that their lives did not matter. This toxic shaping would form into slow forms of suicide, a deep loss of self and authenticity, and the loss of connection and community.

I reflect on how silence and historical amnesia figure largely in how internalized oppression and colonial subjugation are perpetuated among Pilipinxs and the diaspora. The phenomena of "colonial debt" in which Western culture is exalted and maltreatment from the oppressor is the cost for being civilized, and "imperial rationality," which demands the forgetting of colonization, permeated my family system. Any mention of how dominated we were by Empire would lead to intense vitriol and backlash. We didn't have the tools to hold our collective trauma and pain and so we projected it onto each other. My mother fell victim to the worst punishment, because she was female and the eldest. She was responsible for the care of her entire family, according to Spanish socialization. She was made to sacrifice her own needs and longings for the sake of the men in the family. Catholicism made her distrust her body, sensuality, and sexuality. She would struggle to access her body, to feel her desires. She responded to challenges with reactivity and an overexerting control. She was taught that she had no choices. My mother was like the land she lived on. She held the painful traumas of a country that had lost its center. When she exhibited any type of authenticity or individuation, she was violently punished. For the three generations of my family that I know, the cost of this silence and erasure, this undigested rage and grief, manifested into complex PTSD, multiple chronic illness, and survival strategies that included physical, emotional, and sexual abuse.

As a product of this system, I see clearly how my colonial education manifests as "noise" forming a barrier between my body and my intuition, and therefore a barrier between me and my clients. Because I was shaped as a caretaker, as a martyr, as my mother was before me, I feel responsible for caring for and solving my clients' problems. This responsibility feels closely linked to how oppressors rationalize knowing what is better for the other. I believe I embody Empire when I become a problem-solver, a fixer, and an imperialist in how others should heal. My internalized oppression believes that a therapist's job is to "give" personhood. In my zeal to support others I move into the extreme of taking on other people's healing so that they don't have to—just as the colonized brown body has been socialized to do. Succumbing to the "noise" is colluding with oppression and unconsciously using strategies of power over my clients.

My body is split; fragments engaged in a silent war. One side is conquered, old, familiar, brimming with shame and self-loathing. The other is a healer-warrior filled with strength, gall, and a predictably profane tongue. These two sides have been fighting a generations-old skirmish here. My throat, although still narrow and closed, works to find the wind, waves, and force of the Pacific. My eyes that are fetishized, commodified, and exoticized—closed by Spanish, Japanese, and American lenses—filter and bend the light, altering my reality. My ears, that yearn to hear words differently, to redefine and decolonize them. When the oppressive forces throw spears of self-doubt, fear, shame, guilt, anxiety, they aim straight for my head. My aunties remind me that I am also incredibly stubborn and thick-headed, so the arrows don't have to go all the way through. They can break off and fall to the floor.

Like all wounds, apply coconut oil, holy water, and wrap with a warm banana leaf.

Call the hilot.[10] *Say a prayer or send a curse. Or both.*

I grieve the embodiments I have inherited. I grieve for my family, my homeland, and her diaspora. However, as I access more of my body and authenticity through somatic practice, I feel myself respond differently to my pain. I begin to feel agency over it, to shift from helplessness and victimization—to consciously call in the power of my resilience and untold cultural history.

---

10 *Hilot* is Tagalog for the village healer.

Part 2: (My) Somatics of Decolonization

Accessing Depth through Babaylan

According to Pinoy scholar Virgilio Enriquez, *ama ng sikolohiyang Pilipino,*[11] the Babaylan was "the first Filipino psychologist ... she is the foundation of Filipino consciousness" and the sacred keeper of "communal culture, shared history, and collective memory that has developed a community psyche or *kamalayan.*[12] Pinay historian and scholar Leny Mendoza Strobel described Babaylans as mystical women (and men) who wielded social and spiritual power in precolonial Philippine society before the coming of the Spanish imperialists in the sixteenth century.[13] The Babaylan served as mediator between cosmos and earth; a shaman, a culture bearer, "She ... embodies and represents the openness of the culture to the world outside. She represents the notion of *kapwa*[14] (the self in the other) as the fluid, inclusive boundaries of her multiple social worlds. The seeming lack of preoccupation with control belies her ability to do so; her ability to traverse and mediate between worlds is her gift."[15]

The role of the Babaylan is to "guide people through the process of proper grief once they realize that their grief is really a longing for wholeness and connection. It is through the inability to grieve that

---

[11] Translates to "father of Filipino psychology" in Tagalog.

[12] "Awareness" in Tagalog.

[13] Lily S. Mendoza and Leny Mendoza Strobel, *Back from the Crocodile's Belly: Philippine Babaylan Studies and The Struggle for Indigenous Memory* (Santa Rosa: Center for Babaylan Studies, 2010), 164.

[14] *Kapwa* translates to "self in the other" or "shared self, mutual self" in Tagalog. It is a key concept in sikolohiyang Pilipino and one of the concepts integral to the Babaylan's spiritual teachings and practice. An in-depth exploration of this concept will be shared later in this paper.

[15] Leny Mendoza Strobel, ed., *Babaylan: Filipinos and the Call of the Indigenous* (Santa Rosa, CA: Center for Babaylan Studies, 2010), 27.

[causes] violence and cultural and spiritual amnesia, which in turn, [causes] physical and emotional violence."[16] People would often hear the call in a dream or through a life-threatening or chronic illness and be healed by prayers, experiencing a change of consciousness called *sinasapian,* a form of communication from the spiritual or ancestral realm. This communication served as a recognition or awakening that provided meaning, understanding, and connection to the universe outside of their physical bodies. It was pain as initiation, a threshold towards a larger connection.[17]

It seems that Babaylan has been guiding me my whole life. Through my pain and suffering, she deepened my capacity to hold collective pain and suffering. I had been a sickly child, visiting the hospital ER nearly every other week for severe asthma, high fevers, and inexplicable fatigue. Babaylan was in all my moments of escape, dissociation, and play. She was in my free-flowing tears, allowing me to grieve unabashedly at the legacy of violence my family and my body have experienced. As I hear her once again, I realize this is not merely an invitation to healing but a call to action. Babaylan emerges when the person is ready, which is a shedding of the "familiar, illusory safety of colonization," and a sense of coming home to land, nature, and purpose.[18] Strobel asserts that the Babaylan is a "tacit knowing," embedded in between layers of tissues, viscera, and muscles, and manifesting in art, voice, gestures, practices, and movements.

I believe it is through this tacit knowing that Babaylan is more than a healer or culture-bearer; she is an initiation to a path forward, a politicized somatics where the body as a whole is a form of activism and resistance in itself. She moved through the great

---

16 Strobel, 29.

17 Translates to "spirit possession" in Tagalog.

18 Strobel, *Babaylan,* 18.

revolutionaries of Philippine history like Gabriela Silang[19] and Jose Rizal. Her initiation was different from the type of politicization or activist training I had received in the past. My previous political/activist learning focused on decolonizing the mind, whereas the Babaylan offered a decolonizing of the body—an embodied counter-narrative and critique to the white male–focused somatic theories I had studied over the last few years. Her initiation activates the cellular memory of my ancestors' sacred healing and ritual. Most importantly, she demands that I cultivate my own indigeneity and spiritual intuition.

As the Pinxy embodiment of compassion, wisdom, and creative imagination, the Babaylan supports the dignity of the postcolonial Pinxy body and her diaspora in response to the wounds inflicted by empire. Embodying the Babaylan is to recover, to participate in a sacred rite and legacy of wholeness, and healing the split between body, soul, and mind. For me, this is the "dogged strength" that Du Bois alludes to, the sacred resilience that I share in collective with other Pinxys. It is this strength that allows me to do my own Babaylan-inspired work: to support and cocreate authentic personhood through sacred stories and traditions, to weave wholeness and to allow this wholeness back into the world as collective healing.[20]

Under the somato-spiritual guidance of the Babaylan, I yearn to hold the act of therapy as a place for sacred storytelling and the therapeutic relationship as a dance of uncertainty, curiosity, death and dying, aliveness. Our stories become a piece of brilliant choreography of longing, change, and authentic personhood. Integrating indigenous psychology ensures I stay true to my own sacred mission of decolonizing and authentic personhood. By sitting at the intersection of

---

[19] The first Pilipina leader of a movement for independence from Spain. She is a powerful symbol of the current global movement to end the exploitation of the Philippine people. The Gabriela Women's Party is a leftist Pilipina organization that fights for women's issues. Gabriela Network USA is a solidarity mass organization to provide political education and community action.

[20] Strobel, 5.

ancient tradition and postmodern society, I can deepen my capacity to bear witness and hold the fragments of our broken selves with tenderness and sensitivity, to mediate between the different complexities and contradictions that get the way of our deepest longings.

Accessing Width through *Kapwa*

Indigenous psychology is the study of human behavior, i.e., our belief systems, knowledge, and skills in their cultural context. My process of learning about my ancestry, the Babaylan, and *sikolohiyang Pilipino* serves to widen my framework for somatic theory.

Exploring Ignacio Martín-Baró's conceptualization of liberation psychology, which integrates "psychology's core aim, the psychological well-being of people with the stark reality of oppressive systems that undermine this aim" has also been important.[21] Liberation psychology is rooted in the liberation theology founded by the Peruvian priest Gustavo Gutiérrez, which models a form of politicized somatics where we engage with not only a person's systems and constellations, but also with the earth. The ultimate goal is to cultivate a deep sense of justice and liberation for all people. The nature of indigenous psychology is to deeply root healing within a sociopolitical and revolutionary context.

For many Pilipinxs, a comparable healing system to liberation psychology or indigenous psychology is *sikolohiyang Pilipino*. It describes foundational beliefs in dignity, social justice, and emancipation.[22] The beating heart of interpersonal relations included truth-seeking, which in itself is therapeutic. This system of beliefs and practices centers on the core value of *kapwa*.

---

[21] Taiwo Afuape, *Power, Resistance and Liberation in Counseling and Psychotherapy: To Have Our Hearts Broken* (London: Routledge, 2011), 59.

[22] Virgilio Enriquez, *From Colonial to Liberation Psychology: The Philippine Experience* (Manila, PI: De La Salle University Press, Inc., 2004), 41.

Kapwa means "shared identity" or "mutual self" in Tagalog. It symbolizes the central value of personhood, gender neutrality,[23] and seeks to integrate binary concepts. It is a form of shared self, where self is inherently interconnected to other people, myths, time, the earth, and the cosmos. It is at the heart of collective thought, where one is so deeply interconnected to the other that they can feel and read each other's thoughts and needs. *Kapwa* can be a seen as a powerful witnessing of another.

Kapwa is a type of knowing that resides in our DNA. It is a knowing that can be harnessed during times of cultural and spiritual amnesia. Because it is a type of knowing that exists in sacred space and time, it provides a collective consciousness (e.g., myths, dreams, nature, and ancestors) that preserves a sense of continuity for all the lost Pilipinxs who seek to reclaim and free themselves from empire narratives.[24]

In understanding the width of *kapwa,* one needs to understand other critical concepts that are folded into it. A critical concept is called *pakikiramdam* (shared inner perception), which means thinking with the heart or a kind of emotional "a priori" and is the true legacy of the Babaylan. It is a mode of knowing that is beyond empathy; it is a sensing of context, content, emotion, mixed with a desire to maintain balance and harmony in one's universe of relations. It is the most somatic and kinesthetic of all the concepts because it incorporates *loob* (internal experience), which includes heightened sensitivity, intuition, and sense impressions, and *labas* (external experience), which includes physical sensations, touch, and overall body feeling. The last nuance, which feels most important for me, is *pakikiisa. Pakikiisa* is a type of interconnected dignity, and a belief that the person in front of them is an extension of themselves. It is seen as a type of blending in without losing one's individuality.

---

[23] The creation story within the *kapwa* describes god splitting a piece of bamboo into two equal pieces where one piece formed femininity and the other, masculinity. The two qualities were seen as equal, similarly to concepts of yin and yang in Chinese spiritual belief.

[24] Strobel, *Babaylan*, 27.

These concepts intersect into a type of wholeness that is rooted in how communities interacted in precolonial Asia. It allows me to make spiritual contact with a time before imperialism and colonialism. This type of contact with others is inherently dignified and anti-oppressive. It catalyzes in me a fight for a collective space where we are fulfilled and whole. This image brings me awe and a very real and alive conception of somatic healing.

As I reflect on my early adult life, I can see where *kapwa* has emerged as an anchor when I have felt deep grief and despair. *Kapwa* arrived when I came into political consciousness. When I began to understand the role of empire, war, and colonization onto my family, I felt so deeply seen but full of rage and terror on how I use this information. The activist community gave me a place where I can hold my rage and provide a place where I can demonstrate my anger in public, so that I can continue feeling witnessed, and to leverage power toward systemic change. It is through this therapeutic framework that I could widen my capacity for connection and to others; it challenged my edges, my shape of isolation. More importantly, it re-patterned my tendency to isolate, to keep my pain and vulnerability secret. This isolation and secrecy are what strengthen colonialism. Through *kapwa,* my body has a place in this world.

Kapwa came when I would ache from all of the everyday oppression I experienced and came when I used coping strategies that hurt, and helped. It allowed for deep intimacy with my activist community; it allowed me to not be isolated or vulnerable. I was able to rage and grieve collectively, which was powerful healing of my soul and a mighty push against colonialism.

Accessing Length through *Bahala Na*

Growing up, my family would often exclaim *"bahala na"* when we were faced with multiple and compounding racist episodes from microaggressions such as being refused service at a restaurant to structural racism such as the constant threat of losing jobs or housing. They told me that it means, "Leave it to God," which used to infuriate me. It felt like we were giving up and not demanding justice and accountability.

Through indigenous psychology, I realized how wrong I was to be angry with them. Although my family may have had some resignation, there was more than meets the eye when it comes to this expression. According to Enriquez, *bahala na* translates to "determination in the face of uncertainty" and has an interesting history. He writes that in the 1960s Americans compared *bahala na* to American fatalism—where Pilipinxs passively resign to their fate and demonstrate a careless lack of responsibility for their actions.[25] This was rooted in the belief that Pilipinos were lazy, rural, and lacking in Western education. Luckily, Pilipino scholars corrected these misconceptions and defined *bahala na* as an active process, as confrontation. It is "risk-taking in the face of the proverbial cloud of uncertainty and the possibility of failure." It is an active acceptance of the nature of life and as a call to be resourceful, to reorganize one's capacity for change, and to harness creativity to make the situation better. It is meant to rally courage, to cope, and ease in stressful and uncertain situations.

Most of this arose from the indigenous Pilipinx's relationship to uncertain and dangerous weather patterns, from typhoons, earthquakes, and hurricanes, which allowed them the fortitude to survive and thrive. It was then called upon to fight against imperialism during the Spanish-American War.

Exclaiming *"Bahala na!"* takes on new meaning for my personal and collective healing work. I feel it most potently as a gathering energy, keeping my head up, spine straight, and back relaxed. I feel my ancestors' hands on my back, bringing readiness and strength. Whether I am faced with challenging client work, frightening political events, or the despair that often comes in the decolonizing process, I meditate on the history of *bahala na* to access the courage and curiosity I need to face the challenge head on.

---

[25] Enriquez, *From Colonial to Liberation Psychology*, 72.

Conclusion: Collective Dignity, Collective Responsibility

With the power of indigenous memory, I begin to suture the split within my body. The process of decolonizing is about accessing blood, earth, and spirit. It is naming of shared pain and struggle. It is historical revisioning and recovery. It is about truth-telling.

I deeply appreciate *sikolohiyang Pilipino* for bringing forward psychological concepts that integrate colonial history and indigenous healing. It heals the either/or split into a both/and relationship. This methodology illuminates how colonial and indigenous embodiments interact for the sake of dismantling colonialism. Reflection of people's histories in the study of somatic practice and somatic psychotherapy can help reframe the more antiquated and oppressive elements of Western psychology and be more inclusive of global bodies. For therapist practitioners and/or healers, learning cultural competency or humility is not enough. I believe actively investigating and interrogating our shared histories and how they impact our embodiments lead to transformative social change. We are on the edge of a dangerous political time. With fascism around every corner and in every neighborhood, somatic practice and somatic psychotherapy have the potential of healing the split within and collectively.

If I am to be committed to supporting a person's self-determination and liberation, it is required that I support my own. This chapter was a brief inquiry of my own frameworks and how I can use my body as a tool for healing. I have barely scratched the surface and am grateful for the opportunity to unite the somatic explorations of my body, the *babaylan* stories I have yet to unearth, and the interventions within *sikolohiyang Pilipino* to practice. Engaging in this integrated framework invites me to see whole beings, cultivate a continuously relevant sociopolitical analysis, and ultimately contributes to our shared dignity.

Dignity is a bridge. It needs two sides that, being different, distinct and distant become one in the bridge without ceasing to be different and distinct, but ceasing already to be distant. Dignity demands that we are us. But dignity is not that we are only us. In order for dignity to exist, the other is necessary. Because we are always us in relation to the other.... Dignity should be a world, a world in which many worlds fit."

—*Zapatista speech during the March for Indigenous Dignity, February/March, 2001.*[26]

---

[26] Hank Johnston and Paul Almeida, eds., *Latin American Social Movements: Globalization, Democratization, and Transnational Networks* (Lanham: Rowman & Littlefield, 2006),

Bibliography

Afuape, Taiwo. *Power, Resistance and Liberation in Counseling and Psychotherapy: To Have Our Hearts Broken*. London: Routledge, 2011.

Constantino, Renato. *The Miseducation of the Filipino*. Quezon City, Philippines: Foundation for Nationalist Studies, 1982.

Du Bois, William Edward Burghardt. *The Souls of Black Folk*. Mineola, NY: Dover Publications, 1994.

Enriquez, Virgilio G. *From Colonial to Liberation Psychology: The Philippine Experience*. Manila, Philippines: De La Salle University Press, Inc., 2004.

Johnson, Rae. "Oppression Embodied: The Intersecting Dimensions of Trauma, Oppression, and Somatic Psychology." *USA Body Psychotherapy Journal* 8, no. 1 (2009): 6,10.

Johnston, Hank, and Paul Almeida, eds. *Latin American Social Movements: Globalization, Democratization, and Transnational Networks*. Lanham: Rowman & Littlefield, 2006.

Mendoza, Lily S., and Leny Mendoza Strobel. *Back from the Crocodile's Belly. Philippine Babaylan Studies and The Struggle for Indigenous Memory*. Santa Rosa, CA. Center for Babaylan Studies, 2013.

Root, Maria P. P. *Filipino Americans: Transformation and Identity*. Thousand Oaks, CA: Sage Publications, 1997.

Strobel, Leny Mendoza. *Coming Full Circle: The Process of Decolonization among Post-1965 Filipino Americans*. Santa Rosa, CA: Center for Babaylan Studies, 2015.

Strobel, Leny Mendoza, ed. *Babaylan: Filipinos and the Call of the Indigenous*. Santa Rosa, CA: Center for Babaylan Studies, 2010.

Chapter 8

The Void of Experienced Meaning in Japanese Society: Ambivalent Attitudes toward Traditional Bodily Practices

Haruhiko Murakawa

Segment 1: Aum Shinrikyo

More than two decades have passed since the Aum Shinrikyo cult attacked people by dispersing poisonous sarin gas in the Tokyo subway in 1995, but the attack's influence still lingers in Japanese postcapitalist society. It is one of the most memorable incidents in recent history because the target was not a particular group of people but Japanese postcapitalist society itself. Aum Shinrikyo used various spiritual practices such as meditation, yoga, Tantric teachings, psychedelic drugs, and even technological devices based on brain science for their followers ostensibly to achieve personal liberation and the organizational vision to attack society. As a result, Japanese people have become suspicious of anything overtly religious or spiritual in nature. While we still visit temples and shrines, and conduct funerals and weddings in religious ways, any spiritual activity originating in religion to explore the meaning of life became socially unacceptable and was almost banned.

In our premodern societies, such activities were called varieties of "self-cultivation" and provided a basis for various healing modalities before Western medicine gained hegemony all over the world. Moreover, they provided a framework in which people could explore the deeper meaning of life when the agonies of daily living brought the ordinary meaning of life into question. Thus, such practices of self-cultivation have played significant roles, directly or indirectly, in enriching our lives in Japan and indeed all over the world. Yuasa once defined them as "an endeavor to experientially get familiar with the world, which will be opened up from the depth of our interior mind through exploring it with our bodily existence."[1] Don Hanlon Johnson has described such practices in a different way as "methods for luring us out of our divisive, self-centered ideas into the realm of sensing and feeling where we exist together, breathing, pulsing, gesturally interacting; a palpable matrix for the building of a more humane social order."[2]

Although self-cultivation was once esoteric, practiced by a very limited number of people, as our modern society has become more and more secular and technological, it became available to a much wider population. However, self-cultivation has typically been represented and practiced in a rather shallow and fragmented way, as in mindfulness meditation for American people or modern Americanized yoga for Indian people. One of the problems of this social shift was the lack of a framework in which people could openly verify the meanings and pitfalls of such self-cultivation practices, which I believe was the very issue raised by the Aum Shinrikyo incident.

---

1 Yasuo Yuasa, *Shintai no uchusei* [The universality of the body], (Tokyo: Iwanami-shoten, 1996), 6.

2 Don Hanlon Johnson, "Body Practices and Human Inquiry: Disciplined Experiencing, Fresh Thinking, Vigorous Language," *The Body in Human Inquiry: Interdisciplinary Explorations of Embodiment* , eds. Vicente Berdayes, Luigi Esposito, and John W. Murphy (Cresskill, NJ: Hampton Press, 2004), 108.

Segment 2: Somatics and the Social Body

On a hot sunny day I was sitting on a big green lawn at the Esalen Institute in Big Sur, looking out upon the Pacific Ocean. Up above my head was the blue California sky stretching out to the horizon, toward which my nostalgic memories for my beloved homeland across the ocean were hovering with the white clouds. Once in a while, water from the sprinkler would drizzle over my sweating body. The salty smell of the ocean, mixed with the odor of green plants, floated in the air. The mesmerizing sounds of ocean waves together with the songs of unknown birds invited me to a long-forgotten world. I was there, fully experiencing my "body in sensuous nature."

I first landed in the United States in 1986. After staying in San Francisco for a couple of days, I went to the Esalen Institute, the famous center of the human potential movement, and stayed there for two months as a work scholar. Because of my poor English, I was thrown into a situation where I could barely use my verbal communication skills; what I could do was repeat just a few words in any situation. Fortunately, people were generous and brave enough to accept my bold survival strategy. Rather than saying "I feel lonely," I cried in front of people. Rather than saying "I feel sympathy with you," I hugged them. Rather than, "I am uncomfortable with what you said," I stood up and said "no" directly to them.

Instead of my verbal skills and intellect, my whole body expressed who I was. I peeled off the layers of my intellectual armor that had accumulated through my family upbringing and public education and detached myself from my bodily sensations. Finally I reached the layer where my primordial bodily-felt sense was located. All my frustration, sadness, joy, and anger were present before being mediated by words and were expressed through the full sense of my body. The more I contacted that body, the less I identified myself with those social images of my family, educational background, and even my ethnicity. After being stripped of those images, I found my body to be full of sensations, a source of meaning, and a subject of expression. I found my body as myself.

In order to further explore this "body as myself," I have studied various Eastern and Western bodily practices, including Gestalt therapy, Sensory Awareness, Holotropic Breathwork, Process-Oriented Psychology, Continuum, Taiji Quan, Zen meditation, Katsugen Undo, and Qigong. These practices have provided me with deeper experiences to explore my body as myself. However, after taking a master's program at the California Institute of Integral Studies, I realized that bodily practices were rarely valued as themes of academic study. Moreover, I found that the important epistemological issues those bodily practices might open up for us, i.e., the dichotomies of body and mind or subject and object, were totally dismissed in the methodologies we could employ to study such bodily practices. It was a source of great existential frustration since I had found my body-as-myself and again needed to bury it under the mind-separated-from-the-body.

Then I decided to explore a way to articulate the body not as a mere object of study but as a significant subject of inquiry. At that time, Maurice Merleau-Ponty and the theories of radical constructivism gave me a framework for my exploration of the first-person science in which such dichotomies of body and mind, or subject and object, might be overcome. My concern for the methodological issues of studying bodily practices as well as for the significance of the body in a disembodied society has played the central role in my inquiry since then.

After working for several years in Japan as a counselor at an outpatient mental clinic, I returned to the United States to enter the CIIS PhD program. In the second quarter, I took a class to explore our social bodies in which we read *A Chorus of Stones* by Susan Griffin.[3] My classmates from Germany and Israel confessed the burden they had carried from World War II, and I suddenly faced the fact that I did not have a meaningful sense of history. I had some knowledge about the atrocities against Asian people committed by the Japanese army during World War II, and I had felt remorseful about them.

---

3 Susan Griffin, *A Chorus of Stones: The Private Life of War* (New York: Anchor Books, 1992).

Still, they had not been experientially related to my own life. But in that class, for the first time I realized that I was still holding the same social body as my ancestors who had killed hundreds of thousands of Asian people, including innocent women and children; with my own social body, the war was not in the past, but present in myself.

Through this experience, I became aware that my body is multilayered, and that some of those layers had been hidden by social construction processes such as upbringing, education, medical practices, the modernization of life, and so on. Then I realized that, different from the body of my parents' generation, my primordial body had been deeply buried under the externally imposed modern Westernized body and that I needed to intentionally dig into the deeper layers to attain my primordial body. Since then, it has become important to recover the body I myself have lost through growing up in modern Westernized Japanese society. Qigong, among various bodily practices, has become significant to me since it can provide me with clues to recovering the sensual nature of the body.

At the very same time, the act committed by Aum Shinrikyo, killing twelve people and injuring more than five thousand, had a tremendous impact on my inquiry because the cult members had used many Eastern body-related practices, such as yoga and other meditation techniques, to attain their spiritual experiences. It seemed to me that this incident symbolized how the memory of World War II had been built up in layers or "sedimented" in the Japanese social body. Those cult followers, many of whom were intellectuals with a higher education, must have experienced some meaningful moments through their bodily practices, but then they had gone to the extreme of surrendering themselves to the cult leader. I saw myself in them, those who unfortunately had found a terrible guru rather than their authentic Selves in their bodies. Without having been so fortunate as to find my own body as myself, I could have been one of them.

After this, I became concerned with how experiences through bodily practices could be distorted by such powers which eventually led them to their cultic movement. Don Hanlon Johnson defines this issue as the difference between "the technologies of alienation" and "the technologies of authenticity." He describes these two technologies in the following way:

> Some ways of working with our bodies cause us to further estrange ourselves from our direct experience. Exercise … can be taught and performed so that the exerciser struggles so hard to accomplish certain external goals that he or she becomes habituated to give little value to experience. Or it can be taught so that a person can develop his or her sensitivity to experiences of toning, stretching, and vigorous effort, coming to further knowledge and appreciation of oneself.[4]

I realized the importance of discerning the two different directions in which any bodily practices may lead us. One is to direct us toward experiencing the body as an authentic self; that is, we can develop our bodily awareness, transform our state of body and mind, and cultivate our way of being-in-the-world. The other is to direct us toward alienating ourselves from our authentic selves and allowing us to surrender to some extreme authority. These two directions are not simply contradictory to each other, but rather are complicated and interconnected.

Segment 3: The Body as Authentic Self

In a strange historical bifurcation, the traditions of self-cultivation were developed almost exclusively in Eastern cultures until the middle of the last century, while Western cultures have placed little significance on them. The relatively new field of bodily practices called somatics changed that dichotomy. In his seminal article on somatics, Johnson opens up a new pathway to situate it in a broader context of human inquiry.

> Despite their many differences of strategy, demeanor, and professional presentation, all of them share a foundation in core questions: what happens when we learn to turn our awareness in repeated

---

[4] Don Hanlon Johnson, "Body Making," in *Groundworks: Narratives of Embodiment,* ed. Don Hanlon Johnson (New York: The Hampton Press, 1997), 8-9.

> methodical ways toward the intricacies of our bodily experience? What is revealed about the world? About ourselves?"[5]

With this common ground established, somatics focuses on "an inquiry into human experience through exercise of sensing, paying sustained attention to sound-making, breathing, and various ranges and depths of body movement, both voluntary and involuntary." Johnson summarizes the very unique role of these bodily practices as "the cultivation of adult behavior and capacity." Its aim is, according to him, "to awaken people's capacity to discover things themselves, unclouded by the endless mental chatter that clouds our experience."

With this view of bodily practices as self-cultivation for our adult learning, Johnson points out that the fundamental obstacle to reclaim the importance of such self-cultivation specifically lies in an abyss between thought and experience, which is deeply rooted in our social structures, especially academia and education. Our long-held academic prioritization of theory over praxis has influenced the way we approach our experiences and establish a social system to transmit them. Johnson describes this issue in the following way:

> For anyone old enough to read Husserl, there is little likelihood that he or she will have the ample resources of flexibility and sensitivity required to embody his invitation. Those of us who have been schooled enough to approach his arcane texts have typically been successfully educated to feel a primal disconnection between thought and experience, no matter what we think, say, or hope for. Those primal feelings seep into the dissociated climate of academic texts, pedagogy, social structures, and interpersonal behavior, even when they are rooted in phenomenological claims.[6]

To "awaken people's capacity to discover things themselves, unclouded by the endless mental chatter that clouds our experience,"[7]

---

5 Johnson, "Body Practices and Human Inquiry: Disciplined Experiencing, Fresh Thinking, Vigorous Language," 106.

6 Johnson, "Body Making," 1.

7 Johnson, 3.

somatics has developed "methodical, observable, teachable ways of bracketing,"[8] which provide us with "a significant key to articulating a more intelligible model of a science of subjectivity which might address issues of bias and replicability."

This concept of "bracketing" was originally developed in the phenomenological movement that Edmund Husserl initiated. However, Johnson pointed out that this philosophical method of bracketing is not a mental exercise as typically described in qualitative research, but rather a bodily practice in "methodical, observable, teachable ways." In other words, bracketing is not to postpone or eliminate our "subjective biases" but rather to stay with "feeling" before any concrete contents or images, words, symbols emerge; as Isadora Duncan waits for the moment when primordial movement emerges after a long pose. This very subtle but concrete difference between mental bracketing and bodily bracketing needs to be understood, not only practically but also theoretically since we have the tendency to reflect on and think about experiences, not reflect in and think with experiencing.

Besides this primal disconnection between thought and experience, another important issue is our unexamined framework of bodily experiences as "subjective and idiosyncratic as opposed to objective and universal." Following Johnson's proposal of "a significant key to articulating a more intelligible model of a science of subjectivity, which might address issues of bias and replicability," we need to reexamine our epistemological stance to deal with "bias and replicability." In order to do so, I would like to set up a methodological foundation to explore the "intricate sensitivity to the nuances that exist between experience and verbalization," by way of William James's radical empiricism[9] and Eugene Gendlin's approach in *Experiencing and the Creation of Meaning.*[10]

After careful detailed examination of the then-rapidly developed psychological investigations and long history of philosophical debates on the human mind, James proposed an idea on the stream of consciousness to

---

[8] Johnson, 12.

[9] William James, *Essays In Radical Empiricism* (New York: Longmans, 1912).

[10] Eugene Gendlin, *Experiencing and the Creation of Meaning* (Chicago: Northwestern University Press, 1997).

overcome the mind/body and subject/object dualisms, and later elaborated on it to take his stance of radical empiricism based on pure experience and his own pragmatism. I believe that to situate the exploration of bodily experiences, we need to start with a firm standpoint radically different from our normal, deeply imbued dualistic viewpoint. For this purpose, we are going to follow an approach James suggested:

> Experience, I believe, has no such inner duplicity; and the separation of it into consciousness and content comes not by way of subtraction, but by way of addition—the addition, to a given concrete piece of it, of other sets of experiences, in connection with which severally its use or function may be of two different kinds ... a given undivided portion of experience, taken in one context of associates, play(s) the part of a knower, of a state of mind, of "consciousness"; while in a different context the same undivided bit of experience plays the part of a thing known, of an objective "content." In a word, in one group it figures as a thought, in another group as a thing. And, since it can figure in both groups simultaneously we have every right to speak of it as subjective and objective both at once ... dualism ... is still preserved in this account, but reinterpreted ... (as) an affair of relations ... outside, not inside the single experience considered....[11]

Although this "experience as a flow" standpoint asserted by James has been succeeded by many scholars, including Husserl, Bergson, and even Nishida, it was Gendlin who created a new approach for us to think in James's way, to dip ourselves in the flow of experience. Although, Gendlin rarely mentions James in any of his writings, his fundamental concept of "experiencing" can be looked at as an extension of James's.[12] Gendlin (1961) defined and outlined the characteristics of experiencing as follows:

> The characteristics of experiencing that I have mentioned are:
>
> 1. Experiencing is a process of feeling

---

[11] William James, "Does Consciousness Exist?" *The Journal of Philosophy, Psychology and Scientific Methods* 1, no. 18 (1904): 480.

[12] An indirect connection between Gendlin and James could of course be Carl Rogers, Gendlin's teacher in psychology, but Jean Wahl, who introduced Husserl and Merleau-Ponty to Gendlin in his graduate study could be another source since Wahl was also the strongest advocate of James in France.

2. Experiencing occurs in the immediate present

3. Experiencing is a direct referent [clients (people) can refer directly to experiencing]

4. Experiencing guides conceptualization [in forming conceptualizations, clients (people) are guided by experiencing. First rough conceptualizations can be checked against direct reference to experiencing]

5. Experiencing is implicitly meaningful

6. Experiencing is a preconceptual organismic process [experiencing is preconceptual and is a concrete organismic process, felt in awareness].[13]

Segment 4: Toward an Experience-Grounded Peace Education

Anyone who closes his eyes to the past is blind to the present. Whoever refuses to remember the inhumanity is prone to new risks of infection.

— GERMAN PRESIDENT RICHARD KARL FREIHERR VON WEIZSÄCKER, SPEAKING ON THE FORTIETH ANNIVERSARY OF THE END OF WORLD WAR II[14]

The historical sociologist Yoshiaki Fukuma in his "Postwar History of Wartime Experience"[15] describes in detail the process by which

---

[13] Eugene Gendlin, "Experiencing: A Variable in the Process of Therapeutic Change," *American Journal of Psychotherapy,* 15(2), (1961): 233–245. The parenthetical comments are mine.

[14] From a speech that German president Richard Karl Freiherr von Weizsäcker delivered at the ceremony for the fortieth anniversary of the end of World War II. Even now, thirty years after this speech, these words by Weizsäcker remain significant to us Japanese.

[15] Yoshiaki Fukuma, *Senso taiken no sengoshi* (Tokyo: Chukoshinsho, 2009).

conflict over the meaning of wartime experience and a gap between the postwar generation and the earlier pre-war and wartime generations were created. He also points out, "In the postwar period, war experiences formed a kind of 'culture' and functioned as a symbol of violence for the postwar young generation who did not have direct experiences of war. Therefore, the 'culture of wartime experiences' lost support among the younger generation."[16]

As Fukuma clarified, in postwar Japanese society, initially the experiences of the wartime generation were not aligned with the "anti-war" and "peace" movements. Views of the war were complicated. The wartime generation could not easily express their experience with words; sometimes they would criticize the political manipulation of antiwar sentiments by the postwar generation, in turn creating fierce conflicts with them over the experience of war. Such criticism and conflicts show the complicated aspects of passing down wartime experiences, but Fukuma regards this positively, pointing out that "many possibilities emerge through such discontinuities and discrepancies." He asserts the following:

> Wartime experience has been repeatedly worn down and fragmented. However, it does not mean that it is impossible to pass down such memories. Rather, the revival of memory and opportunities for regeneration may dwell in sincerely examining the postwar period's sense of disconnection around wartime history. Our future can be carved out by examining the mistakes and what-ifs of our past.[17]

In this period of time, seventy-nine years after the Nanjing massacre and more than seventy years after the end of WWII, how can we approach thinking about events that took place long before most of us were born and relate them to our current way of life? How can we take responsibility for the war and deal with these wartime experiences? What is the purpose and meaning for us to offer an apology

---

[16] Fukuma, 32.

[17] Fukuma, 262.

as "Japanese people"? To find out the answers to such questions, we need to sincerely examine postwar history, and once more explore approaches to our "worn down and fragmented" experiences of war.

The task given to us as individuals living in the twenty-first century is to figure out how we can carry these wartime experiences without closing our eyes to certain details so we can avoid repeating such events in the future.

De-Historicizing Body

I was born in 1963, eighteen years after the end of World War II. As I shared beforehand, the first opportunity for me to face the issues of history within myself came when I took a class on "The Social Body" while attending graduate school in the United States in my twenties. Our assignment was to read *A Chorus of Stones* by Susan Griffin and to present an essay on it. In the very first session, a German and a Jew born in the same generation as myself spoke about the burden of the history they carried. When I witnessed their confession, I was shocked by the fact that I myself had never felt my own history with the seriousness that they did.

Before this moment, although I had some knowledge about the wartime "incidents" that took place at Marco Polo Bridge, Nanjing, Pearl Harbor, and Hiroshima-Nagasaki, I had never realized that they had any connection with my present self. Dates such as December 13, 1937; December 8, 1941; or August 6, 1945, were not as significant in my mind as the dates of the Taika Reformation, CE 646, and the formation of the Kamakura Shogunate, CE 1192. When I thought of wartime battles, I associated them with the Boshin War of 1868–1869, or the Battle of Sekigahara in 1600, popular scenes that appeared on period television programs. Although I had been to the Nagasaki Atomic Bomb Museum and the Hiroshima Peace Memorial Museum and had seen films on Pearl Harbor and photos of the Nanjing Massacre, these experiences had not changed my way of life. I had never connected the war of my grandparents' and parents' generations with the violence within myself and Japanese society or with the wars that were taking place all over the world in the present time.

In that class, I learned the concept of the "social body," which indicated that social systems such as education and medical care inscribed a particular frame of feeling and thinking, which was sedimented in the bottom of one's consciousness through bodily disciplines. Through the concept, I first realized that the body that did not realize the connection between the past war and my present was my "social body" that was shaped within Japanese society. At this point I came to call my social body, which was disconnected from the past and lived as if only in the present, the "De-Historicizing Body" parodying Kitaro Nishida's famous "Historical Body."

With this social body, if we simply accumulate knowledge about past events, without having sympathy for the pain of others or the imagination to think about the complicated social situation, we may just deepen the degree of de-historicization of the body. That is, even if we increase the amount of description of World War II in textbooks, it will not be enough. If we carry a "de-historicizing body" such as my own, we may not sympathize with the direct voices of those people who went through the agony of the huge historical wave of war. Such voices include the victims of the Japanese invasion, the *hibakusha* survivors who suffered under the atomic mushroom cloud, and the people running to escape the Tokyo blitzkrieg.

In order for me to overcome such a "de-historicization," find living meanings in the past events I was brought up with, and connect with people from other countries at a deeper level, I needed to develop a "historical body" for myself that would honestly face and accept the feelings of others and myself.

In order for us to remember and learn from history, we should develop, through history education, this kind of "social body," which allows us to be aware of the complicated nature of the history we have grown up with—which inevitably raises the issue of the violence within us—and to grasp this history as an extension of this present moment connecting to our lives. Inspired by that lesson in that class, I decided to organize an Asian Worldwork conference in 1996 in San

Francisco with the purpose of exploring how the various atrocities the Japanese army conducted during the World War II in Asia influence us in the present day.[18]

Worldwork

Jungian psychotherapists Arnold and Amy Mindell started Worldwork, which "brings into psychology a new vision of taking individual inner processes and group processes as a dynamic single process...."

> In this Worldwork, with the issues of racial discrimination, gender, and ethnic conflicts, the goal is not reconciliation, by dividing into the good and the evil or the oppressor and the victim. Rather they adopt the view of "the field" as a third viewpoint and try to "heal the field."[19]

They do not make an intellectual analysis or interpret from a third-person objective stance, but rather explore the experiences from each participant's first-person perspective. Therefore, they encourage the participants to accept their own experiences as they are, before making an intellectual judgment or reflection. Since each person's experience is different, they do not make judgments from an absolute standpoint of "good or bad" or "right or wrong." However, needless to say the "experiences" should also not be cast in an absolute position, and their meanings should be explored through a process of reflecting on and analyzing them. In this sense, "experience" in the view of experiential psychology is an "experiment" with actual feeling and is only an opportunity to explore how we can live our lives while communicating and cooperating with others. Therefore, experience and thinking/reflection form a reciprocal process.

---

18 Haruhiko Murakawa, "World Work (b)," in *Introduction for Process Oriented Psychology: Practical Psychology to Connect the Body, the Mind and the World,* eds. Yoshihiko Morotomi and Yukio Fujimi (Tokyo: Shunjyusha, 2001), 157–167.

19 Murakawa,157.

Worldwork emphasizes "field dynamics" as an opportunity to sublate dualistic positions such as individual and group, right and wrong, or victim and a perpetrator. I believe that by taking this new approach where we deliberately deal with complicated issues regarding the war, it might be possible to create "a new history education" which would deal with the above-mentioned "de-historicizing body."

History Embodied: Nanjing

As an individual, I have generally been regarded as a rather nonviolent person, but when I participated in the Worldwork in 1994 for the first time, I became aware that inside myself existed a "violent energy associated with the pleasure of life that rises up from deep within." In that Worldwork, after freely expressing myself in a group of Japanese people, I realized I had strong violent impulses to knock down all the men and women in that room. This realization forced me to question myself as nonviolent, and look at the possibility within me to conduct the same atrocities as Japanese soldiers did during the war. This experience taught me that the atrocities that the wartime Japanese army conducted are not to do with being "Japanese" nor "some other," but rather concern me, a person who has a hidden impulse to oppress others and treat them violently; the very issue is how I face that impulse.

After organizing the Worldwork conference to deal with issues of war in Asia, I started to work as a volunteer for a Chinese-American civil movement, which was growing at that time trying to make American society recognize the history of the Second Sino-Japanese War. Through this work, I became acquainted with Chinese-American war victims, Mrs. Iris Chang and Mr. Shudo Higashinakano, American veterans who suffered from the human body experiments of Unit 731, a covert Japanese chemical and biological warfare plant in Manchuria during the war. I was invited to memorial services for the victims of the Sino-Japanese war in San Francisco, in which I was given an opportunity to offer flowers as a Japanese participant. These experiences inevitably made me realize that the war seventy years ago was not something in the past but "in the present" for many Asian people living now with intense feelings.

A Japanese artist and activist, Kaz Tanahashi, who participated in the Asian Worldwork of 1996 and who also continued to work for this issue with a strong will and passion, initiating a new project. With the help of the late Iris Chang, author of *The Rape of Nanking*, Kaz organized an international conference on Japanese atrocities in Nanjing in 2007. Kaz Tanahashi wrote the invitation letter for this international conference as follows:

> This conference is for people from China, Japan, and other parts of the world, who have had different war experiences and educations, to open their hearts and listen deeply to one another on the issues of the Sino-Japan War and the Nanjing (Nanking) Tragedy.[20]

This conference was unique since it clearly mentioned its nonjudgmental position as follows: "in order to reflect the diversity of historical interpretations, this conference asked to put our fixed ideas aside and allow each person to be open to other viewpoints. We encourage people to listen to the feelings of others and express their own personal feelings."[21]

Another figure who was a participant in the Asian Worldwork of 1996 and who continued to get involved in this issue was Armand Volkas, a drama therapist. Mr. Volkas came to Japan in 2007 and held a workshop at the Ritsumeikan University Peace Museum in Kyoto on "Healing the Wounds of the History," based on his own method of Playback Theater, for members of the Japanese postwar generation to deal with the war experience. At the opening of the workshop, an elderly Japanese man expressed his intense feelings by saying, "You should deal with the fact that the Japanese lost many lives by A-bomb before calling us assailants." His expression, though

---

20 Kaz Tanahashi, "Remembering Nanjing (Nanking): Report on the International conference, 70th anniversary of the Nanjing Tragedy" (Berkeley: A World Without Armies, 2007).

21 Tanahashi.

appearing aggressive, also contained a sense of sorrow, which made me realize that many Japanese people carry both feelings of damage and assault layered upon each other that remain unexpressed. Here I saw how Playback Theater can absorb such strong aggression in a public space, without denying the truth of people's feelings and respecting them as they are.

During the four days of this seminar Volkas conducted, I had several opportunities to speak up actively. On the first day, after a group of several Chinese and Japanese participants discussed the issue of Japanese and Chinese identity, Volkas put two chairs representing Japanese and Chinese people in the center of the circle of all the participants, and then encouraged anybody who wanted to speak for that position to speak. In this exercise, I first sat on the chair representing a Chinese person and spoke to a Japanese chair, to criticize Japan, which was an expression of the voices of Chinese people I had listened to over ten years. Then various participants spoke for each side, and expressed their feelings. At the end, I took a turn on the Japanese side, and expressed a voice of the Japanese "indifferent generation." This was an affirmation that there were various voices inside of me, regardless of whether they were Chinese or Japanese.

Within the frame of experiential psychology, we were encouraged not to identify ourselves as a Japanese or a Chinese, but rather that we embody our Japanese or Chinese history and speak up from that embodiment. Speaking up at the seminar was an experiment for me to explore what kind of presence my voice comes from and to find out how different is the difference between a Chinese and a Japanese, and someone from Aomori or Nara or Yamaguchi or Fukushima prefectures, or to find out whether that difference depended on our language or customs. By the method that Volkas conducts, we could express and share such various voices in a safe space, which provided an opportunity to listen to various voices within others or ourselves and to take them in. However, the experiences in this experimental space do not necessarily lead to the "healing" of the victims, and the experiences and the voices from them might not be connected to the "truth" in a political context. Such connections are unknown to us yet. Manabu Sato criticizes history education under postwar democracy in the following way:

> Through the strategy of erasing the war as a past event and crossing out the voices of the dead, postwar education was able to put in effect a prompt shift to peace and democracy education. Although vivid memories of the war hovered in each person's body, accompanied by agony and cries of pain, in the official history taught by schools, such body memories were erased and a bright and undaunted education geared toward rebuilding the homeland was implemented.[22]

Sato proposed a new approach to history education "whose principle should be to respect as they are the varieties of memories and histories which were held by each person's body."[23] He asserted that it is necessary to establish education that accepts histories lived by each person in this modern Japanese society as the facts of the "history of the Japanese people" rather than lumping them together with labels of "good" and "evil" or "right" and "wrong."

Mai Takahashi also points out that the fundamental problem of modern education in Japan lies in "the continuation of modernity or colonialism," which prevents true meeting or "encountering" with others. A paradigm shift is needed from "self-education for victims" to "self-education for perpetrators" because the existing pedagogical framework is inherently violent against others.

> Even after the war, we merely shifted the boundary between groups, effectively enabling the colonization of Japanese citizens by Japanese elites, and still continuing to eliminate truly "encountering" each other as human beings just as we did during the war, and colonizing others and ourselves as before. We never truly meet or encounter anyone, so we feel isolated—it's a crisis of relationship. Unless we move beyond this modern society, which we maintain by never "encountering" each

---

22 Manabu Sato, "*Ko no shintai no kioku karano shuppatsu* [departure from the individual bodily memory]," In *Beyond National History*, eds. Komori and Takahashi (Tokyo: Tokyo University Publication, 1998), 310.

23 Sato, 310.

> other, that is, a society that forces us to be not individual human beings, but "somebody," the educational problems of the present age will remain unsolved and we will never truly be liberated.[24]

Embodying Myself and "Encountering" Others

On the morning of the last day of the seminar, we went to Yanziji in Nanjing and all of the seminar participants offered flowers at the monument for the victims. The conference participants in 2007 had come to this monument for the same purpose, but this time there was a big difference. Chinese and Japanese seminar participants paired up to offer flowers together. This moment of watching Chinese and Japanese youth taking each other's hands and going up the stairs together inspired me and gave direction to a path that I had walked without a definite direction ever since I had heard the heartbreaking voices of German and Jewish classmates in that class at CIIS years before.

In the afternoon, we came back to Nanjing Normal University and did a closing ceremony for the seminar. At the end, Chinese and Japanese participants stood facing each other and truthfully and openly expressed their requests. Prompted by Mr. Volkas to "take the words of each voice as an individual as well as a collective," Chinese participants expressed thoughts such as

> Please take any action to change—do not use right-wing pressure as an excuse for not taking action.

> Watching a Japanese kneel and apologize makes my heart ache. We do not want to watch such a figure. We want you to take some action.

We could hear these direct, genuine words, which had never been spoken before. In turn, a Japanese participant, a historian who had

---

24 Mai Takahashi, *"Ningenseicho wo sogaishinaikotoni shotenkasuru kyoikugaku"* (Tokyo: KOKO Publication, 2009) 276–77.

struggled with defending the historical truth of the Nanjing atrocities, said,

> Only the voices of the right wing seem to stand out in Japan, but there are many Japanese who have tried hard to educate the young generation for peace since the old days. However, recently more and more of those people are giving up and have developed a negative feeling toward China. We would like you to find a way to come together and lend us your support. Please.

After speaking so openly and exchanging frank responses, Japanese and Chinese participants approached each other, shaking hands and embracing each other. Sitting on the floor between the two groups, I observed the process, wishing to imprint the scene firmly in my mind. It seems that I witnessed a true "meeting" between humans, which was made possible only through spending time together in which each individual touched their unspeakable dark history and felt the pain of each other, and sincerely explored what we should do for the future.

******

The author would like to express the deep gratitude for all the participants of the Remembering Nanjing projects especially Kaz Tanahashi, Armand Volkas, Zhang Lianhong, Aya Kasai, and Kuniko Muramoto. The projects were financially supported by Ritsumeikan University and National JSPS KAKENHI Grant Number JP 23310189. The writing of this article was also supported by Kansai University's Overseas Research Program for the year of 2016.

Bibliography

Abiko, Kazue, Uozumi Yoichi, and Nakaoka Narifumi. *Sensosekinin to wareware—rekishishutai ronso wo megutte* [Responsibility for war and us—on the subject of history]. Tokyo: Nakanishiya Publication, 1999.

Connerton, Paul. *How Societies Remember*. Cambridge: Cambridge University Press, 1989.

Fukuma, Yoshiaki. *Senso taiken no sengoshi* [Postwar History of Wartime experience]. Tokyo: Chukoshinsho, 2009.

Gendlin, Eugene. "Experiencing: A Variable in the Process of Therapeutic Change." *American Journal of Psychotherapy,* 15, no. 2 (1961): 233–45. http://www.focusing.org/gendlin/docs/gol_2082.html.

———. *Experiencing and the Creation of Meaning*. Chicago: Northwestern University Press, 1997.

Griffin, Susan. *A Chorus of Stones: The Private Life of War.* New York: Anchor Books, 1992.

James, William. "Does Consciousness Exist?" *The Journal of Philosophy, Psychology and Scientific Methods* 1, no. 18 (1904): 477–91.

———. *Essays In Radical Empiricism.* New York: Longmans, 1912.

Johnson, Don Hanlon. "Body Making." In *Groundworks: Narratives of Embodiment*, ed. Don Hanlon Johnson, 1–13. New York: The Hampton Press, 1997.

———. "Body Practices and Human Inquiry: Disciplined Experiencing, Fresh Thinking, Vigorous Language." In *The Body in Human Inquiry: Interdisciplinary Explorations of Embodiment*, eds. Vincent Berdayes et al. New York: The Hampton Press, 2004.

Kleinman, Arthur, et al., eds. *Social Suffering.* Berkeley: University of California Press, 1997.

Morimoto, Anri. "Toward a Theology of Reconciliation: Forgiveness from the Perspective of Comparative Religion." In *A Grand Design for Peace and Reconciliation Achieving Kyosei in East Asia*, eds. Yoichiro Murakami and Thomas J. Schoenbaum, 159–75. England: Edward Elgar Publishing, 2008.

Murakawa, Haruhiko. "World Work (b)." In *Introduction for Process Oriented Psychology: Practical Psychology to Connect the Body, the Mind and the World*, eds. Yoshihiko Morotomi and Yukio Fujimi, 157–67. Tokyo: Shunjyusha, 2001.

———. "Reclaiming the Wartime Experience from the First-Person Viewpoint: Toward a History and Peace Education Based on Experiential Psychology." In *Generational Transmission of War Trauma and Approaches to Reconciliation and Restoration: Report on Remembering Nanjing 2011.* Research for Collaboration Model of Human Services 3, 406–18. Kyoto: Institute of Human Sciences, Ritsumeikan University, 2012.

———. "Cultural and National Identity and Responsive Subjectivity." In *An Innovative Peace/History Education Program for the Chinese and Japanese Post-War Generation: Report on "Remembering Nanjing 2013" and Achievement and Prospect of a Seven Year HWH Project*, Studies for Inclusive Society 1, 51–61. Kyoto: Institute of Human Sciences, Ritsumeikan University, 2014.

Muramoto, Kuniko, ed. *Generational Transmission of War Trauma and Efforts of Reconciliation: International Seminar-Remembering Nanjing 2009.* Kyoto: Ritsumeikan University Human Service Research Center, 2010.

Nagahara, Yoko. "*Wakai to seigi-minami afrika shinjitsuwakaiiinkai wo koete* [Reconciliation and justice: Beyond South Africa's Truth and Reconciliation Commission]." In *Rekishi no kabe wo koete* [Beyond the historical barrier] *Irenology for Reconciliation and Symbiosis: Irenology of Global Age 3* eds. Aiko Utsumi and Keizo Yamawaki. Tokyo: Horitsubukasha, 2004.

Sato, Manabu. "*Ko no shintai no kioku karano shuppatsu* [Departure from the individual bodily memory]." In *Nashonaru hisotori wo koete* [Beyond national history], eds. Yoichi Komori and Tetsuya Takahashi. Tokyo: Tokyo University Publication, 1998.

Takahashi, Mai. "*Ningenseicho wo sogaishinaikotoni shotenkasuru kyoikugaku* [Pedagogy focusing on not inhibiting human development: an education necessary for community life]." KOKO Publication, 2009.

Tanahashi, Kaz. "Remembering Nanjing (Nanking): Report on the International conference, 70th anniversary of the Nanjing Tragedy." Berkeley: A World Without Armies, 2007.

Taylor, Eugene. *Shadow Culture: Psychology and Spirituality in America.* Washington, DC: Counterpoint, 2000.

Yuasa, Yasuo, *Shintai no uchusei* [The universality of the body]. Tokyo: Iwanamishoten, 1996.

Zhang, Lianhong. "Healing the Trauma: The Unavoidable Issue between Japan and China." In *Generational Transmission of War Trauma and Efforts of Reconciliation: International Seminar Remembering Nanjing 2009*, ed. Kuniko Muramoto, 66–86. Kyoto: Ritsumeikan University Human Service Research Center, 2010.

Chapter 9

Sankofa: A Journey of Embodied Re-Membering

Muriel Jamille Vinson

The year is 2013. It's a warm California summer day. I am twenty-three. I am walking into the Santa Cruz dance studio with my musician friend who plays djembe for the dance class. We met at a gig of his a few nights earlier. As I walk inside, I look around, gazing upon what would become my sanctuary, my church. I see the large mirrored wall across from where I'd just entered. Adjacent to it, I see men setting up the drumming altar. My friend is the only person I know in the space and I immediately notice that I am surrounded by White women. I am surprised at first, but the surprise quickly fades as the state of this town, and our country, enter my mind. I smile and cordially I say "Hi" to women whose eyes meet mine. I make sure to smile and head-nod toward the few people of color in the room, none of whom are African American. I feel a sense of safety from their presence, glad that they're there.

Identity

I was born in Hampton, Virginia, to Robert Roger Vinson and Julia Yvonne Best in the summer of 1990. As they chose to remain separate, I experienced my parents separately. I lived with my mother during the week in Newport News, Virginia, and visited my father in Hampton on the weekends and holidays.

My Virginia upbringing carries the label of being a Southern girl with (some) traditional southern values, a badge I've learned to cherish. I am a descendant of the Maafa and of the fifth generation after the Emancipation Proclamation. My maternal great-grandmother, Julia Shipman (Big Mama), was born May 10, 1896, thirty-three years after the emancipation of enslaved Africans and African Americans in the United States. My paternal great-great-grandmother, Eliza Lowe, was born around the year 1840, when slavery was still legal. These lineages are also a badge I cherish, as it lends me the ability to stand on the great shoulders of my ancestors whom I thank for being able to sit in front of my computer and tell this story in the twenty-first century, 2018. My mother is currently able to trace our ancestry back to the emancipation and no further. My father's DNA was tested and traced back 2,000 years to the Kota and Tsogo people of the coast and forests of Midwest Africa, present day Gabon.

Mother's Story

Born of Southern Africentric parents, I grew up with values such as: respect your elders, work hard, and be the best at what you do. Growing up in the Jim Crow South, both of my parents had experienced varieties of racism, from extreme to subtle. However, each side of my family experienced and handled racism in very different ways. My mother, an only child, was born in 1948 and raised in Valdosta, Georgia, to a schoolteacher named Odell Shipman Hall, and a first class petty officer (a Navy chef) named Bishop Hall.

My mother grew up on a farm from birth to age fourteen (when she was in the tenth grade). There were basic appliances in her home, a wood stove and electric stove, a fridge and, eventually, a TV and telephone with multiple neighbors on the same line. You could actually hear other people's conversations. There was no running water. They had a well for watering plants and animals and for washing clothes. Clean clothes were hung on a clothesline to dry. They went to town to fill water jugs with clean water for cooking and drinking. When a Laundromat was built in town, they took the clothes there to wash and dry. When my mother was around fifteen years old, her mother and father built a new brick house, which was a well-to-do home for Black folks at that time. Her mother had been embarrassed about the old house and did not allow any visitors there except for close relatives. The family was very proud of the new house. My mother's mother would say, "Now we live in the suburbs." She relished the idea that some Black folk in the neighborhood were jealous of the new house.

My mother's father was deployed on the US Navy ship in various European countries during my mother's early childhood years. Her mother chose to remain in Valdosta to take care of my great-grandfather and great-grandmother. Her father came home during the Christmas holidays. She knew him only as the visitor she called "Daddy." In the old house, she was upset that she had to move out of her room and sleep with Big Mama, and she'd ask, "Why can't Daddy sleep with Big Mama?"

The main activities for the family revolved around church. Services were held every second and fourth Sunday because the preacher conducted services at another church on first and third Sundays. However, there was Sunday School on the first and third Sunday mornings and there was a prayer meeting every Wednesday night. In addition to Sunday services, the church family also participated in activities such as the Big Meeting Sunday, Homecoming Sunday, Easter Sunrise Service, Church Anniversary Sunday, Mother's Day and Father's Day services, Children's Day Sunday, and Christmas programs. My grandmother forced my mother to play piano for the church choir, which she disliked with a passion. She recalls going to church three to four times a week to worship, spy on people, and mostly gossip.

My mother reflects on her family and community feasting on artery-clogging menus, including chitterlings, pig ears, and pig feed, a diet remaining from enslavement, to accommodate the animal scraps given to my enslaved ancestors by their enslaver. Let's also not forget the fried chicken, chicken and dumplings, ham, pork-infused greasy vegetables, potato salad, cornbread, biscuits, sausages, fried fish, hush puppies, tea cakes, jelly cakes, and fried corn.

I enjoy listening to my mother tell the story about the time when she was entering tenth grade and decided to change her diet. She cut back on greasy and starchy foods and started measuring her meals by eating from a small dessert plate the size of a saucer. She also ate more vegetables. My mother started exercising more by riding her bicycle and using large tomato sauce cans to lift as weights. She wanted to look like the girls on the cover of *Seventeen* magazine so people would no longer make fun of her weight. She remembers feeling hungry at the end of the school day from skipping lunch. "I became cute enough to be one of the homecoming queens, "she says in her *"I showed you!"* voice. In school, she joined a dance group and the drill team to get more exercise. My mother is a very determined woman.

My mother lived a sheltered life. Her relationship with her mother, my grandmother, whom I call Grammy, was strained as well as abusive. My mother broke free of my grandmother in her twenties after completing her undergraduate degree at Spelman College. My mother shares a memory of my grandmother squeezing her nose as a child in an attempt to make it thinner, more European. Her story reminds me of a time when she and I were talking about the types of plastic surgery I would have if I were rich. I wanted larger breasts and liposuction, as I was a chubby child with small breasts. My mother expressed her desire for a nose job because she thought that her nose was too wide. At the time, I did not know about her mother pinching her nose. My mother's desire to alter her nose surprised me and I expressed my love for her nose and how beautiful it was, saying that it looked like my nose.

She loves to tell the story of how, while moving out of her dorm after graduation, she escaped my grandmother's trick to lure her back to Valdosta and make her stay. My mother had a fiancé, a job as a teller, and an apartment in Atlanta that she shared with her cousin so she did not want to return to her mother's home. Still, her mother wanted her back under her watchful eye. While visiting Valdosta with her parents, my mother recalls noticing that her dorm room key was different. She knew instantly that her mother had switched her with a different key.

My mother and her parents drove to her dorm in Atlanta to get her things, a four-hour drive. On the way, my mother planned what she was going to do when they arrived. My mother walked to her room door, tried the bogus key knowing it wouldn't work, and then looked at her mother. "She had to take out the real key and use it to unlock the door," my mom would say. My grandmother tried to butter my mother up by helping her pack. While my grandmother was engaged in packing, my mother went to the dorm office and called a friend who lived in the dorm at Atlanta University. My mother told her friend her plan and to look for her soon. When the packing was completed, my mother told her mother that she was going to put her suitcases on the luggage elevator. She left my grandmother in the room, and walked out toward the elevator. In the time it took her to walk to the elevator, she decided that it was time to escape. My mom sent her luggage to the third floor, and ran up the stairs from the first floor to the third floor to meet it. She grabbed her suitcases and stored them in the luggage room where they would be safe until she could get them later. She ran back down to the back of the dorm, peeped out of the back door to make sure her father and mother hadn't moved their car, and ran across the lawn, past the security guard and other students as they stared at her. She didn't care.

A man in a black convertible Cadillac pulled up and asked, "Do you need a ride?" At first, my mother declined, but then said, "Yes!" The man took her where she wanted to go, Atlanta University, then bid her goodbye. When she arrived, her friend met her, and they walked to the friend's dorm room. Once there, both of them kept looking around and peeping out the window every few seconds, keeping watch for her mother and father's car. And sure enough, their car circled into that dorm's parking lot. My mother and her friend called a third friend who lived across town with her parents to come pick them up. When they arrived, my mother and her friend got into the backseat of the third friend's car. As soon as they got inside, my grandmother and grandfather circled into the parking lot, driving right past my mother as she and her friend ducked down in the backseat. My mother called my grandparents the next morning to make sure they were back in Valdosta and to let them know she was not coming back. Her narrow escape of her parents served as one of my mother's sources of liberation of her body from the abuses of internalized oppression.

My mother remembers her mother and paternal grandmother favoring her musically talented cousin while continually chastising and tormenting her, saying "Why can't you be like your cousin?" She also tells stories of Grammy being called a black pickaninny by my maternal great-grandfather's mother, a dark-skinned African American woman whose parents were a few decades out of slavery. My mother chose to pursue her PhD because her mother always said to her that she was going to be nothing, just like her paternal relatives. My mother wanted to prove to her mother that she *was* somebody. She chose to raise her children in a completely different way than how she was raised, as she knew that what she'd experienced was cruel. She took child development classes to learn how to manage the different stages of development properly and constructively. In the process of birthing and raising two children, my mother overcame matriarchal intergenerational abuse, patriarchal absence, and intergenerational dietary imbalance, as well as society's multicentury intergenerational abuse of Black African people. At a young age, she knew she would end the cycle of internalized oppression with her future children: me and my brother, Elliot.

Father's Story

My father's story is quite different. He was born of Christian sharecroppers on a plantation in Franklin, Virginia, to Pearl and Walter Vinson. Born one of seven, my dad was able to witness and interact with his siblings as they grew and created together.

My father and his siblings entertained themselves by playing with each other outdoors, using their imagination and humor to tell stories, and by interacting with the African American elders who lived close by. He reflects lovingly on his experience growing up, referring to himself as a barefoot dusty child with a strong sense of pride and self-worth. I imagine what he looked like as he described himself walking in the woods with a rifle, ready to shoot a deer passing by. He remembers watching his father, Walter, working on the plantation farm and his mother, my Grandmother Pearl, mending clothes, cooking, and managing their garden. They grew tomatoes, beans, cabbages, potatoes, greens, and corn, and had hens. My father shares memories of his family canning vegetables and meat to preserve them. "We definitely didn't have finances," he recalls, "and even though we didn't have money to go to the grocery store, we had food and we never felt what one might call 'abject poverty.'" My father likens his experience to being "more like communal living." They shared with their neighbors the food they had for my father's family. They had the traditional Southern diet of collard greens, greasy foods, neck bones, and pig feet. "My mom wasn't heavy on that stuff, but we ate a lot of it out of necessity," he'd say. When my father was a baby, his father became partially disabled from a stroke of the brain due to hypertension. It was said that the fat and lard from pork caused the stroke.

During his late teens, my father started reading *How to Eat to Live* by Elijah Mohammad, saying that it resonated with him because it talked about eating pork, reminding my father about his father's stroke. At thirty, my father found out that he also had hypertension, due to heredity and too much salt in his diet.

My father recalls his memory of his Uncle Dike and Mrs. Mamie who didn't have any children, who also happened to be my father's neighbors. "They took a liking to me," my father says as he reflects on his time spent at their home enjoying hot biscuits. After staying with his Uncle Dike, my father moved in with his Uncle Joe, who owned a logging business. Eventually, the rest of his family moved in with Uncle Joe. After living with Uncle Joe, the family moved to a farm as sharecroppers on a plantation. My father started first grade at the age of five. His father died when he was eight. The rest of my father's family remained sharecroppers on the plantation until he was seventeen. "Sharecropping was really exploitation of the workers," he'd say. "We did most of the farm work and received little pay in return."

In my father's family, it was custom for the children to emancipate from the family when they were old enough. When my father emancipated himself, he moved to Hampton, Virginia. My father and a friend of his dropped out of high school and got jobs at Hampton Institute, now Hampton University. He continues to reflect on his sibling's experience of their emancipation from the family. "We did what was necessary to help our younger siblings out, that way, Mam could concentrate on the younger siblings and we would get an education to help." My father reflects on his situation as being one without a lot of choices, growing up on a plantation during Jim Crow. He names himself and his family as survivors.

My father stayed in Hampton for about a year and, by that time, his mother had moved off the plantation, and they moved together to Newport News, Virginia. My grandmother did domestic work for European American people like dentists, who paid "slave wages." My father reflects on his mother's understanding of the value of education. Her family started the first African American school in south Hampton, which instilled a sense self-worth. My father was exposed to different people through his siblings and the elders around town. I picture him as a kid that liked to talk to people. He often credits the wisdom of his mother, telling stories about his memories of her. She fostered my father's love for his skin color, for who he is and where he comes from, contributing to his development into an inquisitive, critically thinking, open-minded and loving man.

My father describes his experience of racism as the "overriding cause of traumas" that no one ever got a doctor to help with. My father tells a story about how he used to play with another little boy named Chunkie who was his mother's employer's child. They played together just about every day. Then, after puberty, the boy was no longer allowed to play with my father. When my father asked his mother why this was the case, the response he got was, "That's just the way things are." This was a painful and confusing experience for my father, and one he remembers to this day. He remembers what it felt like not being able to understand that his skin color was why he couldn't play with his friend, his skin being a feature completely out of his control. When he told me this story, he mentioned how reading Dr. DeGruy's *Post Traumatic Slave Syndrome* as an adult was the first healing he'd ever gotten from the trauma caused by racism. My father's brother Roger committed suicide when my father was twenty-five. He remembers being mad, acknowledging the experience as one that helped him understand mental illness.

After going to trade school to be a dental technician, my father worked with a dentist before opening up his own technician lab. Being in business for more than forty years now, he has been making people smile ever since. Due to his family's connection with their self-love, it is apparent to me that my father experienced an upbringing that perpetuated a sense of self-worth and self-efficacy among the daily racism of the Jim Crow era, while my mother's upbringing perpetuated an internalized hatred that she called "slave mentality."

******

After moving to Blacksburg, Virginia, with my mother at age seven, I continued to live in predominantly European American communities until age twenty-four. I accredit my ability to exercise and maintain the level of self-efficacy and self-worth that I embody to my parents and their dedication to educating me about African and African American people, geniuses, inventors, activists, scholars, athletes, and entrepreneurs. They had books authored by prominent Black scholars around the house, including *The Miseducation of the Negro* by Carter G. Woodson, *The Souls of Black Folk* by W. E. B. Du Bois and *Why the Caged Bird Sings* by Maya Angelou. They also lived as an example of what I could achieve, as my mom received her doctorate in education and my dad was a successful business owner since before I was born. My mother and father continue to keep symbols of African Americans and Africa around their houses, including African masks, dolls, paintings and photos with Black people in them, as well as other cultural motifs. My parents aimed for the representation of that which was stolen from us, but not completely lost.

Drummers of various races are seated in a line at a wall adjacent to the long mirrored one, pulling their djembes out of their bags. None of them are African American. They are beginning to slap their djembes, checking the tone of their drums. "Slap slap slap . . . ," one says. "Bidiba!" says another. "Bida bidibada!" says a third. There's a set of three larger drums behind the djembes positioned to be played standing up. These are unfamiliar to me. A large, highly melaninated African man is setting up the drums, tightening the strap that holds them together. It is clear that he is one of the indigenous carriers of this art form. He checks the tone of the largest of three drums, strapped in the middle of the two slightly smaller ones. "Gengen gen gen!" The conversation has started. I've never heard drums like these large ones before. Djembes I was familiar with, recalling my friend picking on me the previous night for the djembe my mother gifted me, calling it a "tourist djembe." I look around for the dance teacher and see her immediately. The moment when my eyes find her, she looks right at me. I smile hard at her as she smiles at me, barely containing my impulse to jump up and down with excitement for being there. The drums are louder now. Their strikes pierce my body, quickening my pulse, shocking my cells into the impulse to move. "Crack!" I feel a pulse in the center of my chest.

When we pay attention, we recognize that the experience of life is through the mind simultaneously with the body. Our embodied experience influences the environments we, or our caretakers, choose to be in, as well as our identity, values, beliefs, overall behavior, perceptions, and thought processes. The reverse is also true, as our embodied experience is also shaped by our environment.[1]

I grew up watching TV shows, including *Xena Warrior Princess, Hercules, Beast Master,* and *The X-Files.* I was fascinated and drawn into the stories of brave warriors who lived in nature, talked to animals, and went on exciting quests. Aliens were cool too. I was fascinated by these stories and watched them daily. However, none of the lead roles in any of these films looked like me. So, every day I'm watching these shows with only White people starring in lead roles. I looked up to a lot of these White people, wanting to be fearless, mystical, and strong like them. Xena was definitely my favorite. I'd

---

1 Rae Johnson, *Oppression Embodied: The Intersection Dimension of Trauma, Oppression, and Somatic Psychology* (The USA Body Psychology Journal, 2009).

fantasize about myself swinging through trees, a chakram at my hip. In my early twenties I awoke from a semi-lucid dream and recognized that the image of myself in my dream was a woman with light skin and black hair, much like Xena. I initially felt shame and confusion when I discovered this. "What's wrong with me?" I thought. "Do I not love myself?" I contemplated the subconscious processes that were at play during the fusion of my subconscious identity with a White woman's in identifying with the characters I watched on TV. Was it seeing this image over and over again as an archetype of my personality that carried it into my imagination? Was it because I didn't have access to models that looked like me who embodied the warrior archetype? Xena also served as a pinnacle in the beginnings of my discovery of my sexuality. I remember being intrigued by Xena and her sidekick Gabrielle's relationship as well as Xena's relationship to Hercules, both of which I experienced as erotic. I continue to consider how this influenced my relationship to mainstream norms of beauty and attraction to European features.

Growing up, I had my own experiences of racism and oppression. In a Newport News preschool, I remember asking a teacher to tie my shoes, as I didn't know how to tie them yet. The teacher, a White man, tied my shoes together and watched as I struggled to walk away. As soon as I sat back in my seat, I untied my shoes and left them that way. I still remember what it felt like to have to make tiny shuffling steps, as I walked by to my seat. Ashamed, I didn't tell my mom about this until years later when I was older. In this same preschool, I continued to encounter my relationship to sexuality. I'd pull my pants down for a White boy who had long hair like Hercules. He returned the favor and, with huge smiles on our faces, we'd go back and forth like this, wholly amused, pulling our pants down for each other before quickly pulling them back up again. One day, as I was pulling up my dress for Herc, a teacher spotted me, chastised me, and forbade me from participating in the school's Halloween walk, where all the teachers were giving out candy. This is when I learned that sexuality, or relating to someone in an erotic way, is something that is shameful. Interestingly, I also learned how to masturbate around this time in a summer

Montessori school. I was taught by another kid during naptime. This boy also happened to be White. I think it went something like this:

White boy: "Hey, if you do this, it feels good!"

Me: "Okay!" ... or something like that.

In kindergarten, I remember having a crush on a light-skinned African American boy in my class. To my dismay, he preferred a White classmate over me. I remember feeling jealous and frustrated that he liked her more than me and wishing I could be more like her, more calm, and wishing I had hair and clothes like her.

When I was seven, my mom and I moved from the Tidewater region of Virginia, inland to the Appalachian Mountains. We lived in an apartment in Blacksburg, Virginia. My mother's goal was to pursue a doctorate at Virginia Tech, five hours away from my two hometowns Newport News and Hampton, and five hours away from my father.

Blacksburg was very different from Newport News. In Newport News, most of my classmates and community looked like me, brown skin with curly or relaxed hair and dark eyes. In Blacksburg, most of my peers had fair skin, thin hair, and light eyes. At the time, there were only two African American first graders at the elementary school. Instead of having us in the same classroom, the school decided to disperse us, putting us in separate classrooms so more children could experience being around a Black child. I was not conscious of the change right away, not until I started getting questions about my hair and requests to touch it. At first, I indulged the requests, enjoying the task of teaching my peers about something they didn't know. This was before the bullying started.

In first grade, a bully grabbed my hand and bent my finger back for no reason. In second grade, a bully kicked my butt while I was swinging on a swing set, again for no reason. Both of these children were boys. Both were white. In fifth grade, at the same elementary school, I remember witnessing one of my friends, an African American boy, lick the spit of a White girl off of a school bus seat. I've never forgotten this. He had a crush on her and her way of getting him to prove his love was, after spitting on the seat, requesting that he lick it up. The crazy thing was he did it ... and I watched. In sixth grade a "friend" of mine decided to spit in my chair without me knowing and watch me sit on it. I sat down as she and several other children, who were White, stood around me and laughed. When I discovered the spit, I hit this girl in the face. She cried. I got lunch detention.

In high school, my mom and I moved to a house in a neighboring town called Christiansburg, which was noticeably whiter than Blacksburg. Blacksburg attracted a somewhat more diverse community due to the university. All Christiansburg had was a Walmart, a Goody's, and the mall. I remember having a crush on one of the only African American boys at my school, who happened to also be in my grade. To my dismay, he preferred a White girl who was also in our grade. I remember feeling resentful of him for choosing this girl who I felt was boring and had no personality. I felt rejected. It reminded me of when the same thing happened in preschool.

My first boyfriend, however, did come along. He was an African American boy who moved to Christiansburg from New York. He was smart, cute, sweet, and he played on our basketball team. Between school, extracurricular activities, and his basketball practice, there was only time to hang out and hold hands between classes. Unfortunately, he had very sweaty hands, which grossed me out. Our relationship lasted about two weeks.

Most of my high school friends were European American, as they outnumbered all other ethnicities. I often got called "Oreo" by both African American and White students, some of whom I believed were my friends. Seeing Confederate flags on hats, T-shirts, and phones was normal in high school, until they were banned. Many students, who I thought were friends but also knew were racist, protested this ban. Wearing camo was also a norm for many of the students I went to school with, as many were hunters. I participated in chorus as well as the marching band, where the population of people of color was mostly Asian, with no other African Americans. At this point, being the only African American or one of two or three in a space, at any given time, was normal for me.

After returning to Christiansburg after spending time over break with my family in Hampton, I remember speaking with my best friends one day after school in a dialect that is culturally African American, known as Ebonics or African American Vernacular English (AAVE). One friend's response was, "You're with your White friends now," laughing and mocking the way I spoke, letting me know that all of me wasn't welcomed. I laughed with them and endured their "jokes" often.

My hair has always been an anomaly to my peers. One day it would be short and permed, the next it would be long and braided, and the next it would be long and straight. I often received the comment, "Your hair grew so fast!" I always enjoyed reveling in the cultural secret of Black hair. Sometimes I would get the question, "Is that your *real* hair?" or, "Is that *your* hair?" I always answered "Yes," while thinking, "none of your damn business." If they knew it was a weave and called me on it, I'd often respond with humor, "It's on my head isn't it?" or "I paid for it, so it's still my hair!" I remember one of my friends, a White boy, blowing in my face and on my hair. He was fascinated by the fact that it did not move when he blew on it, mocking me for what he viewed as abnormal hair behavior. I would sit there as he'd blow forcefully on my hair, making his comments about how it didn't move. I'd respond by rolling eyes or laughing him off and turning away.

A White woman steps to the middle of the mirrored wall and begins stretching rhythmically. The dance teacher speaks to her husband in a language I've never heard before. He speaks back, while hitting the edge of one of the strapped drums with a large mallet. A djembe joins the dancer with a rhythm. The large man joins the first djembe, and the other djembes are signaled to join in. The rhythm is gentle, yet pulsing. The dance teacher chooses a spot in the room and joins the woman in the stretching, mirroring her movements. Other women join, take a spot slightly behind the first woman and join in her rhythmic stretching. I look around and walk to a space to join in the warm-up. As I'm doing the warm-up, I'm scoping the room, feeling big and small at the same time. I'm big, in that I literally feel too big for the space and small in that I feel isolated. I check out the teacher as she stretches. She is petite, compact with dense-looking thighs, calves, and sculpted arms. The rhythm quickens as the movements quicken as my heart rate quickens. I notice my breathing quickening.

When many people think about trauma, they think of war, famine, domestic violence, sexual abuse, and the Holocaust. These intensely negative experiences shake the very core of a human being off balance and can lead to a fragmented sense of body, mind, and sprit. The impact environmental trauma has on the body-mind can be passed down genetically through epigenetic DNA markers that respond to the hormone cortisone released by the adrenal glands during times of stress. Joy DeGruy describes trauma as

> an injury caused by an outside, usually violent, force, event or experience. We can experience this injury physically, emotionally, psychologically, and/or spiritually. Traumas can upset our equilibrium and sense of well-being. If a trauma is severe enough it can distort our attitudes and beliefs. Such distortions often result in dysfunctional behaviors, which can in turn produce unwanted consequences. If one traumatic experience can result in distorted attitudes, dysfunctional behaviors and unwanted consequences, this pattern is magnified exponentially when a person repeatedly experiences severe trauma, and it is much worse when the traumas are caused by human beings. The slave experience was one of continual, violent attacks and traumatization on the enslaved body, mind, and spirit.[2]

Here, Dr. DeGruy alludes to the intergenerational impact of chattel enslavement (and continued oppression) as an experience unique to that of any other human group on the planet. She describes the slave experience as "one of continual, violent attacks and traumatization on the [enslaved] body, mind, and spirit." Post Traumatic Slave Syndrome (PTSS) refers to the "transgenerational adaptations associated with the past traumas of slavery and on-going oppression." PTSS highlights the unconscious adaptations of behavior and beliefs of descendants of enslaved Africans that persist from their ancestors, behaviors, and beliefs adopted for survival of body, mind, and spirit. In recognizing that unconscious forces influence the personality and somatic organization of descendants of enslaved Africans, PTSS can

2 Joy DeGruy, *Post Traumatic Slave Syndrome: America's Legacy of Enduring Injury and Healing* (Milwaukie, OR: Uptone Press, 2005), 13.

be known as a psychodynamic theory. In this case, these forces may include, but are not limited to, epigenetic DNA markers, internalized oppression and self-hatred, and maladaptive survival tactics. It must not be assumed that all descendants of enslaved Africans have PTSS. It must also not be assumed that a descendant of enslaved Africans can be immune or completely unaffected by PTSS.

When we experience trauma, it "is significantly mediated through the body and manifested in embodied experience."[3] Rae Johnson notes that "the nonverbal component of social interaction is the basis of the most common means of social control in the form of oppression." I claim that oppression, used as a form of social control, can be held in our body.

Through this vignette, I seek to bridge the psychological with the biological, highlighting the psychosomatic affects of intergenerational trauma on the bodies, minds, and spirits of descendants of enslaved Africans. Again, the assumption that all African American/black people have this experience and are traumatized should not be made. The assumption that you as the reader are not integrated into the web of experience that encompasses the experiences described in this paper should also not be made.

Oppression lies on the trauma spectrum and can be "understood as chronically traumatic."[4] Since embodiment theory and traumatology theory tell us that trauma lives in and through the body, it can be said that oppression lives in and through the body as an embodied oppression, a type of embodied trauma. What does the embodiment of PTSS look like? How is continued intergenerational, institutional oppression of mind, body, and spirit currently held in the bodies of Africa's enslaved and marginalized brown and black-skinned children?

The warm-up concludes as the dance teacher trades places with the woman facilitating the warm-up, intensifying the movement as the rhythm speeds

---

3 Johnson, *Oppression Embodied*, 465.

4 Johnson, 465.

to its end. The teacher stands facing the mirrored wall. "Mirem," she says. "Watch," I hear. She begins dancing, vocalizing the rhythm as she moves, showing us what to do. Some women watch her; some women try imitating the movements as she shows them to us. I slightly move with her as I try to remember what she's showing us. Soon, everyone is dancing upright, trying the movement as she shows us. I try my best to mimic my teacher's strong compact body. I notice the movement I'm trying requires my feet to move one way with my arms moving another. I sense that I've got it, and then I sense that I am somehow off. I see my teacher's head and hands completing her movement. I try to give my movement a similar flair, but as soon as I do, my feet make a mistake and then the movement is off again. I focus in on my teacher's feet and mimic hers. The rhythm feels backwards, or inside out, but somehow natural. I add movement in my arms, noticing the connection between my arms, torso, neck, legs, hands, and feet. I notice the feeling of thinking about what I'm doing. I notice the feeling of pure joy. I notice feeling oddly uncoordinated. I make a mistake. I study other's feet to regain the correct rhythm and rejoin the movement, starting with my feet.

Body Safety around White People

As a young woman with a brown body, my lived experiences have taught me that I am strong, enduring, innovative, creative, unique, and beautiful. Alongside this, various lived and ancestral experiences have taught me that my body is not safe around White people, and that my body is something that White people want and think they have access to. Childhood experience taught me that White women will act like your friend while diminishing you. And, unfortunately and maybe the most dangerous aspect of all, I have learned that many White people will do this without knowing it, genuinely feeling like everything is okay and/or that there's something wrong with you, gaslighting you for speaking your truth. The descendants of the enslaved, oppressed, and colonized as well as the descendants of the enslaver and oppressor remain the carriers of the intergenerational trauma of enslavement and skin/culture-based oppression. We are symbols of this trauma for each other now, replaying the same story over and over again when in space with each other.

I am able to recognize that it is traumatizing for me to know that somewhere, someone isn't getting a job, access to housing, education, access to feelings of safety or just plain old respect, due to their skin color, style of dancing, the way their body is shaped, the way they dress, or because their name sounds too Black, their skin too dark, physique too African, their hair too natural, their Ebonics too prominent. Meanwhile, White folks are sporting cornrows, locs, and afro-wigs. They're getting lip and butt fillers, twerking and teaching twerking classes! Not only are White folks making money off of these things, they are given credit for it, a strategy of appropriation that dates back to the time of Socrates, Plato, Hippocrates, and Fibonacci, whose genius can be attributed to their study at Egyptian Mystery Schools, otherwise known as Ancient Kemetic Universities. When I see the appropriation and degradation of the Black and Brown body, I receive the following message, "If you want to be acknowledged and make money, you must strive to be like me. European. If you do this, I'll let you feel like you belong. Go ahead and straighten your hair, lighten your skin, and speak and write as I do and I'll let you work for me. But don't forget, all of you is not welcome here. Your body isn't allowed to utilize, display, or express your ancestral culture ... but mine is ... and watch me make money off of it. If you try to be yourself, I'll make everyone think you're a nasty, dangerous, foolish, thug that they can do what they want with."

I'm repeating the same movement over and over again, increasing the intensity, trying to get the movement in my body, trying to re-member. My teacher shows a second movement sequence. This one's even more intense. The movements are fast and it feels like I must fly to keep up with them. I notice my breathing. I notice that my balance isn't that great, but that I've got the movement. Some of the women around me seem to also have the movement, adding their own style to it. I notice other women noticing that I've got the movement. I notice that I'm smiling a lot.

After my first West African dance class, I continued to attend weekly. I'd learn the movements and try to remember the names of the rhythms. My body started to understand the language of the African body in conversation with the drums, the moves and rhythms becoming easier to comprehend, my confidence building. Despite this, it was over a year before I could face the fear that kept me from soloing at the end of my West African dance classes. Other women who'd been dancing for longer went into the circle doing perfectly choreographed sequences, knowing the rhythm and the dance moves that went with it. I was self-conscious. I held back for fear of unwanted attention, with lack of trust in myself and others, feeling as though I wasn't good enough or didn't know enough. Upon hearing the drums, I felt what my soul was capable of expressing, and a battle with my intergenerational demons and my soul ensued. My parents fostered confidence in my abilities, they encouraged me, put me through many extracurricular activities that they were able to access, including ballet and tap dance. I've performed songs and musicals in front of huge audiences in auditoriums and cafeterias. So why did I feel so uncomfortable and unsure of myself in that space? Was it the overwhelm from the raw and new connection to my ancestry? Was it fear? Fear of what? I'd stand on the periphery of the solo circle pushing myself from the inside out to solo, judging myself for not going in and fearing the retribution and embarrassment if I do. I was too afraid to step inside and engage in the experience of integration with my environment's judgment and my judgment of myself.

I am now able to recognize my judgments as a reflection of internalized oppression and the fear of retribution from White women, an intergenerational fear seeded during enslavement. Historically and in the lived experience of many Black folks, including myself, White women have occupied the role of, and, at some point, served as a symbol for someone who acts nice on the outside, but cannot be trusted … even if it seems like she genuinely means well. The intergenerational message, for me, is: *White women are not out for you.* One of the ways this feeling manifested for me was in this dance class. I felt unsafe when surrounded by a large group of pale-skinned women.

I'd like to name an intergenerational dynamic or ghost role at play here: the plantation owner's jealous and abusive wife. Writings from enslaved Africans and African Americans tell stories of plantation owners raping Black women, seeming to prefer them over their wives. This act likely felt truly insulting to their wives as Black folks were considered animals, equating their husband's acts to bestiality. After the Emancipation Proclamation, White women are seen maintaining a scornful manner toward people of color, exemplified in the story of the brutal beating and death of Emmett Till, a simple lie robbing a mother of her child. Portrayed in literature as well as cinema, including *Forty Years a Slave,* I consider the scorn of the jealous plantation owner's wife as an intergenerational dynamic that impacts my feeling of safety around White women.

Dynamics like, but not limited to these, are in the room when White people and Black people occupy space together. When we enter the space, these ancestral dynamics enter in with us, through our body-minds. Just as the avoidance of attention from the scornful plantation owner's wife, or White person in general, was a survival technique utilized by enslaved Africans, so was my avoidance of attention from the many White women dominating the dance class space. The survival technique teaches the oppressed to keep our head down, don't act special or important or confident to avoid being sold away, exploited, harassed and/or murdered. Unconsciously, I utilized this technique, keeping myself small in order to avoid the wrath of the plantation owner's wife, feeling unsafe.

I notice that I'm trying not to do the movement better, bigger, or with more flair than the women around me. I don't want to make them feel bad. I don't want to draw attention to myself and have them looking at me. I don't want them to think they have control over me or my body. I don't have to be good because they expect me to be. Maybe they feel threatened by the fact that I am a good dancer. I am focusing on my body while watching my teacher's. My thoughts melt away as my mind syncs up with my body. I notice that keeping my breathing steady helps the movement. In noticing this, I misstep, my thoughts active again. I focus on my feet, arms, head … I see the other women around me trying the movement.

Embodied Suicide

My experience of the White women throughout my lived and ancestral life contributed to my sense of feeling frozen when beckoned by the drum and my teacher to solo in subsequent dance classes. I thought, "I know I can dance, I know I'm capable, but I can't let all of these White women see me, I'm scared. It'll attract unwanted attention, jealousy, and/or retribution. If I mess up, they'll judge me and feel happy that they're better than the Black girl."

I adapt a concept of a colleague of mine, Diego Basdeo's, "intellectual suicide" into *embodied* suicide. Embodied suicide is the practice of actively preventing the full expression of one's embodiment/expression of self/truth in order to preserve a feeling of safety and/or connection. At the time, I also thought, "They expect me to be really good because I'm Black, but know that they're better than me because they've been dancing for longer." (Keep in mind these are my assumptions, projections, and transferences fostered by racism.) "They're going to think that I'm trying to outdo them or that I think I'm all that." When I mess up a movement, I notice some White women smile and dance harder, and maybe what they perceive as better. Some encourage me to dance and it feels as though they want me to perform for them. Instead, at that time, I chose to keep my magic and my vulnerability to myself until I felt mentally, physically, and spiritually safe. "Would I feel safe in Africa?" I thought.

So we learn to make adjustments of mind and body. To survive. I've witnessed many Black folks continue to display the adaptations of our ancestors. We alter our posture, to protect ourselves, keeping our head down and avoiding making eye contact with a White woman. We accommodate White people by crossing the street to avoid making them uncomfortable and, especially, to avoid giving them an opportunity to take our dignity and/or our body. Rearing practices meant to keep our children safe and alive during enslavement through to today serve as an invisible cage around the expression and exploration for our African American children, due to the combination of our fear and the real threat on their physical and mental well-being. Many of us must navigate what behavior must be exuded (compliance or defiance/confrontation) to avoid humiliation, and feelings of helplessness, or threat of death. In high school, I often chose compliance, laughing at my classmates' backhanded jokes and exoticizing comments. I think back and sometimes wish I could have told them all to go to hell. Instead, I clenched in my buttocks and thighs to make them jiggle less and make them seem smaller. I wanted to take up less space. I also very slightly curled in my lips so I could not see them when I looked down. I did not like them poking out when I looked down. If I could see them, that meant others could really see them, and I didn't want the attention. I did these things to avoid comments about my body that felt uncomfortable and invasive. I liken these experiences to self-policing as a survival technique, meant to withstand the intergenerational objectification and exoticization of African, Black, and Brown bodies throughout history.

We remember Saartjie "Sarah" Baartman's story. If you don't know it, I encourage you to Wiki it right now. Being a Brown body in a predominantly White space feels like being on display, like Sarah Baartman, taking up too much space, doomed to be gazed upon, groped, and dissected by a bunch of pale faces.

My body is learning to create one cohesive movement out of three or four different movements, just as the drums are creating one cohesive polyrhythm out of four distinct rhythms. After learning a few dance sequences, we create lines with other dancers to dance toward the drums, as is the ritual of the class. The feeling in my head is that I don't know what I'm doing and that I don't care. The feeling in my heart and body is that I know exactly what I'm doing and I'm exactly where I'm supposed to be. Our teacher shows us the move she'd like us to do. The first line of dancers joins in and begins dancing toward the drums. The drums are so loud, they fill the room, every object and body in it. Pulsing radiating from behind my sternum out to the muscles in my shoulders, arms, neck, head, thighs, calves, and feet, and finally out to my skin, hair raised into goosebumps. I'm shaking, subtly, internally, all over. Children are laughing and running around. I watch the second line go, then the third, then the fourth. I'm rehearsing the moves in the back as I watch them. Then it's my turn. I step in line and allow my body to take over. I have a HUGE smile on my face. I continue to oscillate between trusting my body and thinking about what I'm doing with my head. I quickly learn that trusting my body is privileged in this space, as when I return to my head, I make a mistake in the movement. I feel that the movement is there, and it's not. I am with the drums, but also in my head. Even though I'm picking up the moves and their rhythmic conversation with the drums faster than many, I noticed that I was still holding.

Learning How to Hold

During my time living in predominantly European American environments, I often received unwanted attention regarding my body from peers and strangers. I remember a high school friend, a White guy, calling me DSLs, an acronym for "dick-sucking lips," in reference to the size of my lips. My response was a shy smile with a hint of attitude, thinking that it was absurd for me to have this nickname without having even kissed a boy yet or seen a penis in real life ... other than a baby's. Despite my dad complimenting my lips and my smile throughout my childhood, experiences like this led to a further attempt to lessen the protrusion of my lips. I altered the way I walked, preventing my hips from swaying while squeezing my buttocks in. As you can imagine, these attempts were futile and resulted in my holding and clenching of my body from the inside out. I was literally holding myself back, making myself smaller, in an effort to avoid attracting unwanted objectifying attention to my body. On the day of my first West African dance class, and the beginning of my body's liberation journey, I recognized how much I had been holding and that I had been living with this tightness, holding and bracing since childhood.

The teacher shows us another move. Again, it is my turn. I start to feel my jaw tighten and saliva build in my mouth. I ignore it and keep dancing. I feel the drums. My stomach feels tight, but my blood is boiling, liberated. I ignore the communication from my body and keep dancing. Eventually, not being able to hold it back anymore, I run outside of the studio and vomit, once, twice, three times. Surprised, I look up to the dusky blue sky, breathing out loud. My skin is buzzing, and my ears are ringing. No one is around, I am alone. I feel the cool of the setting sun and arriving night on my skin. I still hear the drums pounding from inside the studio. I still feel my heart, blood, and skin pounding with them.

Returning to African Ways of Embodiment: Sankofa

When I was a child, I remember watching the movie *Coming to America,* starring Eddie Murphy and Shari Headley. I was obsessed with the wedding scene where a slew of African dancers proceeded to flow into the great hall and perform the most impressive piece of art I had ever seen. I remember wishing I was like the dancers I saw on the screen. Strong, confident, precise, fit, artistic, and proud. Now, when in its presence, the African song and drum pull me out to fill my lungs, my skin, and cradle me like a womb. I feel an ultimate sense of safety, belonging, relaxation, and happiness. After hearing it, sometimes I am motivated to accomplish a task. Other times I am reminded of pieces of myself that I have forgotten. The African drum entices me to face my demons, to be courageous, vulnerable, passionate, and authentic.

I am breathing. The feeling of purging no longer with me, I stand up, walk toward the studio door and swing it open. Immediately, I feel the blast of the drum without the filter of the wall hit my entire body, feeling strongest at my heart, at my core. I enter, smiling softly, my face buzzing, and I look around. I feel calmer, more stable somehow, more clear. When I walk, my feet plant firmly on the floor and I feel the weight of my body pouring into them, stable, as if they are rooting with each step. I return to my line and, when it's my turn, I continue dancing. I notice I feel lighter than before. My chest raised, heart first, more open, energized. I feel powerful. After class, a dancer, a White woman, comes up to me and says, "This is your first class? It took me like two years to get to where you are! I hope you keep coming." I didn't know it at the time, but that was the beginning of my journey for the liberation of my body.

Contextualization and Future Research

The three drums mentioned at the beginning of our journey are called the *dununs.* They are composed of the smallest *dun*, known by the Malinké people of West Africa as the *kenkeni,* the medium dun, known as the *sangban,* and the largest dun, known as the *dununba.*

The player of these drums is the *dununfola.* Now I write about these drums, five years after the journey described above, feeling as if they're old friends that I still barely know. That day, I attended a Senegalese West African dance class taught by Oumou Faye at the 418 Studio in downtown Santa Cruz, California. Unknowingly, I met a woman who would become my teacher, my friend, my sister, and my mentor. I'd just moved to California with the goal of landing a job I liked and finding a graduate program to apply to. I had never been to a West African dance class or heard West African drums in person until the day described to you above. I certainly had not tried any of the dance moves until this day, but still, they felt vaguely familiar and reminded me of how I naturally move when I dance to music I enjoy. During my first experiences engaging in Senegalese West African dance class, I had an experience of my heart feeling like it's being blasted open, as if I were being pulled up and out by a force that is pouring out of my heart. Simultaneously, I noticed all the ways I'd been holding myself, preventing myself from full extension, embodiment, and fullness.

I now reflect on my purging experience as a symbolic purge of mind, body, and spirit during the dance class. Initially, due to years (and generations) of holding, I wasn't able to extend my arms and legs or embrace my full embodiment of a movement, seeking to avoid judgments of being arrogant, out of control, or exotic. This purging served as the kickoff point from which I began the intentional liberation of my body, sexuality, and voice. Since this day, I have attended many more classes including more Senegalese and Guinean West African dance as well as attending West African drum and dance camps. I have built a meaningful community and continue to experience expansion in the motion and expression of my body in connection with rhythm and other bodies.

I did eventually solo at the end of a class. I was at a Fareta, the West African dance camp in Sequoia National Park I attended annually. I listened to my teacher Yousouff Koumbassa relaying a message saying something like, "Feel the rhythm in your body! Don't worry about doing the move right or think about what you're doing!" What I *heard* was, "Fuck that choreographed shit! Do you! If you remember a move, FINE! If you don't remember a move, FINE!" After I heard him say this, I was good. With the help of my teachers, I learned to trust myself and to love my body-self more than I feared judgment from my environment.

I am interested in doing research on the impact of access to African ways of embodiment on *self-efficacy*, *self-worth*, *self-awareness*, and *self-love* of Black-African and African American people in an African context and a Western context. West African song, drum, and dance have provided an avenue for knowing myself in a way that I, and my ancestors, haven't known ourselves in hundreds of years, despite the ancestral traces that remained after enslavement. I want to explore the reintegration of that which has been fragmented due to the intergenerational trauma of Black American people through African ways of being.

In working with intergenerational trauma, my premise is to integrate the fragmented mind, body, and spirit through Africentric somatic psychotherapeutic intervention and psychoeducation that "supports the cultivation of an integrated, embodied consciousness."[5] I have an interest in exploring how to work with intergenerational PTSS using West-African inspired movement clinically through a dance and movement therapy framework utilizing Stanley Keleman's concepts of character structure.[6] I argue that the programming of enslaved minds can be overridden by the movements and ways of embodiment of our ancestors before enslavement. The connection to Africa in the movement can be utilized as a customization of technique to the descendants of the distinctive experience of multigenerational chattel slavery and oppression. Dance and music of Africa and of the African diaspora serve as an embodied connection to the African ancestry of descendants of enslaved Africans. This connection is made manifest in dance styles born in the African American community including the cabbage patch, the twist, the camel

---

[5] Johnson, 465.

[6] Stanley Keleman, *Emotional Anatomy: The Structure of Experience* (Berkeley, CA: Center Press, 1985).

walk, chicken head, running man, the Steve Martin, the lindy hop, krumping, the stanky leg, and so many more. The connection between African-inspired dance and character structure can be used clinically to reverse PTSS, facilitating transformation through intention, mindfulness, psychoeducation, and community.[7]

James Baldwin is quoted as saying "to be Black and conscious in America is to be a constant state of rage." I would amend this sentiment to say that the body has a knowing of this state of rage, regardless of cerebral consciousness, as a form of embodied oppression. Engaging with West African drum and dance has provided me with new, yet ancestral, ways of relating to my body, my sexuality, and my worth. My relationship with expansion from toes to fingertips to hair has grown and now solidified in my sense of self-worth, beauty, safety, and resilience in and of my body. I prioritize and privilege my ancestral ways of knowing and I continue to experience the possibility for liberation through our ancestral ways of embodiment.

Bibliography

DeGruy, Joy. *Post Traumatic Slave Syndrome: America's Legacy of Enduring Injury and Healing.* Milwaukie, OR: Uptone Press, 2005.

Johnson, Rae. *Oppression Embodied: The Intersection Dimension of Trauma, Oppression, and Somatic Psychology.* The USA Body Psychotherapy Journal, 2009.

Keleman, Stanley. *Emotional Anatomy: The Structure of Experience.* Berkeley, CA: Center Press, 1985.

Krantz, Anne M. *Let the Body Speak: Commentary on Paper by Jon Sletvold.* Mortimer Street, London: Routledge Taylor & Francis Group, LLC, 2012.

---

7 Anne M. Krantz, *Let the Body Speak: Commentary on Paper by Jon Sletvold* (Mortimer Street, London: Routledge Taylor & Francis Group, LLC, 2012).

Chapter 10

Somatic Psychotherapy and Gay Men: A Return to Yourself

Kurt Wagner, LMFT, PhD

Working somatically with gay men entails considering the client in a complex paradigm that embraces the impacts of multiple vectors on his physicality.[1] This means the cultivation of an understanding that the world that we inhabit is one that has the body and all its manifestations as a major means of identity, both internally and externally, consciously and unconsciously.

Practically, this translates that the clothing we wear, the places we visit, the ways we use our bodies, how we manifest our sexuality, what communities we associate with and inhabit are impressing upon us an identity that is shaping us daily.[2] We will explore somatic therapy using

---

1 *Gay man*: For the purposes of this paper, a cisgendered (denoting or relating to a person whose self-identity conforms with the gender that corresponds to their biological sex) male who identifies with being sexually and emotionally attracted to other men; not transgender.

2 See V. Clarke and K. Turner, (2007) "Clothes Maketh the Queer? Dress, Appearance and the Construction of Lesbian, Gay and Bisexual Identities," *Feminism and Psychology*, 17(2), 267–76; S. B. Kimmel and J. R. Mahalik (2005), "Body Image Concerns of Gay Men: The Roles of Minority Stress and Conformity to Masculine Norms," *Journal of Consulting and Clinical Psychology*, *73*(6), 1185.

the following ideas: syndemics, epigenetics, origins of gayness, protogays, effemiphobia, chemsex, marginalized community stressors, sexuality, resilience, physicality, and somatic interventions.[3]

Many of the ideas that we will be exploring together are not unique to gay men or to marginalized communities, but I will be investigating them through this discrete lens on a culture that is universal, diverse, and ever-changing. My colleagues in this volume will discuss their own process and work with marginalized populations; my own focus is on gay men and how they manifest themselves. We will be considering some general patterns in how gay men occupy their bodies. These ideas have been cultivated through years of working with gay men and in numerous conversations with other gay therapists who work with gay men.

A few caveats: I'm writing from the place of an urban-dwelling gay man in one of the most protected gay enclaves in the world, San Francisco. It is not wholly representative of other communities, large and small, of gay men and yet the influence of the San Francisco gay community is spread throughout the world. I'm not speaking for all gay men or to even to say that they all have these same experiences; I write to focus on numerous forms and ways of self-expression that I've seen over the years and continue to see with each successive generation of young gay men in their twenties and thirties and that continues with older gay men as well. I am a white gay male who is a transdisciplinary somatic psychotherapist in private practice in San Francisco. This is a population that I work with, am a member of, and have curiously inquired about over the past twenty years. The following section will describe some of how I got to this place.

3 Protogays: Eve K. Sedgwick, *How to Bring Your Kids Up Gay* Social Text, (29), (1991), 18–27; *Effemiphobia:* "The fear of men who are too effeminate in the societal view of what a true man should look, act, and speak like" (Jaye Spot, as cited in Binaohan, 2012); Syndemics: A set of linked health problems involving two or more afflictions interacting synergistically, and contributing to excess burden of disease in a population. Syndemics occur when health-related problems cluster by person, place, or time. Syndemic. (2014). *MedicineNet.com online dictionary*. Retrieved from http://medterms.com.

How I Got Here

I grew up in a small farming town in Watertown, Wisconsin. I was the sixth of nine children, born in 1960. From the age of four, I knew that I was different. My family also knew that I was different. That difference that I expressed is now often referred to as a child who is *protogay*.[4] I didn't have a word for what it was, but I knew that it was bad. My family started calling me a fem then, and that progressed to being called a fag or a girl. I was too sensitive in their eyes. I grew up in an extremely physically violent household. I couldn't play in the same way as my brothers; I was extremely uncoordinated, I was too sensitive, and hypervigilant about objects and fast movements. I didn't know how my body worked, and my feelings were always on the surface. I became skilled at dissociating from my body; however, one part of my body still had some expression. I have a picture of myself as a four-year-old boy with my right fist clenched while I look at the camera.

I was eight when I first began my inquiry about what this being different was all about by looking in the library of my Catholic school. I still remember the smell of the library, the feel of the library cards, and the furtive way that I went looking in the drawers of the card catalog. I first found the word "homosexual" and then, like many protogay boys before and after me, I explored what that meant by reading more; everything that I found was negative, pathologizing, and demoralizing.[5] This continued when I went to junior high school and again in senior high, where I continued to research in a bigger library, where I found material that finally confirmed that I was mentally ill, sick, depraved, and incurable. When I went to university, I had access to larger databases and continued uncovering more and more data. This story is unfortunately

---

4 *Protogay*: A child who is born gay and not yet aware of his orientation as a cognitive experience, but who will grow up homosexual (Sedgwick, 1991).

5 Eve K. Sedgwick, *How to Bring Your Kids Up Gay* Social Text, (29), (1991): 18–27. Kimberlyn Leary, *Passing, Posing, and "Keeping It Real,"* Relational Psychoanalysis," Volume 4 (2014), Expansion of Theory, 31. C. J. Pascoe, *Dude, You're a Fag: Masculinity and Sexuality in High School* (Berkeley: CA, University of California Press, 2007).

intimately familiar to many gay men and boys who look outside themselves for an explanation of who and what they are. At the time of this writing, there are millions of articles, studies, and voices on being gay that a young protogay has access to. I have heard multiple versions of my story many times and this narrative continues with the younger generation in spite of the wide exposure that gay men have come to know. They have often grown up in repressed families, communities, churches, spread out over the whole of the United States, and especially distressingly, in the San Francisco Bay Area.

The Beginning of Embodiment[6]

In 1978, I went to the University of Wisconsin—Milwaukee for premed and met my new roommate, Jack. He was a speed skater during the time when Eric Heiden was the preeminent speed skater in the world, who would go on to win five gold medals at the 1980 Olympics in Lake Placid, New York.[7] Jack was intensely physical, always moving and always training. He embodied for me a way of being in his body that was infectious and also showed me it was something I could obtain as well. I spent many hours at the track with him while he skated and would watch the speed skaters push their bodies to the extreme in freezing cold. There was an intensity and unabashed wildness in their relationship with their bodies that I had never seen or experienced myself.

My roommate began to help me find a relationship with my body from our first days of living together. He took me out running and showed me the speed skater workout routines: sprinting up any staircase and then running down to do it again (over and over again), doing

---

6 *Embodiment:* For the purposes of this chapter, embodiment means the integration of the mind, heart, soul, and spirit, with the physical form holding the space for all of those elements to coexist.

7 "Heiden, Eric." Notable Sports Figures. *Encyclopedia.com.* (February 19, 2018). http://www.encyclopedia.com/sports/encyclopedias-almanacs-transcripts-and-maps/heiden-eric.

fartleks (sprints with random rests) and lunges on the Milwaukee lake front. Through my efforts I found my first runner's high: the pleasure of pushing my mesomorphic self to the extreme, and discovering that exercise moderated my emotional and mental states. I started working out in the gym and found out that I had a body that felt good to move and feel in. It was the beginning of agency—a term we use in psychology and especially in somatic work where a person feels that they can act and have an impact on their world.

If you would look at my body now, I am, depending on the day, a doppelganger for Bruce Willis. It is a daily occurrence that people stop and ask, "Has anyone ever told you that you look like ... Bruce Willis?" Police, security guards, FBI agents, nod at me like I am either one of their own or in some way need to be acknowledged. I'm often told by strangers that I look like a cop. As a gay adult man I have passed more times as straight than gay.[8] This look has afforded me a level of safety, privilege, and agency that a lot of gay men don't experience because of how they are more noticeably different in physicality, movement, and voice. I am often told by gay men that I look like I could be someone who might bash them. Gay clients have often asked in a session if I'm straight or gay.

Beginning to Work with Gay Men

I started working with gay men in 1996, conducting residential retreats, classes, workshops, meditation groups, and psychoeducation with a strong grounding in Bioenergetics and expressive psychodrama styles of working. I began that work after spending three years in Cologne, Germany, doing group work at the Osho Uta Institute and studying in Pune, India, at the Osho Commune. The workshops and groups included breath work, meditation, mindfulness, Bioenergetics, Pulsation, Gestalt, Primal, Tantra, and many esoteric practices. I am

---

[8] K. Leary, "Passing, Posing, and 'Keeping It Real.'" In A. Lewis and A. Harris (eds.), *Relational Psychoanalysis: Volume 4, Expansion of Theory* (New York, NY: Routledge/Taylor & Francis, 2014).

certified as a clinical hypnotherapist, massage therapist, trance dance facilitator, neurolinguistic programming trainer, past life regression therapist, Reiki master, and intuitive counselor. I am also trained as a Core Energetic therapist.

In addition to those trainings, I have participated in more than eighty-five therapeutic processes since the age of twenty-two. This background has allowed me to hear and assimilate hundreds of gay men's diverse narratives professionally as a therapist. In my role as a psychotherapist, I have found through the years that my own narrative from my personal journey joins the narratives of other gay men. I have a bachelor's degree in zoology and a master's degree in counseling psychology with a specialization in somatic therapy, and a doctorate in transformative studies focusing on gay men and somatic resilience.

I have lived in the San Francisco Bay area for almost twenty-five years. Many of the things that I'm talking about are unique to this community. However, this community of gay men is fluid and has many intersections with other gay men throughout the world. It is a well-known place where gay men come to leave the suppressive places where they live and come here to be free to be.[9]

A lot of gay men grow up like bonsai trees, being pruned to act in specific ways and to live in a heterosexual culture that is dangerous to their being; they are taught early to limit their emotional and physical contact with men, to be hypervigilant about their attractions, and to modify their physical movements and emotional expressions to fit the dominant male culture. To use another metaphor, they are like those Japanese square watermelons, which begin their lives in square Plexiglas containers so that they can be harvested shaped as cubes and then stacked, displayed, and sold as better able to fit in small refrigerators.

---

[9] Dan Black, Gary Gates, Seth Sanders, and Lowell Taylor, (2002), "Why Do Gay Men Live in San Francisco?" *Journal of Urban Economics, 51*(1), 54–76. See also A. C. Howe (2001), "Queer Pilgrimage: The San Francisco Homeland and Identity Tourism," *Cultural Anthropology, 16*(1), 35–61. https://doi.org/10.1525/can.2001.16.1.35.

The social and physical containers that gay men often grow up in are limiting in much the same way. While we retain our essence, we have been shaped so profoundly by our environment that we must force ourselves out of our original containers to overcome that early learning. This forcing leads to a kind of embodiment that allows for a reawakening much like Buck's in Jack London's *The Call of the Wild*, to return to ourselves and find our own true north. Reflecting on the bonsai image, it's as if we need to let the plant go unpruned, grow wild, break free from its pot, and find its own agency through the limitations of the cutting that has taken place.[10] Some men never break out and many lead marginalized, thwarted, unrealized lives as a result.

The things we know as somatic therapists that are important for breaking free:

- the earlier one comes out of the closet the better;
- the longer you live a parallel life (closeted), the harder it is to live an authentic life in the future;
- support from the primary caregivers (parents) is vital for long-term health;
- generating self-respect, self-esteem, and self-compassion is important;[11]

---

[10] *Agency:* Sense of agency refers to the feeling of control over actions and their consequences. J. W. Moore, (2016), "What Is the Sense of Agency and Why Does It Matter?" *Frontiers in Psychology,* 7, 1272. http://doi.org/10.3389/fpsyg.2016.01272.

[11] See Nancy J. Evans and Ellen M. Broido, (1999), "Coming Out in College Residence Halls: Negotiation, Meaning Making, Challenges, Supports," *Journal of College Student Development, 40*(6), 658–68. Frank J. Floyd and Roger Bakeman, (2006), "Coming-Out across the Life Course: Implications of Age and Historical Context," *Archives of Sexual Behavior, 35*(3), 287–96. David M. Huebner and Mary C. Davis, "Gay and Bisexual Men Who Disclose Their Sexual Orientations in the Workplace Have Higher Workday Levels of Salivary Cortisol and Negative Affect," *Annals of Behavioral Medicine, 30*(3), (2005), 260–67. Nicole Legate, Richard M. Ryan, and Netta Weinstein, (2012) "Is Coming Out Always a "Good Thing"? Exploring the Relations of Autonomy Support, Outness, and Wellness for Lesbian, Gay, and Bisexual Individuals," *Social Psychological and Personality Science, 3*(2), 145–52.

- a network and community of supportive friends and family (often chosen) makes a profound difference for long-term happiness and thriving;[12]
- and finding a way of expressing your life-force through movement, connection, sexual expression, and uncovering an individual voice in the face of easily adopting an encultured life makes a difference.[13]

Somatic therapy is a way to sort through all of messages of the straight and gay community and find oneself and one's own way of being. Gestalt therapy, which is intensely body-based, could be said to be a search through all the introjections (messages taken in without discrimination), retroflections (all the manifestations of those introjections—such as holding back one's attraction to another man or averting your gaze so as to not be found out), projections (those things we attribute to another that are ours—attractions, gayness, effemiphobia), confluence (merging with the straight or gay environment and losing ourselves), and deflection (not letting people into our world for fear of being found out).[14]

The therapeutic journey is to have gay men find a place of compassion for themselves, that they did not consciously choose the ways in which they have developed and responded to a world that largely hates their existence and sexuality. To help them cultivate a practice of mindfulness that allows enough space between their bodily experience and inner world where they can have distance and perspective

---

[12] K. I. Fredriksen-Goldsen, C. A. Emlet, H. J. Kim, A. Muraco, E. A. Erosheva, J. Goldsen, and C. P. Hoy-Ellis, (2013), "The Physical and Mental Health of Lesbian, Gay Male, and Bisexual (LGB) Older Adults: The Role of Key Health Indicators and Risk and Protective Factors," *Gerontologist, 53*(4), 664–75.

[13] R. H. Hopcke, K. L. Carrington, and S. Wirth, *Same-Sex Love and the Path to Wholeness, First Edition,* (Boston, MA: Shambhala, 1993).

[14] Fritz Perls, *The Gestalt Approach and Eye Witness to Therapy.* (Ben Lomond, CA: Science and Behavior Books, 1973). J. I. Kepner, *Body Process: A Gestalt Approach to Working with the Body in Psychotherapy.* (New York, NY: Gardner Press: Gestalt Institute of Cleveland Press, 1987).

on their lives. To make sense of how they have come to be and what new choices are available for the future and restore access to their authentic self.[15]

How Do Gay Men Come into Being?

Gay men seek to find an explanation for their embodiment. Often upon coming out, even in 2018 at the time of this writing, their parents, family, and friends still say things like, "What did we do to make you gay? Was it the people you were hanging with? What you saw on the Internet?" Though these may not be the major things men and boys hear, they are still an important feature of how the world sees and comprehends *gay*. Despite now clear definitive genetic evidence to the contrary (though ambiguous with two theories positing placeholders for genes), the idea that someone can be born gay has essentially lacked scientific proof. This leads people to epigenetics, which assumes the causality to exist in the influence of the environment on gene expression or suppression.[16]

Genetic Theory and Epigenetics

The intersection of the body and environment comes together in epigenetic theory—the expression or non-expression of genetic material based on environmental influences. On the negative side, our genes are highly influenced by the environment as children and young adults; the positive side is that genes can be turned off and on throughout the life cycle, which is why somatic therapy can make the most difference.

There are forces of nurture that cause expression or suppression of both intracellular and extracellular genetic material, resulting in

---

[15] *Authentic self:* The self that is intrinsic and original to the person from birth. From a Reichian and Freudian perspective, it is the undomesticated human (Freud, 1908/1995; Reich, 1970). This term refers to the natural, unfettered expression of self.

[16] Epigenetics is the process by which patterns of gene expression are modified in a mitotically heritable manner by mechanisms that do not involve DNA mutation. Carrie Deans and Keith Maggert, *Genetics,* 2015.

morphological changes in this lifetime. Bodies change in response to the environment, and epigenetic changes happen within this generation and one or two generations; these changes can find expression in the daily lives of humans in their ability to deal with stress, responses to neglect, and skeletal muscle development.[17]

There has been a long and ongoing discussion about the origins and validity of homosexuality as a genetic and naturally occurring phenomenon.[18] Theories from both the nature and nurture domains have continuously striven to ascribe gayness to a single causative factor as opposed to a more complex source in which multiple factors in relationship are responsible for homosexuality and its theoretical natural place in genetic difference—in other words, epigenetic factors.[19] The neurobiology of sexuality and orientation is still a young science, with theories ranging from the effects of prenatal hormonal disturbances to the influence of number of siblings and other epigenetic changes, and studies remain inconclusive as to any single causative agent.[20] A number of researchers have conjectured that homosexuality occurs through a process termed "canalized sexual development."[21] A simple way to state the theory is that it takes a quantity of genetic material and environmental factors to collectively create a threshold point, after which the genes are then channeled into a phenotypical sexual orientation. How that person expresses his or her identity is still a matter of some choice, depending on the person's environment (nurture) and resiliency.

Although the importance of the environment in which a person is nurtured is not a subject of debate, there remains a question of whether

---

17 Barrès et al., 2012; Naumova et al., 2012.

18 Kinsey et al., 1948; Mondimore, 1996; G. D. Wilson and Rahman, 2005.

19 Hamer and Copeland, 1994; Rice, Friberg, and Gavrilets, 2012; Roughgarden, 2005.

20 Ngun, Ghahramani, Sánchez, Bocklandt, and Vilain, 2011.

21 Rice, Friberg, and Gavrilets, 2012.

a negative environment has an effect on the genetic material. A lack of nurturing parents and past abuse have been linked to a loss of gray matter. Another study finds occurrences of depression in adolescents and long-term damage to adults who were abused, maltreated, and socially isolated as children, and childhood abuses have been shown to result in permanent changes to one's immune system, nervous system, and cardiac health.[22]

The negative environment in which some gay men live and are raised contrasts with the positive nurturing epigenetic influences that heterosexual men might experience: supportive families, food security, healthy attachment, and acceptance of a conforming masculinity. For example, the stress of being bullied as a protogay child can provoke long-term epigenetic and genetic changes that limit a person's ability to live a full and productive life. That stress also has repercussions on his long-term mental health.[23] Likewise, the ongoing effects of living a suppressed and thwarted life appear as physical and mental illnesses.[24]

Epigenetic research demonstrates that genes are turned on or off, or are modulated, by environmental factors such as stress, nutrition, violence, exercise, sleep, community support, acceptance, and rejection, pain sensitivity, and brain functions, among others.[25]

Gay men who resist these negative epigenetic influences do so, in part, by attempting to live recognized lives out in the open. Exercise, sex, artistic expression, and music are a few of the stereotypical tools that gay men use to deal with the negative side effects of living within the straight community. What is it like for a homosexual canalized young boy in this environment?

---

[22] Naumova et al., 2012; Danese et al., 2009.

[23] Moore et al., 2014.

[24] Heim and Binder, 2012; Read, Fosse, Moskowitz, and Perry, 2014.

[25] Heim and Binder, 2012; Supic, Jagodic, and Magic, 2013; Essex et al., 2011; Sanchis-Gomar et al., 2012; Yang, 2012; Feldman, 2012; Bell et al., 2014; e.g., Bohacek, Gapp, Saab, and Mansuy, 2012; Rice et al., 2012.

The Composite Portrait of a Protogay Boy

A protogay baby boy is born in the United States to a set of parents who want a boy—a masculine boy. He is greeted by his parents with happiness and excitement, and dressed in blue clothes.[26] His parents, relatives, and their friends comment on what a tough little guy he is. He will grow up to be interested in sports, they say, because his little grip on their fingers is strong. In his infancy, he is handled a little rougher than his sister was when she was a baby, and his cries are not answered with the same urgency that hers were.

Thus, from the first moments of his life, this baby boy is being raised to fit a socially prescribed masculine mold. If he cries as a toddler, he is told that girls cry and that he should toughen up and be a man. If he displays sensitivity, his father likely ignores him, either overtly or covertly. If he demonstrates attachment or the desire to be around his mother, he is called a momma's boy or a sissy.

As a young child he is directed to play sports, given boys' toys, and socially constructed to be a heterosexual male. If he is uncoordinated or feels that sports are too rough-and-tumble for him, he is either ostracized or bullied into playing sports. As a young protogay child, however, he may also have a feeling from as young as three or four years of age that he is different from other boys; he somehow has an affinity for them that is different than their affinities for each other and him. Somewhere in his developing brain, this protogay child knows, from the multitude of messages sent by his parents, friends, teachers, and schoolmates, that he should not reveal his affinity or difference.

Adolescence brings the flush of hormones and more energy to manifest his attractions for another teen like himself; he also feels the push toward going out with girls because everyone else is. Eventually,

---

[26] J. S. Bridges (1993), "Pink or Blue: Gender-Stereotypic Perceptions of Infants as Conveyed by Birth Congratulations Cards," *Psychology of Women Quarterly, 17*(2), 193–205.

the dissonance becomes too much and he has to choose. Either choice brings with it rejections: rejection of self and/or rejection by others.[27]

What Is Happening to the Protogay Child?

From a neurological perspective, a protogay child's brain is being shaped and pruned by the negative messages that he is receiving about his sexuality, the sexuality of boys and men like him. This shaping begins at birth, continues through his childhood, and becomes part of his identity creation process.

Identity is formed through multiple experiences and throughout a person's lifetime; it is formed in relationship to family, the immediate environment, and one's reflections on and interpretations of life experiences. For a protogay boy, the life experiences he has navigated in his short life so far are often stressful. Depending on the stressors (e.g., saying he likes other boys, coming out, being pointed out for being different), he experiences life through a hypervigilant nervous system that is on the edge of kindling due to a lifetime of assaults—direct and indirect, overt and covert. The protogay boy's relationship to the world and his embodiment are at odds as he attempts to make his body congruent with a heterosexually oriented masculine presentation, while keeping his "true north" identity hidden from view.

The protogay child's suppression of natural inclinations toward touch, attraction, and affinity results in a thwarted existence. His thwarted existence manifests as pruned neurological pathways in the brain, hyperactivity in the amygdala hippocampal complex, the propensity to kindle easily to dysregulating behaviors, and the requirement of more effort in reregulation.

The constant pressure from the outside world to follow conventions of heterosexuality and masculinity and the threats to self for not following those conventions also make themselves known in

---

[27] J. E. Cato and S. S. Canetto (2003), "Young Adults' Reactions to Gay and Lesbian Peers Who Become Suicidal Following 'Coming Out' to Their Parents," *Suicide and Life-Threatening Behavior, 33*(2), 201.

his relationships and dating activities when the protogay boy grows older. He is wary of touching his partner in public not only out of fear of attack, but also that his partner might come to harm because of an affectionate gesture. As a result of the perpetual sense of possible threat, the young man often withholds contact from his partner in public and private.[28] This lack of physical contact translates into a diminished ability to heal his uncontactful childhood, which can lead to insecure or ambivalent attachments with his partner.[29] Lack of physical contact also affects his ability to repair the here-and-now mis-attunements with his partner that are a part of a normal relationship.

When physical contact does happen, it may be highly sexualized and scripted, and not necessarily of the more intimate and tender sort that is often needed and wanted. The sexualized contact also often follows learned behaviors that are part of the dynamics of gay sex acquired from pornography (where the more "masculine" and endowed partner tops, and where the other partner is often treated as less than male), advertisements, primary experiences when he first came out, and from being commodified by (and in turn commodifying) his partners.[30] In addition, the amount and quality of his sexual contact are also dictated by his body—his musculature, his drive toward hyperembodiment, his amount of body fat, his penis size, his race, his own level of body shame for being gay, and the

---

28 Gay men have less physical contact than their straight counterparts. J. Gabb, M. Klett-Davies, J. Fink, and M. Thomae (2013), *Enduring Love? Couple Relationships in the 21st Century.* Retrieved from The Open University website: http://www.open.ac.uk/researchprojects/enduringlove/files/enduringlove/file/ecms/web-content/Final-Enduring-Love-Survey-Report.pdf.

29 M. A. Landolt, K. Bartholomew, C. Saffrey, D. Oram, and D. Perlman (2004), "Gender Nonconformity, Childhood Rejection, and Adult Attachment: A Study of Gay Men," *Archives of Sexual Behavior, 33*(2), 117–28.

30 D. Boyda, and M. Shevlin (2011), "Childhood Victimisation as a Predictor of Muscle Dysmorphia in Adult Male Bodybuilders," *Irish Journal of Psychology, 32*(3–4), 105–15.

degree to which he has expelled related introjected messages about gay sex and who does what to whom.[31]

Those men who learned early on to hide their sexuality and have only furtive anonymous connections are often limited in their ability to form relationships that explicitly value themselves and their partners. For other men, the physical body overrides the emotional self; relationships bring up unprocessed material around intimacy, where the emotional self is not yet ready to be engaged in sexuality. This leads to dissociative sexual experiences or sexual experiences that require intoxicants in order to be successful.

Morin's complexity theory helps explain the impact of life on gay men and how they see themselves in the larger world:

> Self-organizing beings—which on our planet, are essentially living beings—are systems that are not only not closed (protecting their own integrity and their identity) but also open to their environment, from which they derive matter, energy, information, and organization. Self-organizing beings, therefore, are self-eco-organizing beings, which leads to this fundamental complex idea; all autonomy constitutes itself in and through ecological dependence. As far as we are concerned, our ecological dependence is not only natural but social and cultural as well.[32]

The online apps Grindr, Scruff, GROWlr, Recon, and web portals for contact have ensured a continuing homogenization of the experience of gay men around sex, music, culture, identity, and especially embodiment.[33] In 1997 Gabriel Rotello published *Sexual Ecology;*

---

[31] *Hyper-embodiment*: The reduction of the body to one particular site (e.g., the genitals) of imagined difference or variation is a model of what Grabham (2007) proposes as a definition. Another definition is the reduction to a single place on the body where emphasis is placed (Edelman and Zimman, 2014).

[32] Edgar Morin (1992), "From the Concept of System to the Paradigm of Complexity," *Journal of Social and Evolutionary Systems, 15*(4), 371–85.

[33] M. Signorile, *Life Outside: The Signorile Report on Gay Men, Sex, Drugs, Muscles, and the Passages of Life* (New York, NY: HarperPerennial, 1998).

Aids and the Destiny of Gay Men.[34] His work looked at the way the gay community has sexual contact with each other from an ecological perspective. Rotello's idea of an ecological model of disease and vector transmission has significant corollaries to how gay men transmit their embodied selves to each other.

Some simple examples are the normalization of sex without condoms (bareback sex, which is seen as pejorative or erotic depending on which side of the natural skin to skin contact anal sex argument one finds oneself), the way facial hair and hypermasculinity are merged, modifying one's body with tattoos, piercings, personal hygiene and masculine smells (not deodorizing the body) as a way of joining the masculine community and sometimes as a form of masculine protest. These ways of being are spread worldwide through social media, gay pornography, gay men traveling to other countries and becoming inculcated with every new encounter, and gay thematic events like Circuit Parties, sex clubs, and street fairs.[35]

A personal example of this homogenization is from a time when I first lived in Germany in the 1980s. The gym culture for gay men then was small, the gyms more like underground bunkers, and men were engaging with each other socially. But years later when I went back in 2000, the gyms were like any gay gym in the United States. The music, lighting, mirrors, busy and sexualized locker rooms, the way men dressed—all looked to my eyes like any gay gym in Chicago, San Diego, San Francisco, Palm Springs, or New York. This included how men acted with each other—unlike the easy and friendly interactions that I remembered from decades

---

[34] Gabrielle Rotello, *Sexual Ecology: Aids and the Destiny of Gay Men* (New York, NY: Dutton, 1997).

[35] G. Mansergh, G. N. Colfax, G. Marks, M. Rader, R. Guzman, and S. Buchbinder (2001), "The Circuit Party Men's Health Survey: Findings and Implications for Gay and Bisexual Men," *American Journal of Public Health, 91*(6), 953–58.

before, there was a new way of relating: more guarded, cruisier, and body-identity based.

Physical Psychoeducation

Bill Bowen, one of my teachers, often said that when working with people's bodies one should always ask oneself, "What moves and what doesn't move?"[36] This inquiry is vital in my forming a working relationship with my clients, gay and otherwise, and to observe and see where there are places of aliveness and places of low energy or static places. One exercise that I do that is particularly poignant and evocative for gay men is skipping. I'll skip around the room with my clients to see how they allow their body to move or how they restrict it. This is a good example of both reservoir and pattern theory emerging in the session room from an activity. Often there are instant feelings of shame in skipping, reflecting a societal perspective that skipping is a "gay" or feminine thing. Many of my gay clients report and remember when they stopped skipping because it was part of what it was to "be a man" or "grow up" and conflated with that idea that it's a gay thing to skip and, "I'll give myself away if I do it." Homework then becomes skipping up and down the hallway or skipping with their boyfriend or partner to expose this part that has become deadened and to enliven that spirit that is still there.

If we use a current healing paradigm for dealing with trauma—the "window of tolerance," an idea first proposed by Dan Siegel—the work of somatic therapy is to increase that window.[37] We increase the window to better cope with changes in life by using physical exercise, sleep hygiene, contact with other people, mindfulness, meditation, food,

---

[36] Bill Bowen, *Somatic Resourcing: Psychotherapy through the Body* (Portland, OR: PPT Publishing, 2009).

[37] The "window of tolerance" is explained by Dan Siegel (1999).

nature, simple movements like walking, experiences that allow a person to see the horizon and have perspective, release, and expression of emotions from a natural ebb and flow that is more mindful of the experience and allow their natural somatic resilience to help them bounce back.[38]

Somatic Theory

There are two operational theories around how the body remembers its traumas and ordeals and why somatic therapies are useful for dealing with those disturbances: *reservoir theory* and *pattern theory*.[39] Reservoir theory is centered on the idea that the body holds "stuck" energy from the past; pattern theory postulates that specific patterns of action or thought elicit the past. Both of these theories have roots in current psycho-neurobiology and can be explained by physiological changes in the body. Both pattern and reservoir theories have a strong basis in current research on nerve pathways and neuronal sequencing, polyvagal theory, attachment models, psychobiology of post-traumatic stress disorder (PTSD) and neuropsychology.[40]

---

[38] *Somatic resilience:* The conscious or unconscious use of the body to cope with life stressors. This includes physicality in all its forms, nutrition, the physical environment in which the body lives, livelihood, and all the ways that a body interacts with the world. See: M. R. Bartoshuk (2009); G. A. Bonanno (2004); R. Cornum, M. D. Matthews, and M. E. P. Seligman (2011); J. Genke (2004); Gwadz, et al (2006); Herrick et al (2011); S. S. Luthar, D. Cicchetti, and B. Becker (2000); S. R. Maddi (2002); A. S. Masten (2014); B. Mustanski, et al (2011); G. E. Richardson (2002); M. Rutter (1985); B. W. Smith (2013); K. M. Waehler (2008).

[39] *Somatic psychotherapy:* A body-based psychotherapy based on the original work of Wilhelm Reich (1945), which incorporates the use of touch and body awareness in the process of therapy.

[40] Polyvagal theory (Porges, 1995), attachment models (Siegel, 1999), PTSD (Van der Kolk, 1994), Post-traumatic stress disorder (PTSD): diagnostic criteria for PTSD include a history of exposure to a traumatic event meeting two criteria and symptoms from each of three symptom clusters: intrusive recollections, avoidant/numbing symptoms, and hyperarousal symptoms. A fifth criterion concerns duration of symptoms, and a sixth assesses functioning (*DSM-V* code 309.81; see APA, 2014).

Pattern theory stipulates that a pattern of behavior or events will stimulate the nervous system to reproduce the emotions and thoughts that accompanied the original event. A few of the current therapies that access these patterns are Accelerated Experiential-Dynamic Psychotherapy (AEDP), Eye Movement Desensitization and Reprocessing (EMDR), and Brainspotting.[41] Pattern theory more explicitly means that putting our bodies into a particular position will evoke feelings, thoughts, memories, changes in cortisol levels, and the way that we can interact with the world. Simple patterns are kneeling and reaching up, holding out your hand for something or someone, putting your hand on the back of someone's neck, crossing your arms, or putting your hand out to stop something coming at you. This also applies to more complex patterns of movement, thinking, speech, and eye movement.

An easy example of this for a gay man is to have him go to the gym. Some men haven't been in a gym since high school, and even if it's a gay gym, his body can't help but respond to the locker room, the showers, and the men in it without the past somehow being evoked. Sometimes these experiences were good, though often the past experiences of the locker room and gym are embedded with shame and confusion. This experience of the body remembering has been reported to me countless times in session. While being in the gym over time can be a form of exposure therapy, those without body privilege have an extra hurdle to overcome; they must deal with both the internalized (introjected) ideas and feelings about their bodies and the very real rejection of their bodied selves by the other men in the gym.

Body privilege in the gay community is ascribed to height, facial appearance (masculine or boyish), penis size, musculature, amount of fat, and level of muscular definition.[42] This list can also be augmented

---

[41] Accelerated Experiential-Dynamic Psychotherapy (AEDP©; Fosha, 2002), Eye Movement Desensitization and Reprocessing (EMDR©; Shapiro, 2002), and Brainspotting© (Corrigan and Grand, 2013).

[42] D. Duncan, (2007), "Out of the Closet and into the Gym: Gay Men and Body Image in Melbourne, Australia," *Journal of Men's Studies, 15*(3), 331–46. D. Duncan (2010), "Gay Men, Body Identity, and the Politics of Visibility," *Gay and*

by those attributes that fall into the class of commodification in which ethnicity and race are important. For example, being black or Latino has the possibility of carrying the projection that the owner has a big dick and in being the active partner, while being Asian may relegate men into being seen as boyish, soft, hairless, and bottoms.[43]

Reservoir theories are those like Bioenergetics, Core Energetics, Bodynamics,[44] and Somatic Experiencing with the last falling somewhere in between both pattern and reservoir theory. The basic form that the reservoir takes is that of a cathexis point, an event in a person's life where a buildup of energy occurs around an unexpressed emotion. The reservoir is generally seen as holding negative emotions (anger, sadness, rage, resignation, etc.); the role of therapy, in this case, is to provide the right circumstances for this energy to emerge and be expressed.[45] I have found that the techniques from the reservoir

---

Lesbian Issues and Psychology Review, 6(1), 20–30. S. B. Kimmel and J. R. Mahalik (2005), "Body Image Concerns of Gay Men: The Roles of Minority Stress and Conformity to Masculine Norms," *Journal of Consulting and Clinical Psychology, 73*(6), 1185. M. J. Drummond, and S. M. Filiault (2007), "The Long and the Short of It: Gay Men's Perceptions of Penis Size," *Gay and Lesbian Issues and Psychology Review, 3*(2), 121–29. Y. Martins, M. Tiggemann, and L. Churchett (2008), "The Shape of Things to Come: Gay Men's Satisfaction with Specific Body Parts," *Psychology of Men and Masculinity, 9*(4), 248–256. G. Rieger, J. A. Linsenmeier, L. Gygax, S. Garcia, and J. M. Bailey (2010), "Dissecting 'Gaydar': Accuracy and the Role of Masculinity–Femininity," *Archives of Sexual Behavior, 39*(1), 124–40.

[43] A. Carballo-Diéguez, C. Dolezal, L. Nieves, F. Díaz, C. Decena, and I. Balan (2004), "Looking for a Tall, Dark, Macho Man ... Sexual-Role Behaviour Variations in Latino Gay and Bisexual Men," *Culture, Health, and Sexuality,* 6(2), 159–71. R. Fung "Looking for My Penis: The Eroticized Asian in Gay Video Porn." In K. A. Ono (ed.), *A Companion to Asian American Studies.* (Malden, MA: Blackwell, 2005).

[44] M. Bentzen, S. Jorgensen, and L. Marcher (1989), "The Bodynamic Character Structure Model," *Energy and Character, 20*(1), 1–17. A. Lowen, *Bioenergetics* (New York, NY: Coward, McCann and Geoghegan, 1975). J. C. Pierrakos, *Core Energetics: Developing the Capacity to Love and Heal* (Mendocino, CA: LifeRhythm, 1975).

[45] A. Lowen, *Bioenergetics* (New York, NY: Coward, McCann and Geoghegan, 1975). J. C. Pierrakos, *Core Energetics: Developing the Capacity to Love and Heal* (Mendocino, CA: LifeRhythm, 1975).

somatic tools are very helpful in having gay men express themselves. There is often a deep well of hurt, resentment, anger, and fear in my clients that needs a voice and a physical manifestation. The point is to drive toward a cathectic event and allow the layers of oppression and suppression both internal and external to have voice and expression often leading to a cathartic experience.

The same techniques are used to manifest joyful, sexual, and "positive" emotional states, by increasing the intensity of laughter, joy, movements that let all the parts in "what doesn't move" move with dramatic and an unfiltered self. The simple act of dancing, without a club environment, which might have demonstrative aspects as well as substance-influenced behaviors, can provide an opening to the suppressed parts of self that are still waiting to be expressed. It is also to have men move positively toward each other without the overarching feelings of possible rejection, but more of acceptance in how they are. To paraphrase Wilhelm Reich, *"When the life force is suppressed there is no limit to the amount of (perversions) distortions that will arise from that suppression."*[46]

Revisiting Epigenetics

Everything in the physical environment influences the expression of our genetic material, from the air that we breathe to the food that we eat, the chemicals we use to clean ourselves and our homes, our places of work, the other substances we put into our body, the pathogens we are exposed to, and the biomes of the people we come in contact with.

An exploration of gay somatic life needs to include looking at the influence of drugs, both illicit and licit. Antiviral medicines (ART) to treat HIV and AIDs and protocols like PEP (post-exposure

[46] Wilhem Reich, *The Mass Psychology of Fascism* (New York, NY: Farrar, Straus & Giroux, 1970); *The Function of the Orgasm: Sex-Economic Problems of Biological Energy,* V. R. Carfagno, trans. (New York, NY: Farrar, Straus and Giroux, 1973); *Character-Analysis: Principles and Technique for Psychoanalysts in Practice and in Training, trans.* T. P. Wolfe, trans. (New York, NY: Orgone Institute Press, 1945).

prophylaxis) and PrEP (pre-exposure prophylaxis) as well as various STI treatments, ED treatments have both physical and psychological influences. Other drugs in the illicit category are substances such as crystal meth, mephedrone ("bath salts"), pot, alcohol, cocaine, MDMA ("Molly" and "ecstasy"), hallucinogens in general, gamma hydroxybutyrate (GHB), and ketamine. Many men participate in sexual experiences that are enhanced or prolonged—through the use of drugs, sometimes for days at a time—often involving lack of consent, rape, violence, and psychotic breaks known as Chemsex. These men are polysubstance users. Most of the drugs reduce inhibitions and generate euphoric feelings that translate into having lots of sex.[47]

While not all participate in Chemsex, this drug use impacts the entire gay community. I have had many clients in my practice who find it difficult and challenging to have "sober" sex once they have experienced drug-influenced sex. Being sober makes them feel more exposed. The intensity of sober sex is so much less than than that of Chemsex; participants compare it to being like the difference between a rollercoaster and walking down the street. In being exposed, the old introjected messages reemerge. Often they have to relearn how to be in their bodies, having direct conversations about what they like sexually, and communicate in a more direct way, both physically and psychologically.

Another thing to consider when working with gay men is the hypervigilance that they have been living with since they were protogay. This is a pattern of being in the world that is especially significant for those men who did not pass for straight and who have body movements that might be more gender-fluid than those of a typical heterosexual male or who have vocal intonation that "sounds gay."[48]

---

[47] Patrick Strudwick, "Inside the Dark, Dangerous World of Chemsex." December 3, 16. Accessed April 9, 2018. https://www.buzzfeed.com/patrickstrudwick/inside-the-dark-dangerous-world-of-chemsex?utm_term=.ygVN1gMZR#.txr48lKer.

[48] Brooke Kroeger, *Passing: When People Can't Be Who They Are* (New York: PublicAffairs, 2005). F. Fasoli, A. Maass, M. P. Paladino, et al. (2017), "Gay- and Lesbian-Sounding Auditory Cues Elicit Stereotyping and Discrimination," Archives of Sexual Behavior 46: 1261. https://doi.org/10.1007/s10508-017-0962-0.

Often there is anger or a sense of betrayal that these body movements "tell" that this person is not a typical male; hand gestures and more fluidity in hip movements, for example, are often beyond their conscious control. These early life stressors for vulnerable gay men and the impact of the environment and everything we come in contact with influence the expression of our genes in an on or off direction.[49]

Our thinking about ourselves also shapes our genetic expression—stressors from the environment change the way our brains and bodies work.[50] For gay men who swim in a sea of stressors for being gay, the influence can be seen in the same way that it is seen in other marginalized communities.

A point I try to make in working somatically is that all of the gene expressions that are available to a human being are available to a gay man. I explicitly etch out that almost all of our genetic material comes from the X chromosome, so that all the feelings, moods, and ways of being have their origin in the X. This paradigm is designed to create a permission structure that lets my clients see that genetically they have all possible expressions within them.

Therapeutic Embodiment and Working with Gay Men Somatically

My goal in working with gay men is to first assess what resources they have cultivated in their lives. Specifically, how they find themselves embodied from their physical activities, sexual expression, emotional

---

[49] Christine Heim and Elizabeth B. Binder, (2012), "Current Research Trends in Early Life Stress and Depression: Review of Human Studies on Sensitive Periods, Gene–Environment Interactions, and Epigenetics," *Experimental Neurology, 233*(1), 102–11.

[50] H. Adam, and A. D. Galinsky, (2012), "Enclothed Cognition," *Journal of Experimental Social Psychology*, *48*(4), 918–25. J. P. Aguinaldo, (2008), "The Social Construction of Gay Oppression as a Determinant of Gay Men's Health: 'Homophobia Is Killing Us,'" *Critical Public Health, 18*(1), 87–96; S. Ahmed, (2006), "Orientations: Toward a Queer Phenomenology," *GLQ: A Journal of Lesbian and Gay Studies, 12*(4), 543–74. A. Noë, *Out of Our Heads: Why You Are Not Your Brain, and Other Lessons from the Biology of Consciousness* (New York, NY: Hill and Wang, 2009).

connections, mentors, and life experiences. From that pool of experience, we can then augment those resources that we know make a difference: community, exposure to other gay men in nonsexual physical settings, and self-expression in relationship to past thwarts of self.

We continue with sexual expression in the areas that Jack Morin describes in *Erotic Mind*: power, overcoming prohibitions, ambivalence, and anticipatory states.[51] Jack's work is vitally important to gay men and how they allow their sexualized selves to express. Each of the four domains that he describes for erotic charge has potential for both freedom and hindrance when it comes to sexuality and gender expression. Overcoming prohibitions range from the simplest expression of public displays of affection: holding hands with one's partner in public, kissing in public, being seen as a couple, and referring to your partner in conversations and naming his gender.

In session, clients have described overcoming prohibitions as having a freedom to be that they could only imagine in other places in the United States and the world. The simple act of going to a "gay" gym and being able to look, interact, and be physically tonic is a corrective emotional experience for the years of being suppressed. Larger expressions of prohibitions include living together as partners, putting oneself online to be seen and to engage with other men, nonbinary and binary expressions of movement pushing against effemiphobia, pushing against their internalized homophobia (more appropriately named homo-hatred).

Some of my clients don't see themselves inside the binary, but view themselves as more fluid with a myriad ways to express themselves. Holding to the binary of masculine and feminine often presents the problem for gay men of how they see themselves in those stereotypical roles. This shows up in session with a gay man who says because he's the active partner he's the "man," or that being receptive is "feminine." This is changing and I see it less and less with younger gay men in their twenties and thirties. Older gay men

---

[51] Jack Morin, *The Erotic Mind: Unlocking the Inner Sources of Passion and Fulfillment* (New York, NY: HarperCollins, 1996).

as a generalization of my experience often have the former view and this shows up as "bottom shaming"—the receptive partner being made to feel that he is less than for his sexual preference and expression. Phrasings such as "He's a big bottom," "He's a bottom, he-she is a power bottom" are often said with derision and sometimes contempt. This is the place in therapy where I encourage the expression and ownership of a man's preference/orientation and reveling in the pleasure his body brings to him. Conversely, "He's a top" or "I only top" is often expressed with pride, power, dominance over the bottom, or commodification and subjugation of the receptive partner. There is a long history of being pejorative against the receptive partner in sex regardless of orientation, gender, or sexual manifestation.[52]

When a clinician meets his gay client for the first time, the areas that he should be assessing are the levels of internalized and introjected hatred of self, how he expresses himself with his body in the room—but not by looking at the body as an object, as often happens with somatic work—instead, the clinician should join with the client in his embodiment. This collaboration can be done by walking around the room together, while having the client observe the clinician's body and movement, and vice versa. This kind of activity creates a shared experience of embodiment and a joining with the client following Martha Stark's two-person model of therapy.[53]

Resilience can be therapeutically assessed by taking a thorough history to find out what the client's innate resiliencies are, what resiliencies he has learned, and what obstacles he has overcome. Other pertinent information to know includes the age at which he came out, the level of acceptance from his family and friends, his sexual expression history, his relationship dynamics, when he became aware

---

[52] David A. Moskowitz and Trevor A. Hart (2011), "The Influence of Physical Body Traits and Masculinity on Anal Sex Roles in Gay and Bisexual Men," *Archives of Sexual Behavior, 40*(4), 835–41.

[53] M. Stark, *Modes of Therapeutic Action: Enhancement of Knowledge, Provision of Experience, and Engagement in Relationship* (New York, NY: Jason Aronson, 1999).

of himself as gay, how much hiding he did in his life, and how long he has suffered with his hidden self. Even details about a life well hidden can assist the therapist in devising salutogenic strategies based on the client's strengths by validating the protection that hiding provided and using those resources for his new life.

Gay identity often has its origination in sexuality, which is where a protogay often has his first experiences of sex whether they are thwarted or met. From there he forms an identity around his body. It is his body that then is socially constructed to either express or sublimate that sexuality in a process involving a complex matrix of events that also begins to shape his own resiliency.

Innately, the protogay young man has his own resilience from his genetic material and the ways in which he expresses himself. His learned resiliency comes from experiences in dealing with a straight world. For example, his first gay experience could take place when he acknowledges to himself that he is gay, and either fights or accepts that realization. That process in itself is like building a muscle—it does not build all at once, and in many cases the process takes a lifetime. Ideally, the man arrives at a level of acceptance that allows him to integrate his gayness into his life. The next experience, in turn, might be sharing that he is gay with someone close and dealing with their acceptance or rejection. In either case, the young man's coming-out process (to himself first, then to others) is a movement toward more resiliency, either by increasing his level of trust in people, or by generating more self-reliance in response to rejection and integrating that self-reliance into his life.

A gay man expresses his embodiment through communities of association; through his intimate relationships; through the exercise of his body, his work, his spiritual life; and through the different venues that are available to him based on his own level of agency, social capital, and privilege. The term agency refers to his conscious application of resiliency strategies that are innate, acquired, or learned in a given situation. His social capital and privilege are intertwined; for example, the way in which he is embodied (e.g., attractive, well-built, young) may gift the gay man with a level of privilege within the gay community and social capital to spend there. A gay man who possesses a taller than average or muscular body or a model's face may be able to access other men and garner more attention, which means more possible partners—a reflection of his privilege and social capital.

For therapists who work with gay men, it is important to start healing work with the body. A gay male client's body presence determines the way that he has been received into his community through sexuality and sexualization; his body is the location where he has been commodified, either positively or negatively. Those men who are of the right size, the right hairiness, the right sexual parts, and the right archetypal look—the acceptance of their body self by the community grants them privileges in, and access to, gay life. These men may be unconscious of the mental cost of those privileges, but they are often very conscious of the attention that they get from that hyper-embodiment.

Whether the client is (or has been) privileged or not privileged, the therapist should guide him to work on self-acceptance and self-compassion on every level. All layers of injury and insults to the gay male self—from sexual assaults and violence to homophobic microaggressions—can and do cause epigenetic changes in a gay man and impinge on his ability to thrive.

Fortunately, the therapist has many avenues to offer toward creating personalized plans to foster resiliency. Repairs to the self can be made by association with communities, having acceptance from family members, exercise in all its forms, increased nutrition, sleep hygiene, positive regard from a therapist, self-acceptance of one's gayness, mindfulness, and so on.

I am speaking about the body as integrated with the mind, heart, soul, and spirit, and take the approach that the physical form holds the space for all of us, as humans, to exist. This physical, body-centric approach is one that most current somatic therapies are attempting to adopt as they become aggregates of theories and trends. Hardiness and resilience are becoming key elements of this embodied idea. The place to start with therapy is with the body; almost any body intervention affects the whole system and activates what was previously thought to be immutable.

To return to the metaphor that I used early on in this chapter: gay men are bonsai trees that started with the genetic capacity to be towering pines, but have been pruned to be smaller and less than what we could have been through our life experiences. A gentler metaphor is that of a tree on the edge of a cliff that has been shaped by the wind into a bent shape, roots exposed, that grows differently from tall and "straight" neighboring trees, which are protected by the lee side of the cliff.

We are molded by our environment into different shapes, and yet we thrive and grow. To move into simile, gay men are like succulents: some turn colors when under stress, some dry out and appear dead, but a piece of them survives to thrive when the right conditions are provided. They grow when watered and given sunlight, and they thrive in contact with others. Like the thriving succulent, gay men in life-giving communities enhance their environment through healing, nurturing, and beauty. The movement from arid, stressful ways of experiencing the world to joyful, sustainable community is my hope and dream for gay men. It is my wish that all gay men find a way to restore their vital natures so that they can thrive and grow fully into their beautiful selves.

Bibliography

Adam, H., and Galinsky, A. D. (2012). "Enclothed Cognition." *Journal of Experimental Social Psychology, 48*(4), 918–25.

Aguinaldo, J. P. (2008). "The Social Construction of Gay Oppression as a Determinant of Gay Men's Health: 'Homophobia Is Killing Us.'" *Critical Public Health, 18*(1), 87–96.

Ahmed, S. (2006). "Orientations: Toward a Queer Phenomenology." *GLQ: A Journal of Lesbian and Gay Studies, 12*(4), 543–74.

American Psychiatric Association. *Diagnostic and Statistical Manual of Mental Disorders* (5th ed., text rev.) Washington, DC: American Psychiatric Association, 2015.

Barrès, R., Yan, J., Egan, B., Treebak, J. T., Rasmussen, M., Fritz, T., … Zierath, J. R. (2012). "Acute Exercise Remodels Promoter Methylation in Human Skeletal Muscle." *Cell Metabolism, 15*(3), 405–11.

Bartoshuk, M. R. (2009). "Minority Coping: The Role of Interpersonal Resiliency Factors in Gay Men's Experience of Minority Stress and Depression." *Dissertation Abstracts International: Section B: The Sciences and Engineering 69*(12), 0779.

Bell, J. T., Loomis, A. K., Butcher, L. M., Gao, F., Zhang, B., Hyde, C. L., ... Spector, T. D. (2014). "Differential Methylation of the TRPA1 Promoter in Pain Sensitivity." *Nature Communications, 5*. DOI: 10.1038/ncomms3978

Bentzen, M., Jorgensen, S., and Marcher, L. (1989). "The Bodynamic Character Structure Model." *Energy and Character, 20*(1), 1–17.

Binaohan, B. (2012, 22 August). "Effemiphobia? (Or, Why Gay White Cis Men Make up Shit and Stay Trans/Misogynist.)" [Web log post]. Retrieved from https://b-binaohan.herokuapp.com/blog/effemiphobia-or-why-gay-white-cis-men-make-up-shit-and-stay-transmisogynist/.

Black, D., Gates, G., Sanders, S., and Taylor, L. (2002). "Why Do Gay Men Live in San Francisco?" *Journal of Urban Economics, 51*(1), 54–76.

Bohacek, J., Gapp, K., Saab, B. J., and Mansuy, I. M. (2012). "Transgenerational Epigenetic Effects on Brain Functions." *Biological Psychiatry, 73*(4), 313–20.

Bonanno, G. A. (2004). "Loss, Trauma, and Human Resilience: Have We Underestimated the Human Capacity to Thrive after Extremely Aversive Events?" *American Psychologist, 59*(1), 20–28.

Bonanno, G. A., and Mancini, A. D. (2012). "Beyond Resilience and PTSD: Mapping the Heterogeneity of Responses to Potential Trauma." *Psychological Trauma: Theory, Research, Practice, and Policy, 4*(1), 74–83.

Bowen, B. *Somatic Resourcing: Psychotherapy through the Body*. Portland, OR: PPT Publishing, 2009.

Boyda, D., and Shevlin, M. (2011). "Childhood Victimization as a Predictor of Muscle Dysmorphia in Adult Male Bodybuilders." *Irish Journal of Psychology, 32*(3–4), 105–15.

Bridges, J. S. (1993). "Pink or Blue: Gender-Stereotypic Perceptions of Infants as Conveyed by Birth Congratulations Cards." *Psychology of Women Quarterly, 17*(2), 193–205.

Carballo-Diéguez, A., Dolezal, C., Nieves, L., Díaz, F., Decena, C., and Balan, I. (2004). "Looking for a Tall, Dark, Macho Man ... Sexual-Role Behaviour Variations in Latino Gay and Bisexual Men." *Culture, Health and Sexuality, 6*(2), 159–71.

Cato, J. E., and Canetto, S. S. (2003). "Young Adults' Reactions to Gay and Lesbian Peers Who Become Suicidal Following 'Coming Out' to Their Parents." *Suicide and Life-Threatening Behavior, 33*(2), 201.

Clarke, V., and Turner, K. (2007). "Clothes Maketh the Queer? Dress, Appearance and the Construction of Lesbian, Gay and Bisexual Identities." *Feminism and Psychology, 17*(2), 267–76.

Cornum, R., Matthews, M. D., and Seligman, M. E. P. (2011). "Comprehensive Soldier Fitness: Building Resilience in a Challenging Institutional Context." *American Psychologist, 66*(1), 4–9.

Corrigan, F., and Grand, D. (2013). "Brainspotting: Recruiting the Midbrain for Accessing and Healing Sensorimotor Memories of Traumatic Activation." *Medical Hypotheses, 80*(6),759–66.

Drummond, M. J., and Filiault, S. M. (2007). "The Long and the Short of It: Gay Men's Perceptions of Penis Size." *Gay and Lesbian Issues and Psychology Review, 3*(2), 121–29.

Duncan, D. (2007). "Out of the Closet and into the Gym: Gay Men and Body Image in Melbourne, Australia." *Journal of Men's Studies, 15*(3), 331–46.

———. (2010). "Gay Men, Body Identity and the Politics of Visibility." *Gay and Lesbian Issues and Psychology Review, 6*(1), 20–30.

Edelman, E. A., and Zimman, L. (2014). "Boycunts and Bonus Holes: Trans Men's Bodies, Neoliberalism, and the Sexual Productivity of Genitals." *Journal of Homosexuality, 61*(5), 673–90.

Elzinga, B. M., Schmahl, C. G., Vermetten, E., van Dyck, R., and Bremner, J. D. (2003). "Higher Cortisol Levels Following Exposure to Traumatic Reminders in Abuse-Related PTSD." *Neuropsychopharmacology, 28*(9), 1656–65.

Essex, M. J., Thomas Boyce, W., Hertzman, C., Lam, L. L., Armstrong, J. M., Neumann, S., and Kobor, M. S. (2013). "Epigenetic Vestiges of Early Developmental Adversity: Childhood Stress Exposure and DNA Methylation in Adolescence." *Child Development, 84*(1), 58–75.

Evans, N. J., and Broido, E. M. (1999). "Coming Out in College Residence Halls: Negotiation, Meaning Making, Challenges, Supports." *Journal of College Student Development, 40*(6), 658–68.

Feldman, R. (2012). "Oxytocin and Social Affiliation in Humans." *Hormones and Behavior, 61*(3), 380–91.

Fine, C. *Delusions of Gender: How Our Minds, Society, and Neurosexism Create Difference*. New York, NY: W.W. Norton and Company, 2010.

Floyd, F. J., and Bakeman, R. (2006). "Coming-Out across the Life Course: Implications of Age and Historical Context." *Archives of Sexual Behavior, 35*(3), 287–96.

Fosha, D. "The Activation of Affective Change Processes in Accelerated Experiential-Dynamic Psychotherapy (AEDP)." In F. W. Kaslow (Series Ed.) and J. J. Magnavita (Volume Ed.), *Comprehensive Handbook of Psychotherapy: Vol. 1. Psychodynamic/Object Relations*. New York, NY: John Wiley & Sons, 2002.

Fredriksen-Goldsen, K. I., Emlet, C. A., Kim, H. J., Muraco, A., Erosheva, E. A., Goldsen, J., and Hoy-Ellis, C. P. (2013). "The Physical and Mental Health of Lesbian, Gay Male, and Bisexual (LGB) Older Adults: The Role of Key Health Indicators and Risk and Protective Factors." *Gerontologist, 53*(4), 664–75.

Freud, S. "Civilized" Sexual Morality and Modern Nervous Illness (J. Strachey, trans.). In J. Strachey and A. Freud (Eds.), *The Standard Edition of the Complete Psychological Works of Sigmund Freud, Volume 9 (1906–1908): Jensen's "Gradiva" and Other Works*. London, England: Vintage, 1995. (Original work published 1908.)

———*Beyond the Pleasure Principle* (T. Dufresne, ed., and G. C. Richter, trans.) Buffalo, NY: Broadview Editions, 2011. (Original work published 1920.)

Frith, H., and Gleeson, K. (2004). "Clothing and Embodiment: Men Managing Body Image and Appearance." *Psychology of Men and Masculinity, 5*(1), 40–48.

Fung, R. "Looking for My Penis: The Eroticized Asian in Gay Video Porn." In K. A. Ono (ed.), *A Companion to Asian American Studies*. Malden, MA: Blackwell, 2005.

Gabb, J., Klett-Davies, M., Fink, J., and Thomae, M. (2013) *Enduring Love? Couple Relationships in the 21st Century.* Retrieved from The Open University website: http://www.open.ac.uk/researchprojects/enduringlove/files/enduringlove/file/ecms/web-content/Final-Enduring-Love-Survey-Report.pdf.

Genke, J. (2004). "Resistance and Resilience: The Untold Story of Gay Men Aging with Chronic Illnesses." *Journal of Gay and Lesbian Social Services, 17*(2), 81–95. DOI: 10.1300/J041v17n02_05.

Gevonden, M., Selten, J., Myin-Germeys, I., de Graaf, R., Ten Have, M., van Dorsselaer, S., Veling, W. (2013). "Sexual Minority Status and Psychotic Symptoms: Findings from the Netherlands Mental Health Survey and Incidence Studies (NEMESIS)." *Psychological Medicine, 44*(2), 1–13.

Grabham, E. (2007). "Citizen Bodies, Intersex Citizenship." *Sexualities, 10*(1), 29–48.

Gwadz, M. V., Clatts, M. C., Yi, H., Leonard, N. R., Goldsamt, L., and Lankenau, S. (2006). "Resilience among Young Men Who Have Sex with Men in New York City." *Sexuality Research and Social Policy, 3*(1), 13–21.

Hamer, D. H., and Copeland, P. *The Science of Desire: The Search for the Gay Gene and the Biology of Behavior*. New York, NY: Simon and Schuster, 1994.

Hans, J. D., Kersey, M., and Kimberly, C. (2012). "Self-Perceived Origins of Attitudes toward Homosexuality." *Journal of Homosexuality, 59*(1), 4–17.

Heim, C., and Binder, E. B. (2012). "Current Research Trends in Early Life Stress and Depression: Review of Human Studies on Sensitive Periods, Gene-Environment Interactions, and Epigenetics." *Experimental Neurology, 233*(1), 102–11.

Herrick, A. L., Lim, S. H., Wei, C., Smith, H., Guadamuz, T., Friedman, M. S., and Stall, R. (2011). "Resilience as an Untapped Resource in Behavioral Intervention Design for Gay Men." *AIDS and Behavior, 15*(Suppl. 1), S25–S29.

Hopcke, R. H., Carrington, K. L., and Wirth, S. *Same-Sex Love and the Path to Wholeness* (1st ed.). Boston, MA: Shambhala, 1993.

Howe, A. C. (2001). "Queer Pilgrimage: The San Francisco Homeland and Identity Tourism." *Cultural Anthropology, 16*(1), 35–61. DOI: 10.1525/can.2001.16.1.35.

Huebner, D. M., and Davis, M. C. (2005). "Gay and Bisexual Men Who Disclose Their Sexual Orientations in the Workplace Have Higher Workday Levels of Salivary Cortisol and Negative Affect." *Annals of Behavioral Medicine, 30*(3), 260–67.

Kepner, J. I. *Body Process: A Gestalt Approach to Working with the Body in Psychotherapy*. New York, NY: Gardner Press: Gestalt Institute of Cleveland Press, 1987.

Kimmel, S. B., and Mahalik, J. R. (2005). "Body Image Concerns of Gay Men: The Roles of Minority Stress and Conformity to Masculine Norms." *Journal of Consulting and Clinical Psychology, 73*(6), 1185.

Kinsey, A. C., Pomeroy, W. B., and Martin, C. E. *Sexual Behavior in the Human Male.* Philadelphia, PA: W. B. Saunders, 1948.

Kroeger, B. *Passing: When People Can't Be Who They Are.* New York, NY: PublicAffairs, 2005.

Landolt, M. A., Bartholomew, K., Saffrey, C., Oram, D., and Perlman, D. (2004). Gender Nonconformity, Childhood Rejection, and Adult Attachment: A Study of Gay Men. *Archives of Sexual Behavior, 33*(2), 117–28.

Leary, K. "Passing, Posing, and 'Keeping It Real.'" In A. Lewis and A. Harris (Eds.), *Relational Psychoanalysis: Volume 4, Expansion of Theory.* New York, NY: Routledge/Taylor and Francis, 2014.

Legate, N., Ryan, R. M., and Weinstein, N. (2012). "Is Coming Out Always a 'Good Thing?' Exploring the Relations of Autonomy Support, Outness, and Wellness for Lesbian, Gay, and Bisexual Individuals." *Social Psychological and Personality Science, 3*(2), 145–52.

Levine, P. A. *Waking the Tiger: Healing Trauma, the Innate Capacity to Transform Overwhelming Experiences.* Berkeley, CA: North Atlantic Books, 1997.

Lowen, A. *Bioenergetics.* New York, NY: Coward, McCann and Geoghegan, 1975.

Luthar, S. S., Cicchetti, D., and Becker, B. (2000). "The Construct of Resilience: A Critical Evaluation and Guidelines for Future Work." *Child Development, 71*(3), 543–62.

Maddi, S. R. (2002). "The Story of Hardiness: Twenty Years of Theorizing, Research, and Practice." *Consulting Psychology Journal: Practice and Research, 54*(3), 173–85.

Mansergh, G., Colfax, G. N., Marks, G., Rader, M., Guzman, R., and Buchbinder, S. (2001). "The Circuit Party Men's Health Survey: Findings and Implications for Gay and Bisexual Men." *American Journal of Public Health, 91*(6), 953–58.

Martins, Y., Tiggemann, M., and Churchett, L. (2008). "The Shape of Things to Come: Gay Men's Satisfaction with Specific Body Parts." *Psychology of Men and Masculinity, 9*(4), 248–56.

Masten, A. S. (2014). "Global Perspectives on Resilience in Children and Youth." *Child Development, 85*(1), 6–20.

Moore, J. W. (2016). "What Is the Sense of Agency and Why Does It Matter?" *Frontiers in Psychology, 7*, 1272. http://doi.org/10.3389/fpsyg.2016.01272.

Morin, E. (1992). "From the Concept of System to the Paradigm of Complexity." *Journal of Social and Evolutionary Systems, 15*(4), 371–85.

Morin, J. *The Erotic Mind: Unlocking the Inner Sources of Passion and Fulfillment.* New York, NY: HarperCollins, 1996.

Moskowitz, D. A., and Hart, T. A. (2011). "The Influence of Physical Body Traits and Masculinity on Anal Sex Roles in Gay and Bisexual Men." *Archives of Sexual Behavior, 40*(4), 835–41.

Mothes, H., Klaperski, S., Seelig, H., Schmidt, S., and Fuchs, R. (2014). "Regular Aerobic Exercise Increases Dispositional Mindfulness in Men: A Randomized Controlled Trial." *Mental Health and Physical Activity.* Advance online publication. http://doi.org/10.1016/j.mhpa.2014.02.003.

Mustanski, B., Newcomb, M. E., and Garofalo, R. (2011). "Mental Health of Lesbian, Gay, and Bisexual Youths: A Developmental Resiliency Perspective." *Journal of Gay and Lesbian Social Services, 23*(2), 204–25.

Naumova, O. K., Lee, M., Koposov, R., Szyf, M., Dozier M., and Grigorenko, E. L. (2012). "Differential Patterns of Whole-Genome DNA Methylation in Institutionalized Children and Children Raised by Their Biological Parents." *Development and Psychopathology*, 24(1), 143–55. DOI: 10.1017/S0954579411000605.

Ngun, T. C., Ghahramani, N., Sánchez, F. J., Bocklandt, S., and Vilain, E. (2011). "The Genetics of Sex Differences in Brain and Behavior." *Frontiers in Neuroendocrinology, 32*(2), 227–46.

Noë, A. *Out of Our Heads: Why You Are Not Your Brain, and Other Lessons from the Biology of Consciousness.* New York, NY: Hill and Wang, 2009.

Perls, F. *The Gestalt Approach and Eye Witness to Therapy.* Ben Lomond, CA: Science and Behavior Books, 1973.

Pierrakos, J. C. *Core Energetics: Developing the Capacity to Love and Heal* (Paperback ed.). Mendocino, CA: LifeRhythm, 1990.

Porges, S. W. *The Polyvagal Theory: Neurophysiological Foundations of Emotions, Attachment, Communication, and Self-Regulation.* New York, NY: W. W. Norton, 2011.

Reich, W. *The Mass Psychology of Fascism.* New York, NY: Farrar, Straus & Giroux, 1970.

———. *The Function of the Orgasm: Sex-Economic Problems of Biological Energy.* V. R. Carfagno, trans. New York, NY: Farrar, Straus and Giroux, 1973.

———. *Character-Analysis: Principles and Technique for Psychoanalysts in Practice and in Training.* T. P. Wolfe, trans. New York, NY: Orgone Institute Press, 1945.

Rice, W. R., Friberg, U., and Gavrilets, S. (2012). "Homosexuality as a Consequence of Epigenetically Canalized Sexual Development." *Quarterly Review of Biology, 87*(4), 343–368.

Richardson, G. E. (2002). "The Metatheory of Resilience and Resiliency." *Journal of Clinical Psychology, 58*(3), 307–21.

Rieger, G., Linsenmeier, J. A., Gygax, L., Garcia, S., and Bailey, J. M. (2010). Dissecting "Gaydar": Accuracy and the Role of Masculinity–Femininity. *Archives of Sexual Behavior, 39*(1), 124–40.

Rotello, G. *Sexual Ecology: AIDS and the Destiny of Gay Men.* New York, NY: Dutton, 1997.

Rutter, M. (1985). "Resilience in the Face of Adversity." *British Journal of Psychiatry, 147*(1), 598–611.

Sanchis-Gomar, F., Garcia-Gimenez, J. L., Perez-Quilis, C., Gomez-Cabrera, M. C., Pallardo, F. V., and Lippi, G. (2012). "Physical Exercise as an Epigenetic Modulator: Eustress, the 'positive stress' as an Effector of Gene Expression." *Journal of Strength and Conditioning Research, 26*(12), 3469–72.

Sedgwick, E. K. (1991). "How to Bring Your Kids up Gay." *Social Text, 1991* (29), 18–27.

Shapiro, F. E., ed. *EMDR as an Integrative Psychotherapy Approach: Experts of Diverse Orientations Explore the Paradigm Prism.* Washington, DC: American Psychological Association, 2002.

Siegel, D. J. *The Developing Mind: How Relationships and the Brain Interact to Shape Who We Are.* New York, NY: Guilford Press, 1999.

Signorile, M. *Life Outside: The Signorile Report on Gay Men, Sex, Drugs, Muscles, and the Passages of Life.* New York, NY: HarperPerennial, 1998.

Smith, B. W., Epstein, E. M., Ortiz, J. A., Christopher, P. J., and Tooley, E. M. "The Foundations of Resilience: What Are the Critical Resources for Bouncing Back from Stress?" In S. Prince-Embury and D. H. Saklofske (eds.), *Resilience in Children, Adolescents, and Adults: Translating Research into Practice.* New York, NY: Springer, 2013.

Stall, R., Friedman, M., and Catania, J. A. "Interacting Epidemics and Gay Men's Health: A Theory of Syndemic Production among Urban Gay Men." In R. J. Wolitski, R. Stall, and R. O. Valdiserri (eds.), *Unequal Opportunity: Health Disparities Affecting Gay and Bisexual Men in the United States.* New York, NY: Oxford University Press, 2008.

Supic, G., Jagodic, M., and Magic, Z. (2013). Epigenetics: A New Link between Nutrition and Cancer. *Nutrition and Cancer, 65*(6), 781–92.

University of California Los Angeles Center for Health Policy Research. (2014, March) California Health Interview Survey, 2011–2012. [Database]. Los Angeles, CA: UCLA Center for Health Policy Research. Retrieved from the Ask CHIS website (account required): http://ask.chis.ucla.edu/main/DQ3/geographic.asp.

Van der Kolk, B. A. (1994). "The Body Keeps the Score: Memory and the Evolving Psychobiology of Posttraumatic Stress." *Harvard Review of Psychiatry, 1*(5), 253–65.

Vilain, E. (2006). "Genetics of Intersexuality." *Journal of Gay and Lesbian Psychotherapy.* Vol. 10, 2006.

Waehler, K. M. (2008). *Resiliency in Lesbian Women and Gay Men after Negative Therapy Experiences with Heterosexual Therapists.* Doctoral dissertation. Retrieved from the ProQuest PSYCHinfo database. (Dissertation No. 3324385).

Whitelaw, E. 2006. Epigenetics. Sins of the Fathers, and Their Fathers (commentary). *European Journal of Human Genetics, 14*, 131–32. Retrieved from http://www.nature.com/ejhg/journal/v14/n2/full/5201567a.html.

Yang, I. V. (2012). "Sleep, Immunology, and Epigenetics: Tip of an Iceberg." *American Journal of Respiratory and Critical Care Medicine, 185*(3), 243–45.

INDEX

Numbers

A

B

C

CONTRIBUTORS

Authors

tayla ealom: an Earth and Water protector working to weave the worlds of social and ecological justice in an embodied way as a somatic counselor and bodyworker. As a multiracial cisgendered woman of color with lineages ranging from West Africa to Europe and the Americas, she works in the worlds of cross-cultural women's work that offer access to powerful healing modalities for all genders. She strives to bring these practices into activist spaces so healing can remain at the forefront of social and ecological movements. Over the past year, through workshops in the larger Northern California community, she has been exploring the theme of how the human body both shapes and is shaped by contemporary society. Her contribution is a reflection on these experiences and how embodied exploration is the key to moving toward a more just society.

STEPHANIE FRANCIS-ECOFFEY: at the time she wrote this piece, she was a second-year graduate student at the California Institute of Integral Studies pursuing her master's in Counseling Psychology with a focus in Somatic Psychology. She received her undergraduate degree in Africana studies with a psychology minor from Bowling Green State University. She writes from the perspective of her biracial identity with particular interest in her embodied experience and is interested in exploring the impacts of navigating two or more racial identities in America, as they relate to the family and other systems, belonging, and one's sense of self. She believes that writing can be a tool for social change and writes from an embodied and vulnerable space. Stephanie Francis-Ecoffey enjoys practicing Reiki, running, and spending time with her wife.

ROGER J. KUHN: a somatic sex therapist and a member of the Poarch Band of Creek Indians. His work is informed from a social and sexual justice perspective. His current academic and activist focus centers on decolonizing sexuality. He is currently completing a PhD in Human Sexuality and is an active participant in the Two-Spirit community in the Bay Area of California.

HARUHIKO MURAKAWA: professor of somatics in the Department of Health and Well-Being, Kansai University, Osaka, Japan. His academic interest is to reclaim the East Asian mode of bodily experiences, especially in the fields of medicine, education, and social welfare. He is a vice president of the Japan Association of Somatics and Somatic Psychology and a past president of the Japanese Association of Transpersonal Psychology/Psychiatry. He is currently working on a project with local people in Kumano, one of the oldest spiritual places in Japan, famous for its ancient pilgrimage routes and mountain-based asceticism, to establish a learning center in which people can revitalize their earth-based wisdom, embodied in their daily lives.

JULES PASHALL: a white, Jewish, fat, and genderqueer artist, activist, and somatic therapist, whose work is grounded in the belief that as individuals we are connected and accountable to the collective body. Jules focuses on highlighting the wisdom of the fat, queer embodied experience.

ANTOINETTE SANTOS REYES: a queer cisgender Pinay who comes from a long line of healers and resisters. With a master's degree in somatic psychology, they are currently pursuing a PhD in women's spirituality to center indigenous and decolonized praxis in psychotherapy. They support the healing of collective trauma by framing human relationship through an intersectional, feminist, and somato-spiritual lens.

MURIEL JAMILLE VINSON: an African American scholar, dancer, musician, writer, activist. As a descendant of enslaved Africans and a practitioner of West African drum and dance, Muriel has personally engaged with the dynamics and healing potential present in Africentric embodiment practices including song, drum, and dance. Currently training as a somatic psychotherapist, Muriel seeks to highlight Africentric somatic practices, including practices of the African Diaspora, and contextualize their potential use in addressing intergenerational trauma.

KURT WAGNER: a somatic psychotherapist, researcher, and activist within the gay community. His doctoral research on the possible hormonal variations in the body of birth has led to his articulating the groundwork for understanding the multiplicity of variants in one's erotic proclivities and gender identity.

NICK WALKER: an autistic aikido teacher, author, speaker, educator, and somatics practitioner, faculty member at California Institute of Integral Studies, and managing editor at Autonomous Press. Nick holds a 6th degree black belt in aikido and is senior instructor at the Aikido Shusekai dojo in Berkeley. His eclectic work explores the intersections of somatics, spirituality, neurodiversity, empathy, and creativity. Books in which his writings appear include *Loud Hands: Autistic People Speaking, The Real Experts: Readings for Parents of Autistic Children, The Spoon Knife Anthology, Spoon Knife 2: Test Chamber,* and *Spoon Knife 3: Incursions.* He has been featured in the documentary films *Orphans of Delirium, Dreambody/Earthbody,* and *Spectrum: A Story of the Mind.*

ALYSSA N. ZELAYA: a first-generation Nicaraguan-American woman and San Francisco "native," somatic psychotherapist, a Lukumi priestess (Olosha) crowned to Shango in 2002, a certified massage therapist and health educator, master-level Reiki practitioner, and former Aztec and Polynesian dancer. Under the exposure of religious initiation, folk practices, spiritual dance disciplines, and professional training coloring her current approaches to mental health and healing, she became interested in exploring ways through spiritually integrated somatic practices to resolve the constant "disconnection to self" and imbalances that result when traumas occur, whether on an individual or community-wide level. From this perspective, she specializes in various forms of trauma work, which include navigating through physical, emotional, and sexual abuses, community trauma, and inter-generational trauma, specifically, and not limited to, children and adolescents of color.

Editor

DON HANLON JOHNSON: founder of the Somatic Psychology program at the California Institute for Integral Studies. For several decades, his writing and teaching have focused on the role of the body in crafting a more just and inclusive social order.

About North Atlantic Books

North Atlantic Books (NAB) is an independent, nonprofit publisher committed to a bold exploration of the relationships between mind, body, spirit, and nature. Founded in 1974, NAB aims to nurture a holistic view of the arts, sciences, humanities, and healing. To make a donation or to learn more about our books, authors, events, and newsletter, please visit www.northatlanticbooks.com.

North Atlantic Books is the publishing arm of the Society for the Study of Native Arts and Sciences, a 501(c)(3) nonprofit educational organization that promotes cross-cultural perspectives linking scientific, social, and artistic fields. To learn how you can support us, please visit our website.